"Most of us struggle to have skilful conversations, and it's partly our lack of self-awareness and skill in this arena that's got humankind in the trouble it's in today. Lee lives up to his description of coach as 'wilderness guide', mapping out the territory of skilful dialogue, and accompanying us on a journey to discovery of what it takes to have meaningful courageous compassionate conversations. A generous treasure trove of resources, from accessible explanations of the underpinning science, to case studies, nifty tools and techniques, this timely book can transform our world, one mindful conversation at a time."

Liz Hall, author of *Mindful Coaching*, editor of *Coaching at Work* magazine, leadership coach and mindfulness teacher

"Graham Lee is at once a safe and an exciting pair of hands to be in, when you are navigating the choppy but rewarding territory of breakthrough conversations. His thinking is structured and clear, and his writing so transparent that you are struck, viscerally, by the powerful ideas that it carries. Lee's intent is more than positive: it is transformational. He provides a trusty framework for the novice and the unsure, and a compendium of delights for the experienced and the confident."

Alison Hardingham, Executive Professor at Henley Business School, Fellow of the British Psychological Society, APECS accredited Master Executive Coach and Coaching Supervisor, Psychodynamic Psychotherapist (Oxford)

"Our shared future relies more than ever before on conversations that break down division, build trust, and generate collaboration. Graham Lee provides organisational consultants and coaches with a profound methodology for enabling their clients to engage in such conversations. Drawing on key ideas from the worlds of psychology and mindfulness, he presents practical tools that can be applied immediately in the workplace, so that conversational participants can remain resourceful and constructive, even in the toughest of situations."

Peter Young, Leadership Coach and Consultant, Bladon Leadership Ltd.

"Graham Lee sets out a coherent and worthwhile theory of human functioning that provides a particularly convincing account of how we deal with emotions. I am of the opinion that Lee's position has sufficient psychological depth even if the obligatory references to neuroscience are removed. The book is full of insightful ideas for practitioners that are based on robust knowledge and the rich professional expertise of the author. I will certainly be recommending it, not only to students of coaching but also to seasoned and discerning practitioners."

Prof Tatiana Bachkirova, Professor of Coaching Psychology, Oxford Brookes University

"Given the complexity of today's world, developing the capacity to have breakthrough conversations is more important than ever. Graham provides us with a map that has both clarity and depth. In a digital age effective collaboration is becoming a key competitive advantage. Breakthrough Conversations is a rich and skillful guidebook that shows the way. For those interested in vertical development, it provides a beautifully accessible pathway into observing and transcending habitual and reactive patterns and in doing so, finding the balcony and expanded perspectives. These are important developmental moves for us all in navigating complexity and enabling transformational change."

Mark McMordie, CEO, The Conscious Leader and co-author of *Mindfulness for Coaches*

Breakthrough Conversations for Coaches, Consultants and Leaders

Conversational effectiveness is a barometer of human thriving and facilitating insightful conversations is a powerful method for accelerating psychological change and collaboration. This ground-breaking professional book provides a map of Breakthrough Conversations together with a practical toolkit for enhancing awareness, emotional resilience and creativity.

Neuroscience, mindfulness, and psychological research shows that awareness is pivotal to skilful conversations. By supporting clients to observe and manage their own body–brain states during conversation, they can learn to employ the physiological systems that support more authentic, agile and attuned interactions. Three body–brain states; reactive, habitual and reflective – characterised as Red, Amber and Green (RAG) – are differentiated in terms of bodily sensations and behaviours, and these correspond to predictable interactive patterns. Facilitated to experience more emotionally resilient conversations, clients access their natural capacities for collaboration, compassion and shared creativity. This journey, through the five stages of Breakthrough Conversations which draws on the RAG states and a number of other practical models, is richly illustrated with case studies from working one-to-one to working as a pair.

Coming to see conversations as a dance driven by the interactions of underlying needs and emotions enables clients to make paradigm shifts in their self-awareness and interpersonal effectiveness. This book, and the approach it outlines, will be essential reading for coaches, consultants, leaders and all professionals seeking to choreograph more insightful conversations.

Graham Lee is a leadership coach, psychotherapist and mindfulness teacher. By integrating the domains of neuroscience, psychology, mindfulness and leadership, he offers a unique blend of pragmatism and depth in facilitating change in individuals, pairs and teams.

Breakthrough Conversations for Coaches, Consultants and Leaders

Graham Lee

LONDON AND NEW YORK

First published 2022
by Routledge
2 Park Square, Milton Park, Abingdon, Oxon OX14 4RN

and by Routledge
605 Third Avenue, New York, NY 10158

Routledge is an imprint of the Taylor & Francis Group, an informa business

© 2022 Graham Lee

The right of Graham Lee to be identified as author of this work has been asserted by him in accordance with sections 77 and 78 of the Copyright, Designs and Patents Act 1988.

All rights reserved. No part of this book may be reprinted or reproduced or utilised in any form or by any electronic, mechanical, or other means, now known or hereafter invented, including photocopying and recording, or in any information storage or retrieval system, without permission in writing from the publishers.

Trademark notice: Product or corporate names may be trademarks or registered trademarks, and are used only for identification and explanation without intent to infringe.

British Library Cataloguing-in-Publication Data
A catalogue record for this book is available from the British Library

Library of Congress Cataloging-in-Publication Data
A catalog record has been requested for this book

ISBN: 978-0-367-51587-4 (hbk)
ISBN: 978-0-367-51588-1 (pbk)
ISBN: 978-1-003-05454-2 (ebk)

DOI: 10.4324/9781003054542

Typeset in Times New Roman
by MPS Limited, Dehradun

Contents

List of Figures	x
List of Tables	xi
List of Case Studies	xii
Acknowledgements	xiii

1 The power of conversations   1
Breakthrough conversations 2
Breakthrough in relation to four conversational purposes 5
Origins of this approach 14
Distinctive elements of this approach 15
Who is this book for? 15
The ladder of capabilities for facilitating change 16
The structure of the book 18
Summary 23
Worksheet 1: Understanding relational patterns in four domains of conversation 23

2 Developing a breakthrough body–brain   25
What is the body–brain? 26
The skull-based portion of the brain 27
Polyvagal theory 28
Heart rate variability 31
Hormones and emotional regulation 32
Three body–brain systems 33
The RED/reactive system 33
The AMBER/habit system 35
The GREEN/reflective system 37
Diagnosing body–brain states 38
Signifiers of the RED body–brain system 38
Signifiers of the AMBER body–brain system 41

Signifiers of the GREEN/body–brain system 42
Summary 46
Worksheet 2: Identifying body–brain states 47

3 Awareness is the key to breakthrough   **50**
What is awareness? 50
Taking an observer perspective 53
Practical models for enhancing conversational awareness 56
PACES – deconstructing experience 57
The Five-Eyed Model of Conversations 66
Summary 73
Worksheet 3: Deconstructing body–brain states using PACES 73

4 A Map of Breakthrough Conversations   **76**
Research evidence 79
The Breakthrough Conversations approach in context 80
A Map of Breakthrough Conversations 81
Summary 85
Worksheet 4: Recognising conversational stages and capabilities 85

5 Preparing the ground   **88**
Introducing a conversational lens 88
Constructing purpose in terms of conversation 89
Character habits and personal intentions 93
Practical considerations 103
Engaging client reflectiveness 104
Summary 106
Worksheet 5: Checklist of areas for exploration during Stage 1: preparing the ground 107

6 Managing emotional states   **108**
Establishing a space for mindful, embodied inquiry 109
Awareness of RAG body–brain states 109
The two stages to mindful inquiry 110
Deconstructing states using PACES 114
Emotional regulation during conversations 116
The 9-Minute Form 118
Formal practices to deepen emotional regulation 124
Summary 126

Worksheet 6: The 9-Minute Form 127

7 Loosening habit and reactivity 129
Self-disclosure 129
Identifying core relational needs 130
Personality 132
Attachment patterns 138
Using attachment patterns to foster skilful conversations 139
Cultural and social conditioning 144
Summary 149
Worksheet 7: Summary of underlying factors impacting conversations 150

8 Seeing the dance from the balcony 153
Disidentifying, attunement, and both-and thinking 154
Vertical development 154
The potential space between self and other 157
Identifying the conversational dance 161
Primary and secondary emotions 162
Organising the interactive cycle 165
Summary 169
Worksheet 8: Seeing the conversational dance 170

9 Harnessing Expanded Perspectives 172
The stage of playfulness 173
Awareness amidst interaction 174
Celebrating positive cycles of interaction 178
Fostering change and acceptance 181
Agreeing pragmatic goals 185
Planning to fail 185
Ongoing development 187
Summary 188
Worksheet 9: Harnessing expanded perspectives 189

Index 190

Figures

1.1	The Four Purposes of Conversation	6
1.2	The Ladder of Capabilities for Facilitating *Breakthrough Conversations*	16
2.1	Three body–brain Systems Shape Conversations	33
2.2	Diagnosing RAG body–brain States	39
3.1	The PACES Framework	57
3.2	Grounding *PACES* with Sensations	59
3.3	Mapping Emotions	64
3.4	The *Five-Eyed Model* of Conversations	67
4.1	*A Map of Breakthrough Conversations* - Stages and Capabilities	81
5.1	The *Character Compass*	94
5.2	*Character Compass* Summary for Rana	101
6.1	Opening from Interior to Relational Presence	117
8.1	Spirals of Development Arising from the Conversational Space	159
8.2	The *ACES* Aspects of RED/AMBER and GREEN Interactive Cycles	165

Tables

1.1	Limiting and Enabling Conversational Behaviours	7
3.1	Illustration of a Completed *ACES* Worksheet	61
3.2	*RAG* States in Terms of *ACES* Patterns	74
5.1	*Character Compass*: Qualities and Terms	97
7.1	Core Relational Needs	131
7.2	Habit and Reactivity for the Big Five Factors of Personality (with MBTI labels)	134
7.3	Indicative Habits and Reactions for Defiant and Compliant Attachment Positions	142
7.4	Summary of RAG Behaviours Shaped by Three Underlying Factors	150
8.1	Three Levels of Agility and Their Impact on Conversations	156
8.2	Summary of Elements Driving RED, AMBER and GREEN Interactive Cycles	170

Case Studies

1	Neil and Rosa	19
2	Julia, Lucy and Amir	45
3	Kulinder	58
5	Doug and Frasier; Rana; Jess	90
6	Stuart; Mick and Stuart	113
7	Jeremy; Julia, Lucy and Amir; Liz and Fiona; Bina; Leah	131
8	Lara; Roger; Mick and Stuart	159
9	Julia; Mick and Stuart; Neil and Rosa	175

Acknowledgements

This book is the product of numerous conversations and I want to thank the many people who consciously or unconsciously, professionally and personally, have enriched my understanding of conversations. First, I want to thank my clients without whom none of these practical ideas would have emerged. Second, I want to thank my coaching colleagues, too numerous to mention, but I particularly appreciate a period of monthly meetings with Peter Young, Emma Donaldson-Fielder and Jane Brendgen. Third, the many psychotherapy colleagues, and especially Helene Igwebuike, Sandra Taylor, Sarah Clevely, and Sarah McConnell for their support and insights. Fourth, I want to thank my mindfulness teachers, including Stephen Batchelor, Gregory Kramer, Ajahn Sucitto, Tara Bach, and Chris Germer. Fifth, Gayle Creasey for being a stimulus and sounding board for my early thinking on some of the models in this book.

And finally, my acknowledgement to my young-adult-children. Cameron for engaging so whole-heartedly in reflective conversations, and Maddy, for being an energising source of sanity, sustenance and outdoor companionship during the first coronavirus lockdown, when much of this book was written.

Chapter 1

The power of conversations

The power of conversations is evidenced by their consequences. Great conversations lead to profound insights, deeper trust, collaboration and creative breakthroughs. Reactive conversations lead to hurt, confusion, distrust and relational breakdowns. Conversations are the medium through which we shape our lives. If we facilitate effective conversation, our approach can be pivotal to the lives of others. By evoking hope, containing fear, and deepening inquiry, we have the means for fostering paradigm shifts in how people understand themselves and their choices. By choreographing their interactions with others, we can elevate mutual understanding, open hearts and create the conditions for startling breakthroughs. In this book I share many case studies of *Breakthrough Conversations*: Rosa uncovering the fear beneath her controlling style, and opening the door to new innovations with her colleague Neil; Julia supporting Lucy and Amir to resolve long-held frustrations; Kulinder finding the confidence to assert himself, and leading a game-changing initiative with Mike. In these and many other examples, I show how facilitating conversations has the power to deepen awareness and bring about significant shifts in personal and interpersonal insight.

If we want to be effective facilitators of change through conversation, we need to know what we are aiming to do. I like to think of our role like that of a wilderness guide. Our goal is to take people on a journey of discovery, to traverse challenging territory, to access hitherto unrealized potential, and assist people to arrive at their destination with an enlarged view of themselves and their place in the world. In what follows I share a *Map of Breakthrough Conversations*, describing the key stages of exploration and challenge that we need to pass through in order to deepen awareness and realise significant change. And like the wilderness guide who not only needs a map but also a good set of equipment, I also share a toolkit of frameworks for supporting people on their sense-making journey.

The approach I share in this book is intended for those facilitating change through conversation, and so is primarily focused on the application of these

DOI: 10.4324/9781003054542-1

ideas to supporting others. But, as Gandhi is often quoted as saying, *we need to be the change we want to see in the world.* The depth and richness of the conversational journey we can facilitate will be commensurate with our own willingness and experience of negotiating the complex array of conversations in our own lives. So, as you engage with these ideas, I invite you to explore them and apply them as much in your own life as in your potential use of them with others. I will begin by elaborating what I mean by *Breakthrough Conversations*.

Breakthrough conversations

In this book I present an approach to facilitating *Breakthrough Conversations* – conversations that are designed to support others to deepen their awareness, to gain insights, to strengthen their connection to others and to find creative solutions to challenges. *Breakthrough Conversations* enable us to shift our perspective and to see the world through new eyes. We confront a limiting mindset and step towards more enabling viewpoints; we own our vulnerabilities and foster deeper intimacy; we build on ideas with others and co-create new possibilities.

Implicit in what I have said already is the idea that we all have a view. We see the world through a particular lens, based on our blend of genetics and experience. When we examine our beliefs, say about politics or the environment, and discuss these with another, we discover areas of similarity and difference. Our implicit assumptions are brought out into the open. If we don't become defensive, our assumptions will be available for examination, challenge, and possibly a change in view. Conversation can literally change our minds. This book is concerned with techniques for supporting others to make explicit their implicit views – to discern if their ways of thinking and relating are serving their deeper intentions, and to support them in finding ways of relating most skilfully. *Breakthrough Conversations* are a journey and a destination; a journey in the sense that it is through shared exploration that previously uninterrupted aspects of experience are brought into awareness – buried emotions, unacknowledged needs, limiting beliefs – and understood at a personal and interpersonal level; a destination in the sense that they yield tangible outcomes – sustainable shifts in how we relate to ourselves and others, a deepening of trust and collaboration, and practical results in terms of creative ideas and shared solutions. In *Breakthrough Conversations* there is a co-arising of personal and interpersonal insight, a revealing of relational dynamics, a disrupting of personal mindsets and a stretching of personal paradigms beyond self-limiting boundaries by the challenge of being relational.

We might think the task of having productive, insightful conversations to be simple. After all, it only requires people to listen to each other, to express their views openly and through discussion to find common ground. That doesn't sound too difficult, does it? And yet if it were that easy, we would not have wars. The need for *Breakthrough Conversations* is evidenced by the many conversations that are either unproductive or even destructive. Although conversations are ripe with creative potential, they can also evoke hurt, pain and division. The course of our lives depends on the quality of our conversations and supporting others to have skilful conversations is a conduit for enabling them to live happier, more productive lives.

In distinguishing *Breakthrough Conversations* from less productive interactions, I will introduce a simple classification that I will subsequently build on throughout the rest of the book. Using the metaphor of traffic lights, conversations can be classified as RED, AMBER or GREEN (*RAG*), corresponding to what I describe as *reactive, habitual* and *reflective* conversations. Most of our conversations are AMBER or habitual, and some of them are RED or reactive. GREEN, or reflective conversations are the ones where potential for breakthrough is found. As we shall see later, RED, AMBER and GREEN conversations are underpinned by corresponding RED, AMBER and GREEN body-brain states and interactive behaviours, and it is by identifying and managing these states that we have the potential to cultivate GREEN states. For now, I want to be explicit about what I mean by *Breakthrough Conversations* by drawing out the difference between RED, AMBER and GREEN conversations.

RED conversations

RED, or reactive conversations, refer to those that are governed by emotional reactivity – emotions such as anger, fear, hurt and shame. When reactive emotions are to the fore, conversational behaviours are usually unskilful. We might become more forceful and controlling, or in contrast become more appeasing and compliant. Or we may move between these extremes depending on the context or the person; sometimes being more demanding and confronting, and sometimes being more distant and avoidant. You will readily recognise RED states in yourself when for example you feel your body tense, notice your tone of voice change, and recognise a shift in your choice of words. Similarly, with clients we can see a change perhaps in their body posture, facial expressions, gestures and language, and we may notice a tension in our own bodies in response to what we are picking up from them.

RED conversations are rarely a source of breakthrough. Instead, RED conversations tend to undermine safety and trust, increase the need for people to protect themselves and reduce the potential for awareness, insight and creativity. When clients complain about friends, partners or colleagues, they may seem possessed by their exasperation. When clients are swamped by the volume of their work, they seem caught by their stress and anxiety. When clients describe a loss, they seem to be overwhelmed by grief. These are natural emotional responses, and in working with ourselves, or clients, we need to tune into these emotions to acknowledge them and to find ways to shift or accept them. So, we are not in any sense wanting to deny or dismiss such emotions, but we need to recognise that psychological change is unlikely to occur when we or our clients are in RED states, and breakthrough is unlikely to result from RED conversations.

AMBER conversations

Our routine day-to-day conversations are usually conducted on automatic pilot. We greet others, we interact with people in shops or restaurants, we converse with colleagues and we talk with family or friends. Most of our conversational patterns are usefully habitual, enabling us to converse fluently and effectively with others without having to reflect consciously about the process of conversation. AMBER/habitual conversations result from our unconscious competence, programmes embedded into our implicit, mental operating systems, optimising our effectiveness in routine situations. However, AMBER conversations become limited when we are addressing new situations that require more reflection. Perhaps a partner is confronting us about something, or a challenge at work needs a different solution from those that have been successful in the past. Perhaps a conversational habit that was effective in prior contexts or relationships is now out-of-date and is no longer leading to positive outcomes. AMBER conversations limit the effectiveness of interactions that require a more reflective exploration, and over time, ineffective AMBER conversations can trigger emotional reactivity and RED conversations.

AMBER conversations are more difficult to recognise than RED conversations because the emotional and behavioural markers are less distinct and universal. Each person's conversational habits are subtly different from another person's, and for example, an abrupt style may be the result of reactivity or the result of a learned habit that is effective in many situations. But we can come to learn about habitual styles, our own and those of others, by noticing patterns of interactions that repeat over time. We can also gather feedback from colleagues or use psychometric measures of personality. We may discover that one person is habitually more friendly and warm, while another is habitually more direct and business-like. Those tendencies in either direction may be effective in some conversations, but we are also interested to notice if and when either of those habitual tendencies is less effective.

Like RED conversations, AMBER conversations are unlikely to be a source of breakthrough. Their automatic nature means they operate beneath reflective awareness and so are not accessible to the shifts in perspective and insight characteristic of breakthrough.

GREEN conversations

When we are able to pause and observe the process of conversation, we can use that awareness to inform how we then engage with others. A GREEN/reflective conversation is characterised by reflective awareness. We might experience GREEN states as a sense of ease and flow, or as a quality of presence. It is as though a part of our minds can observe our experience, without being overly identified with that experience. Being in a GREEN state does not mean that we won't experience RED emotions or AMBER tendencies. Habit and reactivity are intrinsic and essential parts of the human experience. However, in GREEN conversations there is access to a capacity for reflective awareness, which allows RED or AMBER tendencies to be seen and identified, so that the resulting conversational behaviour can be governed by conscious choice. For example, we may notice we have been triggered, perhaps by being aware of tension in some part of the body, or by noticing our eagerness to interrupt a person who is speaking. When this experience arises in a GREEN state, we have the capacity to notice the signals indicating that we have been triggered, and so make a conscious choice to manage our emotional state before responding. We might think of the GREEN state as transcending and encompassing RED or AMBER states. By bringing the observational stance of our GREEN state to bear, we can convert a potentially RED or AMBER conversation to a GREEN conversation.

The key point to make at this stage is that GREEN conversations are the ones most likely to give rise to breakthrough. GREEN states support conscious reflection, and so underpin the attunement, listening, self-expression and mutual exploration essential to *Breakthrough Conversations*. With these distinctions between RED, AMBER and GREEN conversations in view, I now consider the purpose of conversations and the potential targets for breakthrough.

Breakthrough in relation to four conversational purposes

Conversations have many different purposes: some aim for practical outcomes and others for personal connection, some are superficial without obvious purpose, while some others seek much needed discoveries or solutions. In talking about the concept of breakthrough we need to understand which conversations are our potential targets. To do this I will introduce a further distinction, this time between four types of conversational purpose. Conversations can be distinguished in terms of the degree to which they are 'results-focused' or 'relationship focused'. A results-focused conversation is one where the primary concern is about achieving an outcome. A relationship-focused conversation is one where the primary concern is about achieving connection. Considering if a conversation is high or low on each of these dimensions gives rise to four types of conversation (see Figure 1.1).

I have found this model to be a very useful starting place for introducing clients to a conversational approach to coaching because it is a relatively safe place to start, and because it provides a container for our initial, diagnostic inquiry. I describe the model to clients, usually showing them a version of Figure 1.1, and then ask them to identify conversations in their own lives that fit into each of the four domains. I then ask them to consider which of these interactions are most or least effective, and to consider the behaviours they use that are enabling or limiting in each of these contexts. This exploration draws out the areas, and the specific relationships, where clients are most motivated to develop their conversational effectiveness. Worksheet 1 at the end of this chapter describes this process, and the checklist below provides a basis for assessing enabling and limiting conversational behaviours (Table 1.1). I will describe each of these domains of

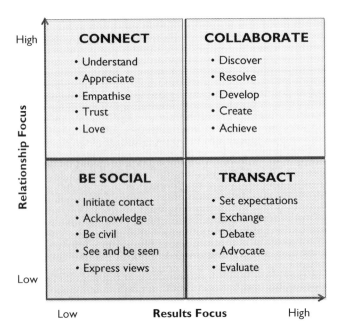

Figure 1.1 The Four Purposes of Conversation.

The power of conversations   7

Table 1.1 Limiting and Enabling Conversational Behaviours

Limiting Behaviours	Enabling Behaviours
• Not listening/monologues/telling • Opting out/withdrawal • Low inquiry • Passivity or silence • Imbalance of speaking and listening • Sarcasm/humour used inappropriately • Ignoring emotional agendas • Approval seeking/appeasing • Seeing views as right/wrong • Avoiding feedback • Blaming or scapegoating • Attacking, threatening, shouting, accusing • Cynicism/scepticism • Win-lose debating • Making assumptions about intentions • Knowing what to say in advance • Venting about historical frustrations • Emotional outbursts • Avoiding conflict	• Active listening • Being open/self-disclosing • Being curious/inquiring • Sharing views • Balancing speaking and listening • Validating others • Reading and expressing emotions • Authentic expression and challenge • Valuing differences • Giving, receiving and inviting feedback • Suspending judgement • Owning emotional triggers • Respectful responses • Win-win dialogue • Naming intentions, yours and theirs • Letting the conversation emerge • Keeping the conversation on purpose • Calm tone, even if content is difficult • Unpacking what underlies conflict

purpose, and as you will see, argue that all of them can be considered to be a potential domain for breakthrough.

Be social

The most basic conversations are concerned with 'being social', where both the relationship-focus and the results-focus is low. The purpose of these conversations is to initiate contact with people we don't know, to acknowledge others in a civil way, to see and be seen by others, and possibly, to express our views. We might say something to someone in a queue, or on a train, or whilst waiting to be served. These interactions are not results-focused, they are not designed to achieve a specific outcome, and they are not necessarily relationship-focused in the sense of trying to build a deeper connection. Nevertheless, these social interactions enable us to share, albeit briefly, in a moment of shared experience. For example, talking about the weather is often a low-risk way of finding common ground with another person. Through reciprocal acknowledgement of the cloudless sky or the relentless drizzle we make a rudimentary link to our shared, everyday humanness. Or, we might routinely say 'good morning' to someone we pass in the park, or to a neighbour with whom we have little contact. These small, social interactions can seem inconsequential, and so we might dismiss them as a domain for breakthrough. However, one of the virtues of the *Be Social* domain is that the stakes are low. Since there is little riding on these interactions, they can be a great place for cultivating the very awareness and skills that we will need to use for more significant conversations. They are like the nursery ski slopes, providing the chance to practice gentle snowplough turns before taking on parallel turns on steeper slopes.

To explore this domain with clients we ask them to consider what conversations they have that fit into this domain, and to notice how conscious they are of their behavioural choices during these interactions. Whether clients are friendly, chatty, distant or brusque, the aim is that they bring their tendencies into view. What is their habitual (AMBER) style, and what is the impact of this approach on their sense of connection?

One manager doing this exercise noted that he rarely interacted with the security staff he passed every day at the entrance to his building. He would be absorbed in his own issues and would walk past without a glance. Realising this, as an experiment he decided to greet the security staff warmly when he passed them. Over time he observed how this small shift in style led to him sometimes stopping for a few minutes to converse with security staff. He learned their names and gleaned snippets about their lives. This seemingly modest shift was a breakthrough for this manager because he was an introverted man who had been uncomfortable talking informally with colleagues, and he was viewed as insular and parochial by some departments. The experiment with security staff led to him recognising the power of being interested in others, and he began to connect more with a wider range of stakeholders.

The 'Be Social' domain and social media

A further element of the *Be Social* domain that has become more prevalent in recent years is social media. Many clients are active on social media and, inviting them to consider how they approach this domain provides further insight into their relational style. For example, a manager very active on social media described how she used social media to connect with clients and colleagues across her industry but noted how she felt uncomfortable with her sense of competition when she read about the initiatives and achievements of others. She realised that comparing herself to others on a daily basis was undermining her confidence and was making it harder for her to discern what was most important in her role. She decided to become more selective in her approach to social media, and to balance it with more face-to-face and telephone conversations with colleagues. The realisation for her was how much she needed a more authentic connection with others, where the relationship allowed for expression of doubts as well as triumphs, vulnerabilities as well as strengths. After these reflections she still viewed social media as invaluable but used it more consciously.

Invited to reflect, many clients are ambivalent about the role that social media plays in their lives. On the one hand they enjoy the ease of connection to others, the potential to sustain contact when geographically distant and the richness of ideas that can be shared. On the other, they may notice the pressure it brings to be available and responsive, to have a view or to be funny, and the experience of creating a public self that is very different from how they truly are. They may also acknowledge how they can get drawn into barbed exchanges and their concerns or regrets about exchanges that have escalated. Taking time to explore their relationship with social media offers clients an opportunity to think deeply about this dimension of social exchange, and to make more conscious choices about how they wish to engage with it in the future.

In summary, many conversations in the *Be Social* domain satisfy a basic need for acknowledgement and for being seen, and provide an important, low risk opportunity to examine a client's relational motivations and tendencies. The *Be Social* domain is also important because it is the starting place for interactions that will subsequently shift to one of the other three domains, and so sets the foundation for the quality of interaction when the purpose is to *Transact*, *Connect* or *Collaborate*.

Transact

Many of our routine conversations are designed to achieve a result in a context where there is little or no relationship with another person, such as when we order food in a restaurant, pay for petrol, ask for directions or give professional advice. As we move through our lives, we interact with numerous people to supply or receive goods or services. There may be a convivial, social component to the conversations we have with these people, but we would not engage in the conversation unless there was something we wanted. In large organisations it is not uncommon for people in one department to have mostly transactional conversations with people in another department, or for a supplier to have mostly transactional relationships with its customers. When we interview someone for a job, the main purpose of the conversation is to decide if he or she is able to handle the responsibilities of the position. Through being social we may also be curious about the potential for this person to fit into a team and to assess how the relationship may develop over time. But, at the interview stage the relational component is part of the transaction designed to evaluate the person's fit for a role.

To explore this domain with clients we ask them to consider how they approach some of the key elements of transactional relationships. These include setting expectations, agreeing what they will give or receive in exchange for money, time, products or services, debating issues where the goal is typically to win an argument, advocating for a position and evaluating something or someone against expectations or standards.

Some clients are comfortable setting expectations and will be direct in holding others to account, whilst others may be somewhat heavy-handed. One manager, who joined from a company with a more autocratic culture, applied the same transactional style in his new company, only to find himself faced with widespread disgruntlement and unwanted resignations. At the other extreme some clients avoid direct discussion of expectations, hoping that a more implicit understanding will yield the outcomes they want. For these clients the breakthrough in awareness occurs when they realise that all relationships, personal as well as professional, have a transactional component. A lack of explicit transaction is a potential forerunner to resentment and conflict because one or both participants in a transaction are bound to fail, at some point, in meeting unspoken expectations. For example, clients who put off feedback to colleagues about shortfalls in performance often find their frustration gradually building over time, until they finally burst with a disproportionate tirade of critical comments.

In the *Transact* domain a discussion often takes the form of a debate, where people advocate for their different positions. The word debate, from the French 'debatre', means to fight, to contend, or to beat down. The implicit goal is to knock down the other person's argument. Many clients believe that a conversational breakthrough would be when they have convinced someone that they are right. However, this is not what we mean by breakthrough. The breakthrough is more likely to be an acknowledgement of the limitations of the transactional domain, because getting people to do what we want without their buy-in is a recipe for demotivation.

Other clients may notice that rather than being forceful or controlling, their transactional tendency is to be compliant or appeasing. They look for others to set the rules and seek to conform. A manager working in a customer service role, reviewing how she approached the transactional domain saw that the high workloads and multiple demands from different departments were not being managed well by her. Her substantial team was overwhelmed, and some team members were absent due to stress. She realised how crucial it was for her to be more assertive in her negotiation with colleagues, and to be explicit in her transactions around priorities and resourcing. For this client, our initial review of the domains of conversation showed us that a key part of the coaching for her was to manage the *Transact* domain more actively.

Like the *Be Social* domain, the *Transact* domain does not, on surface-level, look like an area for *Breakthrough Conversations*. However, many clients find it useful to explore how their approach to transactional conversations can have a big impact on their effectiveness. Whether they need to be more assertive or more accommodating, or a flexible balance between the two, they become more attuned to the means-to-an-end component of conversations, and the relational tendencies that limit or promote smooth transactions. Also, enhancing awareness of conversational styles in the

Transact domain supports clients as they go on to explore the other two conversational domains: *Connect* and *Collaborate*.

Connect

People usually associate the *Connect* domain most strongly with their personal lives. Conversations in this domain are concerned with a focus on building, deepening, and maintaining the relationship for its own sake, with little emphasis on shared outcomes. These are the conversations we typically have with friends, partners and family members. If the *Transact* domain is primarily concerned with logic, then the *Connect* domain is primarily concerned with emotion. As clients consider their patterns in this domain, they begin to explore how comfortable they are with expressing emotion, or with responding to the emotional expressions of others.

For this domain clients typically consider the conversations they have with partners, siblings, parents, children and close friends. They look at these relationships from two perspectives: the degree to which they themselves feel understood and appreciated, and the degree to which they believe they understand and appreciate others. Most clients will identify one or more challenging personal relationships. Observing how they talk about their interactions with these people can tell us a great deal about their styles of reactivity. For example: a manager talks about her husband's lack of thoughtfulness around the sharing of the household duties (a transactional context), but as we explore further, she talks about a deeper longing to be more understood by him, for him to empathise with the challenge of her balancing a demanding work role with her responsibilities at home. She describes how the sense of not being valued by her husband can also arise in relation to her boss and other colleagues. When I ask her how she addresses this apparent lack of understanding, she describes herself as becoming frustrated and angry. At home this takes the form of an argument with her husband. When I ask her whether the argument leads to her feeling more understood, she says, '*sometimes ... for a while ... but then it all happens again a few weeks later*'. At work she feels disempowered and silenced and starts to question if she wants to continue working in that organisation. From a conversational perspective we can see that her relational moves are not working. At this stage in the *Breakthrough Conversations* approach, rather than getting her to think about how to have more effective conversations with her husband or colleagues, I hold the mirror up for her to see her own conversational tendencies, and invite her to tune into the emotional needs that underlie these habitual and reactive styles. Our goal is to begin the process of enhancing awareness; a process that we may subsequently deepen into a significant breakthrough.

One of the biggest breakthroughs for clients exploring the *Connect* domain is to realise that they need to do less than they think to cultivate a sense of understanding, trust, and love. For example, in my work with a married couple, the man described how his son from a former marriage was emotionally distant from his new family. At times he would get angry with his new wife, expecting her to do more to heal the tensions. But when I supported him to speak about his deeper feelings, he acknowledged that he was heavy with sadness. In the past his wife would talk about her sense of guilt or she would make suggestions for things they could do to bring the son closer, but these conversational responses did not help the situation. However, when her response to her husband's sadness was to look at him silently and compassionately, with tears rolling down her cheeks, she met his need for care and understanding more profoundly and eloquently than any conversation. The breakthrough occurred because he was able to step back from his anger and speak about his sadness, and she was able to resist a rush to offering solutions and instead showed, through her non-verbal response, how much she cared.

By exploring relational patterns in the *Connect* domain we support clients to see how their ways of conversing with others is linked to underlying emotions. Even if we decide it is not appropriate to delve more deeply into these emotions, perhaps because the client does not wish to, or because we don't feel we have adequate training, touching into underlying emotions can be essential if we are to facilitate significant breakthrough. One of my goals in this book is to show how this can be done in a safe and contained way with clients. If they feel overwhelmed with RED emotions, and we don't feel comfortable handling these, then we will not be serving the development of our clients. But, as I aim to show, if we take clients through the gradual process of learning to observe and manage their emotional states amidst their interactions, it becomes much safer to approach vulnerable emotions, and to begin to integrate experiences that hitherto evoked reactive escape strategies.

Collaborate

The *Collaborate* domain is concerned with conversations that combine emotional connection and practical transactions. When conversations flow in the *Collaborate* domain, they enable people to work together to discover new things, to resolve difficult issues, to create and develop new approaches and to achieve outcomes unreachable on one's own. At work, most clients recognise the need to work collaboratively with others, and often see the need to build trust and understanding as an important complement to shared transactional goals. At home many clients recognise that their emotional commitments to family and friends need to be coupled to the practical goals of managing money, health, education, housing, schooling and so on. Many of our most important conversations occur in the *Collaborate* domain.

Breakthrough Conversations are usually concerned with shifting to the *Collaborate* domain, harnessing trust and connection in order to work together in achieving mutual outcomes. In some coaching assignments the focus is more on deepening the relational aspect of conversations, and in others the focus is more on increasing the transactional aspects of conversations. For example, a manager whose team was faced with high rates of turnover wanted to understand whether there was anything he could do to retain some of his best team members. A feedback process revealed that he was good at managing expectations, setting clear goals and where necessary stepping in to solve difficult issues. But the workloads were high and team members felt that they had little respite from gruelling days in front of their computer screens. When they asked for flexibility in their work schedules he was discouraging, and when he reviewed performance, he paid little attention to their broader ambitions and personal development. He could see that almost all of his conversations with team members were in the *Transact* domain. He realised that he needed to relate to his team members as people, to understand their hopes and concerns, and to find ways to balance task outcomes with cultivating a more connected team environment. The coaching led to him putting in place a series of one-to-one meetings with his team members specifically to explore their motivations and suggestions for how to manage the workloads most effectively. Over a period of just a month or so, he felt he had shifted his *Transact* conversations to *Collaborate* conversations.

It is worth noting that the shift to *Collaborate* conversations does not always move from the *Transact* domain. For example, a project in a large, public sector organisation found that the staff, many of whom had worked there for a long time and who had established strong, trusting relationships, were reluctant to hold each other to account. The warmth and understanding they had for each other meant that they were not confronting issues and productivity had fallen. A performance management programme was initiated, and a central part of this programme was to support the staff to have more transactional conversations with each other. It was by enhancing the level of transaction in their conversations, alongside their established warmth and connection, that led to a return to fuller productivity.

Looking at these four dimensions of purpose as a whole, we can see that clients can gain value from breakthroughs in any or all of these domains. Recognising the subtlety of automatic behaviours in the *Be Social* or *Transact* domains, although not necessarily problematic, sparks the curiosity of clients to be self-observing. By showing interest in these tendencies, and by noticing and reflecting them back to clients in our conversations with them, we are aiming to establish an investigative working alliance, where small behavioural observations are doorways into a deeper inquiry. Moving into the *Connect* or *Collaborate* domains where emotions are more to the fore, we are usually beginning to work with deeper issues and approaching areas where the potential breakthroughs are more profound.

Origins of this approach

So far, I have set the scene for what I mean by *Breakthrough Conversations* by making a distinction between three types of conversation; RED, AMBER and GREEN, and by identifying the potential for breakthrough in relation to four conversational purposes; *Be Social, Transact, Connect* and *Collaborate*. These two classifications provide the broader definitional territory for *Breakthrough Conversations*. The following statement talks about the origins and development of this approach as a basis for then laying out a fuller picture of its distinctive elements.

This approach draws on my almost 40-year experience that spans roles as a manager, coach, psychotherapist and meditator. During this time, I have been testing and honing what helps or hinders people to change, and the role that can be played by conversations. My approach to change encompasses two somewhat disparate tracks: on the one hand business leadership, strategy consulting, and executive development, and on the other, psychology, psychotherapy, and mindfulness. Working as a coach and leadership development consultant in organisations, conversations are the medium through which managers and their teams find common purpose, engage others and deliver results. Working as a psychotherapist with individuals and couples, conversations are both the primary tool for discovery, and also the method by which clients learn to connect more fully with themselves and the people who matter to them the most. Working as a meditation and mindfulness teacher, both in organisations and in the community, I have witnessed how simple techniques can readily deepen awareness and enable more insightful interactions. And at a personal level, like all of us, conversations have been the essential conduit through which I have navigated the highs and lows of my life; friendship, marriage, family and community, as well as setback, divorce, illness and loss.

This particular array of professional and personal experiences has, over the years, shifted and clarified what I perceive to be the most effective ways of facilitating change. The approach presented in this book is informed by different frames: psychoanalysis, solution-focused therapy, cognitive-behavioural therapy, future leadership potential assessment, relational team development, systemic constellations, attachment-based couple therapy, mindful leadership, brain science, somatic experiencing and other body-based approaches to treating trauma. The approach that has emerged and become honed into what I present in this book uses conversations as the potent constellating frame for these varied perspectives. This approach is used by me and my colleagues in coaching individual managers, pairs of managers, and teams, and we have also trained managers in the approach using a combination of workshops and facilitated conversations. I also use many aspects of this approach in my psychotherapeutic work.

Distinctive elements of this approach

Drawing together the various avenues that have contributed to the *Breakthrough Conversations* approach, I will highlight six distinctive elements:

1. *Conversations are a powerful domain for emotional insight.* They provide diagnostic data through the way people think and talk about their challenges, and they provide a practical basis for making radical shifts in emotional awareness and productivity.
2. *Observing oneself is key to change.* Mindfulness skills, or other techniques to step back and observe oneself, provide an essential observer perspective for making more conscious, skilful choices.
3. *Body awareness is a key doorway to self-awareness.* By awakening awareness to the myriad of sensations arising and passing through the body we can learn to regulate ourselves and attune to underlying emotions and needs.
4. *Neuroscience validates and normalises unfamiliar techniques.* Research into neurophysiology and the role of relationships in shaping and managing body-brain states provides scientific rationale for our approach and reassures many clients.
5. *Change is accelerated by working with pairs as well as individuals.* The heightened relational potency of paired conversations, combined with individual coaching sessions, can accelerate change that is slow or difficult to achieve in a purely one-to-one context.
6. *Visual frameworks support observational sense-making.* Many clients feel supported by visual models, maps, or frameworks because they provide a cognitive container for organising personal and interpersonal experiences.

This book seeks to draw together these elements into a practical and coherent way of fostering change; both in ourselves and in our clients.

Who is this book for?

The book is intended for anyone who facilitates others through the medium of conversation: coaches, consultants, leaders, mediators, psychologists, social workers, therapists, counsellors, teachers and other professionals. The book is targeted to professionals in the sense that the approach draws on blending a depth of psychological and practical techniques. Having said that, I have clients who also make use of these techniques in their personal contexts: with their partners, children or friends. I think this has occurred because clients seem to enjoy the simplicity of the frameworks, such as the RED, AMBER, GREEN distinction discussed already, and so they become part of their language for making sense of their experiences and for talking with others. I have endeavoured to find a balance between offering simplicity in the framing of the approach, whilst maintaining sufficient richness for us to fully embrace the challenge of fostering profound change.

The ladder of capabilities for facilitating change

In order to make optimal use of these techniques, we need to consider the capabilities and skills required to facilitate this process, whether you are a coach, consultant, leader or other professional. I propose five core capabilities, each building on those that come before, like the steps in a ladder (Figure 1.2).

Motivation

The first step in any process of change is to identify the gap between where we are and where we want to be, that is, the *motivation* to change. *Motivation* derives from having a clear sense of *purpose* about the outcomes we are aiming for and clear *intentions* about the qualities we wish to embody

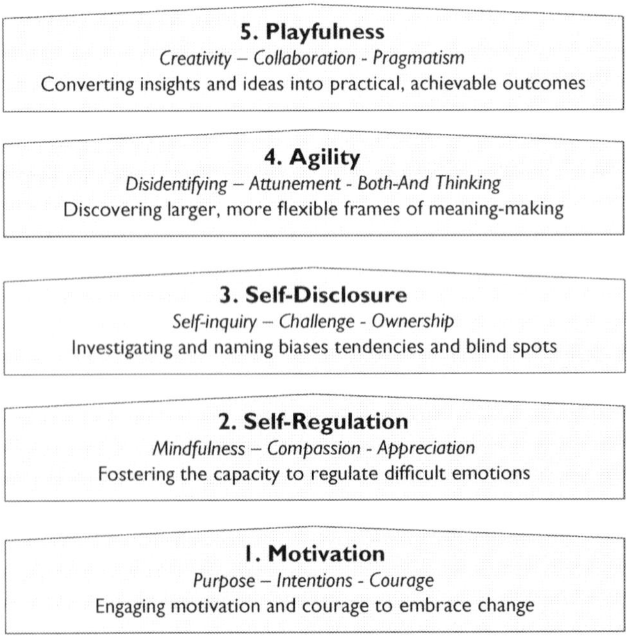

5. Playfulness
Creativity – Collaboration - Pragmatism
Converting insights and ideas into practical, achievable outcomes

4. Agility
Disidentifying – Attunement - Both-And Thinking
Discovering larger, more flexible frames of meaning-making

3. Self-Disclosure
Self-inquiry – Challenge - Ownership
Investigating and naming biases tendencies and blind spots

2. Self-Regulation
Mindfulness – Compassion - Appreciation
Fostering the capacity to regulate difficult emotions

1. Motivation
Purpose – Intentions - Courage
Engaging motivation and courage to embrace change

Figure 1.2 The Ladder of Capabilities for Facilitating *Breakthrough Conversations*.

in our work. This purpose and intentions, if they are concerned with core emotional shifts and insights, will take us outside our comfort zone, and so we also need the *courage* to choose to step towards the unknown.

Self-regulation

The second step is the need for *self-regulation*. Change is difficult to achieve because we are seeking to disrupt embedded habitual (AMBER) or reactive (RED) behaviours, and those behaviours will contain strategies learned early in life to keep difficult emotions at bay. Unpacking relational behaviours tends to bring up vulnerable or difficult emotions, and so we need the self-regulatory capacity to observe and experience these emotions without retreating into our habitual, self-protective strategies. *Mindfulness* practices, including those cultivating *compassion* and *appreciation*, provide a practical set of techniques for enhancing self-regulation. Sustaining *self-regulation*, and so maintaining GREEN/reflective forms of relating lies at the heart of *Breakthrough Conversations*.

Self-disclosure

The third step in this ladder of capabilities is *self-disclosure*. Using *self-inquiry*, we direct our curiosity to our own patterns and tendencies. We *challenge* ourselves to confront our seemingly intrinsic and unquestioned patterns, and rather than blaming our habits or reactions on external circumstances, we take *ownership* for these tendencies, thus reinforcing a sense of agency, and empowering ourselves to make changes.

Agility

The fourth step that emerges from the preceding stages is *agility*, the flexibility and adaptability of mind to embrace different perspectives, *dis-identifying* from one's own fixed viewpoints, and showing *attunement* with the viewpoints of others. When we have this fluidity and agility, we can hold two or more perspectives in mind at the same time and sustain *both-and thinking*. Our meaning-making frames are enlarged, and we have the basis for fostering greater agility in others.

Playfulness

The final step that arises from agility is what I describe as *playfulness*. At this stage we can approach conversations with a genuine sense of *creativity* and *collaboration*, seeking out and valuing contrasting perspectives, and sustaining an openness to new discoveries. There is a quality of flow and ease characteristic of trust. The creative energy at this stage not only gives rise to new ideas or breakthroughs, but is carried forward into identifying *pragmatic* ways to translate ideas into tangible outcomes or next steps.

We might think of these five steps as archetypal stages of human change, whether referring to the development of ourselves as facilitators of change, or as developmental steps we are supporting clients to take. As we shall see, these five steps also correspond directly to those in the *Map of Breakthrough Conversations* (see Figure 4.1).

In addition to reading about this approach and trying out some of the ideas, one of the most effective ways of learning this approach is to go through the experience first-hand: first to experience being coached or supervised from this perspective, individually and as part of a pair, and then being supervised in relation to coaching individuals and pairs. My colleagues and I have used these techniques extensively in face-to-face and online contexts, both with coaches and with clients in organisations. In training coaches and other facilitators, where possible we make use of video-recordings of sessions with clients as a basis for individual and group supervision sessions. These have proved to be especially beneficial learning environments, once people have got over the initial embarrassment of having their work observed by others.

The structure of the book

Following this introductory chapter, Chapters 2, 3 and 4 cover three central, underpinning aspects of the *Breakthrough Conversations* approach. Chapter 2 focuses on the role of body-brain awareness as a fundamental capacity for enhancing self-awareness by distinguishing RED, AMBER and GREEN body-brain states. By teaching clients to attune to their own body-brain states, and learning to switch to more conscious, GREEN states, we support them to experience a more spacious way of being whilst in conversation, whether with themselves or with others. It is the enhanced spaciousness within and between people that gives room for new learning, skilful choice, and the emergence of novel ideas and solutions. Chapter 3 builds on the body-brain awareness discussed in Chapter 2, exploring the concept of awareness more broadly and offering practical tools: the *PACES* framework, the *ACES* worksheet for deconstructing patterns of *Actions*, *Cognitions*, *Emotions* and *Sensations* when relating to others, and also the *Five-Eyed Model of Conversations*. Chapter 4 provides an overview of the five stages of the *Breakthrough Conversations* approach, which is also captured in the *Map of Breakthrough Conversations* together with the corresponding capabilities we are seeking to develop at each stage. I set this approach in the context of a number of other recognised models of conversation from the worlds of negotiation, conflict, couple therapy and mindful communication.

With these three core areas in place, the subsequent chapters describe in detail each of the five stages of the *Breakthrough Conversations* approach.

Chapter 5 focuses on *Preparing the Ground* for conversations, where, in addition to exploring the purpose of coaching, we invite clients to identify their personal intentions. The *Character Compass* is offered as a possible framework for supporting this inquiry. Chapter 6 focuses on *Managing Emotional States* and how we support clients during conversations using the already discussed *RAG* frame and *PACES* model, and introduces the *9-Minute Form* as a structured approach for fostering self-reflection and awareness amidst the conversational experience. Chapter 7 focuses on taking clients towards a deeper self-inquiry by *Loosening Habits and Reactivity*, and I consider four aspects that play a significant role in shaping behaviour, core relational needs, personality, attachment patterns, as well as cultural and social conditioning. Chapter 8 explores how we can use the steadiness and awareness gained at earlier stages to observe conversational experiences from a larger perspective, or, as I describe it, *Seeing the Dance from the Balcony*. I link this stage to the concept of vertical development and suggest that facilitated conversations constellate precisely the conditions that encourage such paradigm shifts in perspective. In the final chapter, *Harnessing Expanded Perspectives*, I discuss how the relative ease and flow emerging from the work at earlier stages supports increased relational creativity, collaboration and translation of new ideas into practical solutions.

Case illustrations

Case studies are included to illustrate the application of the ideas and techniques. These case illustrations are from my own work, the work of colleagues I supervise, or of leaders who have used this approach in coaching team members. The cases are disguised to maintain the confidentiality of clients.

I will end this chapter with an illustrative piece of coaching that combined individual and paired sessions with Neil and Rosa.

Neil and Rosa: Fostering Collaboration between Central and Regional Offices

Neil was responsible for an important region within a multinational business. He had built the success of his region over many years and he had a strong and loyal team. Although highly valued by the organisation, he could be resistant to initiatives or changes imposed by the central office, and he had for some time been allowed more independence than other regions. However, as the business grew there was a need to streamline key processes in order to harness economies of scale, to cut out duplication, to share innovations across the business and to ensure that all regions operated on similar standards. Rosa operated within the corporate headquarters with responsibility for shaping and implementing business processes across the different regions. She had the support of the executive team to drive change in the organisation, but she found herself struggling in trying to engage with Neil. At first, he challenged her remit, emphasising that she did not understand the specific needs of his region. At other times he was slow to respond to her emails or he would cancel prearranged meetings. When she did travel to meet with him in his region, he would quickly pass her on to other team members who did not have the authority to implement the changes she was seeking to make. She felt as though she was being undermined, and that her competence was being called into question. After some time, they were each asked if they would engage in a combination of individual and paired coaching in order to explore how the central and regional offices could operate more collaboratively. They each agreed, and I began with three individual sessions for each of them prior to moving to a blend of individual and paired sessions.

In the individual sessions they each explored their approach to conversations and were open to noticing their body-brain states and its impact on their interactions. Considering the distinction between the four purposes of conversations (see Figure 1.1) they independently identified themselves as operating in the *Transact* domain. They also recognised that they had not managed to set mutually agreed expectations. They were at cross purposes and so were each evoking frustration in the other. Neil acknowledged that he was quickly triggered into a RED body-brain state (see Chapter 2) by Rosa, whom he saw as controlling and as someone who knew little about the subtleties and nuances of doing business in his region. As he talked about some of the interactions with Rosa, her emails, and the way issues had been escalated to senior managers, he became quickly angry. At these times it took a while for him to calm down. We talked about his capacity for self-regulation and he acknowledged that he needed to be better at managing his stress. He had found the sporadic use of a mindfulness app useful and was very open to being guided in some mindful practice and using mindful inquiry as a way of noticing his own body-brain states, and of developing skills to access a calmer, steadier, GREEN state. He was particularly impressed by how, with guidance, a mindful pause could interrupt a dysregulated state. These experiences reassured him about having paired conversations because he was concerned that he would get angry with Rosa and then say something he might regret later.

At first Rosa portrayed herself as resilient and was reluctant to show how upset she was by Neil's lack of co-operation. But as she talked about previous roles, she noted that her driving style had caused waves with some of her colleagues. She also spoke about the difficulties arising from being made redundant in a previous role. She said she wanted to do a good job and if she felt someone was not addressing issues then she would take action. She presented her approach as logical and reasonable and showed relatively little self-awareness about what might be underlying her drive. Like Neil, she found it useful to be introduced to the concept of body-brain awareness and mindful inquiry, and this allowed her to be more emotionally curious. Her habitual, AMBER style was highly transactional and efficient, and to outsiders she could seem tough and resilient. But this polished exterior hid a more fragile side of her. As we explored, it emerged that she had a strong need to be perceived as competent and reliable, and she had a terror of failing. She wanted to make herself indispensable and to minimize the risk of further redundancy. She also realised that she felt caught between the objectives set her by her manager to implement organisation-wide processes, and the need to collaborate with colleagues, such as Neil, who were resistant to these changes and whose influence in the organisation enabled them to challenge already agreed guidelines.

Having prepared the ground in relation to the purpose, intentions and goals of the work in individual sessions, they agreed to a number of paired sessions, interspersed with further individual sessions. A hallmark of the paired work in *Breakthrough Conversations* is to slow down interactions using a structured form (i.e. the 9-Minute Form described in Chapter 6), so that the personal and interpersonal processes can be observed and shared, alongside a discussion of a specific issue or topic. Mindful pauses allowed Neil and Rosa to tune in to their own emotional states as they engaged in conversation with each other. Agreeing that the goal of the paired conversations was to foster productive collaboration in the service of the business, I invited them each, in turn, to speak about their experiences, alongside a noting of the body-brain states (RED/AMBER/GREEN) prior to and after speaking or listening to each other. When Neil spoke or listened he quickly became loud and angry, but, with strong and repeated support from me to pause, to notice what was happening in his body and to describe his body-brain state, he was gradually able to step back from his reactive state and to talk about his deeper emotional experience. Eventually he then talked about how much he valued autonomy in his role. His region was on the other side of the world from the head office and he enjoyed the sense of being in charge of his own area. He felt his independence was being eroded by the changes that Rosa was implementing, and he recognised that he was 'shooting the messenger'. But he also told Rosa that he felt she had not taken time to understand their local challenges and how the new processes would undermine the business.

Rosa listened to Neil and remained calm in the face of his reactivity. She reflected and empathised with Neil's need for independence, but also went on to talk about how she felt misunderstood. Her primary goal was to support the business to succeed, and she believed that there were things that she was offering that would be beneficial to Neil's region, as well as the wider business. Supported by the slower pace of the interactions, and the invitation to tune into her body-brain states, Rosa was also able to talk about her underlying fear of failure, and to acknowledge to Neil that this could drive her to be controlling and interpersonally insensitive. She felt as if people often misinterpreted her approach as trying to undermine them or to take over their roles, whereas she believed she was simply trying to protect herself from being made redundant. Neil found it helpful when she talked about her fear of failure, and her redundancy. These conversations were a turning point, and I noted how they initiated a shift toward a warmer emotional tone and a greater willingness to listen to each other. We dropped the structured, speaker-listener form to the conversations as they went on to identify mutual goals and to explore how they could co-create solutions together.

By managing their body-brain states and sharing personal insights about the emotions and needs underlying their behaviour, Neil and Rosa realised that much of the difficulty in their relationship arose from misunderstandings and implicit projections from other situations. As they listened more to each other, they found themselves more aligned in the challenge of building the business – in terms of the four conversational purposes, they were shifting from the Transact domain to the Collaborate domain. They started to think creatively together about how to harness the great ideas from across the organisation and to explore how to blend flexible, local initiatives with global consistency. They set up a new steering committee with representatives from each region, as well as from Rosa's team, and over time this became a hub of innovation-sharing across the organisation. Supporting Neil and Rosa to deepen their personal and interpersonal awareness through individual and paired sessions allowed them to have a breakthrough in mutual understanding. This in turn led to them having breakthrough ideas about how to address their challenges, and these led to significant achievements within the organisation in terms of the sharing of commercially valuable ideas.

Summary

The *Breakthrough Conversations* approach is designed to facilitate others to deepen their awareness, to gain insights, to strengthen their connection to others and to find creative solutions to challenges. In this approach conversations are viewed as a powerful place to focus our attention, both for understanding the challenges clients face and for accelerating personal and interpersonal development. Distinguishing three types of conversation, RED/reactive, AMBER/habitual and GREEN/reflective, *Breakthrough Conversations* correspond to GREEN conversations, whereas less skilful conversations correspond to RED or ineffective AMBER conversations. By supporting clients to recognise these different states in themselves and others, we support them to enhance their self-awareness and their capacity to engage in more consciously skilful conversations. A further classification differentiates the targets for *Breakthrough Conversations* in terms of four purposes: *Be Social, Transact, Connect,* and *Collaborate*. There is potential for breakthrough in each of these domains, but the more significant developmental shifts occur as a result of the enhanced emotional awareness associated with the *Connect* and *Collaborate* domains.

This approach originates from a pluralistic integration of developmental ideas from psychotherapy, coaching, neuroscience and mindfulness, and has been honed through the pragmatic experience of one-to-one, paired, team and group sessions with managers and coaches. Principles intrinsic to this approach include a focus on conversations as the agent and target of change, an increase in the client's capacity for self-regulation, body-awareness as a basis for self-awareness and the benefits of working with individuals and pairs. The skills required to apply this approach correspond to the capabilities we are seeking to develop in clients and can be represented as a ladder of five, accumulating capabilities: *motivation, self-regulation, self-disclosure, agility,* and *playfulness*.

Worksheet 1: Understanding relational patterns in four domains of conversation

The purpose of this worksheet is to enable clients to distinguish four domains of conversation as a basis for exploring their relational styles and tendencies. It can provide structure during individual or paired sessions, or as part of a workshop, or it can be given to clients to review in their own time. The exercise provides coaches with an initial picture of how clients approach conversations and encourages clients to consider their conversations as a useful focus for inquiry.

Describe the four domains of conversational purpose to clients, using a sketch or copy of Figure 1.1. Then ask clients to respond to the following questions:

Think about the many types of conversations you have in your life and make notes of how each of these examples of your conversations fit into one of the four domains.

For each domain:

1. Identify examples of your conversations that are most effective
2. Identify examples of your conversations that are least effective
3. Which, if any, conversations would be more effective if they shifted to another domain? (E.g. *Transact* conversations that would be more effective if there was a more relational component, represented by the *Collaborate* domain.)
4. In which domains do you feel most and least comfortable, and why?
5. How would others describe your limiting and enabling conversational behaviours? Consider some or all of those shown in Table 1.1.
6. Reviewing your answers to these questions, where, if anywhere, are you most motivated to develop in your approach to conversations?

Chapter 2

Developing a breakthrough body–brain

The cultivation of emotional regulation is fundamental to *Breakthrough Conversations*. When we are emotionally stretched our communications are less likely to be optimal – we will probably adopt either habitual conversational patterns that are expedient, or reactive patterns that are self-protective. But when we are feeling emotionally steady and positive, we will naturally tend to use more thoughtful, reflective conversational patterns. So, in this approach, we are less concerned with identifying the specific words and conversational skills for optimal conversations. Our aim is to support clients to cultivate the capacity to observe and shift emotional states, and to foster those states that naturally generate more collaborative ways of relating. A central technique for observing and managing emotional states is to be attuned to one's body–brain state. Emotions are expressed through the body, and noticing body sensations is one of the most reliable ways of noticing emotions. If we notice a tension in the belly for example, we may come to associate this with worry or frustration. Conversely, if we notice a sense of lightness and ease in the body, we may associate this with relaxation or happiness. For me, one of the routinely amazing discoveries about people, myself included, is that most of the time we are largely unaware of our body sensations. Most people live most of their lives in their heads and so are relatively out of touch with the nuances of their sensations and their emotional states. Learning to pay attention to body sensations is a relatively simple thing to do, and it can provide a refined barometer to the arising and changing nature of emotions. The body is a doorway to emotional awareness, and such awareness is fundamental to skilful relating.

A method I have developed for inviting clients to attend to body sensations that has proved to be very useful is to distinguish three body–brain states, RED, AMBER and GREEN. I already introduced this distinction in the first chapter in relation to three corresponding types of conversation: reactive, habitual and reflective. In this chapter we travel upstream, as it were, to examine the interior body–brain experiences that underlie different conversational patterns. The goal of this chapter is to provide a clear distinction between RED, AMBER and GREEN that enables us, and our clients, to subjectively attune to different body–brain states and the characteristic non-verbal and verbal behaviours that go with those states. This accessible distinction, that on the surface might seem simplistic, is in fact anchored in the synthesis of key discoveries from brain science and neurobiology. Coaches and clients vary in the degree to which they value or are interested in research findings, but in my experience presenting a scientific rationale for attending to body–brain states increases the willingness and commitment from clients to make time for these techniques. It is as if the science can earn us the credibility to take them on an unfamiliar, experiential journey by reducing scepticism and encouraging experimentation. I begin this chapter by describing the human body–brain and the key systems that influence our emotional states, and then show how we can use this research to distinguish three body–brain systems corresponding to three characteristic conversational patterns. I then shift focus to consider how we, and our clients, can learn to observe and distinguish RED, AMBER and GREEN body–brain states: subjectively by attending to body sensations, and objectively by attending to non-verbal and verbal behaviours.

What is the body–brain?

I use the term body–brain to emphasise that the body is not separate from the brain inside the skull. They're both parts of an interdependent whole. Signals from the brain in the head influence the body, and vice versa. By reading body signals we can monitor our own body–brain systems, and this conscious monitoring activates different body–brain networks, which in turn changes the subjective experience of body sensations. Taking this picture of interconnectedness further, Siegel defines the mind as: 'an embodied and relational process that regulates the flow of energy and information'.[1] It is the emphasis on relationship in this definition of mind that is striking, and of key relevance to our focus on conversations. The mind regulates energy and information between the internal milieu of the body and the external context of relationships, each shaping and influencing the other. According to this way of conceiving the mind, conversations are a central conduit for fostering change because they are the software of connection between the body–brain and relationships.

The following overview of body–brain processes gives more detail than what I share with most clients but is included because it is important for coaches to feel comfortable talking about the science underpinning the approach. I describe the skull-based portion of the brain, polyvagal theory, heart-rate variability, and key hormones associated with emotional regulation, and these four elements are then used as indicative ingredients for differentiating the RED, AMBER GREEN body–brain systems underlying conversations.

The skull-based portion of the brain

It is estimated that the skull-based portion of the human brain is made up of more than 80 million brain cells (neurons) with each neuron having connection to perhaps 10,000 other neurons, giving rise to close to one trillion connections. Energy and information travels between neurons through a mixture of electrical and chemical signals. The neuron sends an electrical impulse along its length, which releases a neurotransmitter into the synapse, the space between one neuron and its thousands of connections to other neurons, which then triggers an ongoing flow of electrochemical signals through other neurons. The complex patterns of electrochemical flow cluster together to form functional wholes, movements of energy that come to represent meaningful information. A person's name or the image of a person's face will have a distinct neural representation in the form of energy moving through a complex array of connectivity. Each time we say that name or see that face a similar neural network will be activated.

Neuroplasticity refers to the capacity of neurons to continually form new connections. When we have a new experience, new synaptic connections are formed, and if we rehearse or repeat that experience, a new functional neural network will be created. Consequently, rather than being a static set of connections, the brain is always changing and evolving according to how it is being used. The capacity to learn comes from neuroplasticity, new connections being formed from the energetic encoding of experience, creating a neural network that when accessed leads to the recollection of knowledge or the performing of a skill. Every thought and emotion corresponds to an electrochemical pattern, and when we try to think about something in a new way or seek to relate to our emotions in a different way, these new intentions, thoughts and feelings will create new connections and pathways. Neuroplasticity gives rise to an astonishingly dynamic, adaptable system, marshalling ever changing bundles of information stemming from within and from outside the body.

An important aspect of neuroplasticity is the potential for change to reinforce change. The conscious use of the mind to think warmly about others for instance, will lead to new neural pathways representing the thoughts and feelings associated with warmth. If this mental attitude is repeated and practiced, the pathways will become an established neural network, and that embedded network will in turn enhance and accelerate the immediacy of the experience of warmth. Conversely, if the mind is used routinely to think negative thoughts, the neural networks for negativity will be reinforced. Thus, neuroplasticity is the neural basis for the notion: 'you are what you think'.

Primary structures of the brain

Neuroscientists differentiate different parts of the skull-based portion of the brain according to their anatomical placement in the lower, central and upper areas of the brain. The lower area contains the brainstem and the cranial nerves, and is responsible for such activities as arousal, alertness and, via the pituitary, the physiology of bodily equilibrium. The central area houses the limbic structures responsible for mediating emotions, motivation and the engagement of the attachment system. Two limbic structures, the amygdala and the hippocampus, are particularly relevant to our discussion of human interactions. The amygdala, known as the threat response system, combines with the contextual memory of the hippocampus, to trigger a protective response to perceived threats. It is these triggered, fight or flight behaviours, unchecked by reflection, that often lead to difficulty in conversations. Another important structure in the central area with strong interconnections to both the lower and upper brain regions is the basal ganglia. This structure is key to habit formation and for understanding the challenge of supporting clients to change unhelpful conversational habits to more productive relational styles.

The upper area of the brain contains the cerebral cortex responsible for mediating complex functions such as perception, thinking and reasoning. The prefrontal cortex is considered to be the most advanced and complex part of the cerebral cortex. Sitting behind the forehead, it is responsible for abstract thinking, the directing of attention, and the capacity to make choices. It is the prefrontal cortex that has the potential to modulate limbic reactivity to perceived threat, and fostering its role in conversations is an important ingredient to *Breakthrough Conversations*. Another important structure in the upper area of the brain is the insula. Its many functions include providing a map of body sensations, and so is key in self-awareness, and developing such awareness is also linked to the capacity for empathy.

Polyvagal theory

Polyvagal theory, developed by Stephen Porges,[2] is concerned with our non-conscious evaluation of safety, and the relationship between the Autonomic Nervous System (ANS) and social behaviour. The theory identifies an evolutionarily ordered hierarchy of neural platforms that activate automatically depending on whether we feel safe or in danger. In our evolutionary past, danger would have involved physical threat or a risk to life, and so autonomic systems developed to respond. In the context of present-day conversations, the threat is usually psychological – the potential to experience feelings such as shame, guilt, rejection or the loss of self-esteem. The triggering of these autonomic systems is often disproportionate to the threat posed by the circumstances of a conversation, and, if unchecked by other neural capacities, disrupts conversational effectiveness. Understanding the different components and functions of the polyvagal system gives insight into how social engagement and reactivity manifest differently in the body, and so underpins our approach to reading body–brain systems during conversation. In polyvagal theory there are three main parts of the nervous system, the ventral vagal system responsible for social engagement, the sympathetic system responsible for fight/flight responses, and the dorsal vagal system responsible for freeze or shut-down responses.

Ventral vagal/social engagement

When we experience safety, the nervous system triggers the ventral vagal complex, or the social engagement system. Porges chose the term *social engagement system* because the ventral vagal nerve affects the middle ear, which filters out background noises to make it easier to hear the human voice. It affects facial muscles and thus the ability to make communicative facial expressions. It also affects the larynx and thus vocal tone and vocal patterning, helping humans create sounds that soothe one another. By evoking a calm state that allows us to attune to the voices and gestures of others it sends a message to others that we feel safe, and is more likely to evoke a sense of safety in others. The social engagement system produces an implicit array of bodily signals that evoke trust and connection and is consequently central to fostering *Breakthrough Conversations*.

Sympathetic system/fight-flight

The sympathetic system mobilises us to respond to danger or threat with fight or flight behaviours. The fight mode is underpinned by anger, and so sympathetic activation manifests as aggression, frustration or confrontation. The flight mode is driven by fear, and so sympathetic activation takes the form of running away, escaping or hiding. The face and voice change when the sympathetic system is triggered. The face loses the ability to express warm and positive emotions, the voice loses its natural rhythm and fluctuations, and the auditory system becomes attuned to threatening, low frequency sounds. We can readily recognise conversations dominated by sympathetic system arousal in the form of raised voices, angry gestures or moves to escape the confrontation.

Dorsal vagal system/freeze – shutdown

Our most primitive response is driven by the dorsal vagal system. This system drops our metabolic rate and immobilises the body, plunging us into shutdown and numbness. In the body there is decreased muscle tone or a sense of collapse, reduced cardiac output and alterations in bowel and bladder function. The face may appear impassive or blank, and the tone of the voice can seem flat. In conversation, clients whose dorsal vagus has taken over may appear distant, absent-minded, unresponsive or disengaged, and the way they speak may seem unemotional, robotic or weary. We can also readily observe a shift from sympathetic to dorsal vagal system arousal when someone who is in heated debate suddenly disengages or appears to 'glaze over'.

The dorsal vagal system and PTSD

The dissociation and shutdown of the dorsal vagal system is central to the experience of post-traumatic stress disorder (PTSD). If a person has a history of trauma it is possible they are perceiving threats from within, or from their environment, that are not actually occurring in the here and now. Such confusion between past and present is a common symptom of PTSD. In inviting clients to attend to the body, it is important to watch out for signs of dissociation. These are signals that the client is overwhelmed, and encouraging them to attune to body sensations, feelings and memories can be retraumatising. If we pick up the sense that we may be in the territory of trauma through evidence of dissociation, the key is to go very slowly, and, unless you have clinical training in working with trauma, to shift discussions back to areas of comfort and resourcefulness, and to consider if it is appropriate to refer clients to trauma specialists.

For those who have undergone training in treating trauma, clients are supported to engage the social engagement system, so they can recognise that they are not in imminent danger. This allows them to access the positive, relaxing elements of the parasympathetic nervous system to "rest and digest." For some clients, turning towards a warm connection with another person is enough to activate the vagal brake of social engagement, and so dissolve the impact of a traumatic experience. This is what happens when someone talks to a friend about a frightening incident, such as a car crash or a physical injury. However, more deep-seated trauma, or developmental trauma that arises from childhood experiences, typically requires a more skilled approach that guides clients to move between gradually increasing doses of the traumatic experience and experiences of feeling resourceful, titrating the capacity to be with what is most difficult and so gradually enabling clients to acclimatise and integrate the embodied trauma with awareness and social engagement.[3]

Links between ventral, sympathetic and dorsal systems

The three systems in polyvagal theory operate hierarchically. When the ventral system is dominant, prosocial behaviours and emotional states of trust and connection are most likely to emerge. When the sympathetic system is the primary defence strategy, the social engagement of the ventral system is inhibited and the mobilising strategies of fight/flight come to the fore. If the immobility response of the dorsal system is the defensive strategy, then the active strategies of the ventral or sympathetic systems are inhibited, and the response is to shut down.

The ventral vagal system has other attributes that enable blended states with the sympathetic and dorsal vagal systems, and these attributes are very important for our approach to conversations. If the ventral vagal system remains accessible it can harness the mobilising energy of the sympathetic system, supporting such activities as work, play, sport, art and sex. In the context of conversations, I suggest that the ventral-sympathetic blended state also opens up interactive possibilities such as noticing and communicating about body sensations, naming reactive tendencies and emotions, soothing oneself in the face of activation and finding constructive ways of working through emotionally charged differences. If the immobilising energy of the dorsal system is blended with the social engagement of the ventral vagal system, it supports rest, rejuvenation, sleep and meditation. It is this kind of safe immobilisation that perhaps underlies the ease and intimacy of a shared silence, the capacity to pause and reflect during a conversation, being present for another without having to comment and engaging in mindful dialogue.

Heart rate variability

The third line of research that contributes to our understanding of the body–brain in conversation concerns heart rate variability (HRV).[4] The time interval between consecutive heartbeats is constantly changing, so for example, an average heart rhythm of 70 beats per minute, is actually oscillating up and down, perhaps between 50 and 100 beats per minute. This variation is called heart rate variability, and the pattern of variability has a powerful impact on the coherence of electrical signals sent from the heart to the brain. When we experience stress, such as anger, frustration or anxiety, the HRV pattern is irregular and erratic, and is described as incoherent. If we are feeling calm the pattern of variability is smooth and regular, and is described as coherent. These differences are the result of the relationship between the sympathetic and parasympathetic branches of the autonomic nervous system. When they are out of balance there is incoherence and a low vagal tone, and these correspond with activation of the threat systems of the amygdala and the polyvagal system, and a decreased capacity to manage emotions. When they are in balance there is coherence and a high vagal tone meaning threat systems are less activated and there is a greater capacity to engage socially.[5]

The great value of HRV in coaching is that clients can readily learn how to enhance their HRV coherence by regulating the pace, depth and smoothness of their breathing and by making a conscious choice to evoke and savour positive emotions. Using a biofeedback device attached to ear, finger or chest, they are often amazed to see feedback on their mobile or other device showing increased coherence within 30–60 seconds, and at the same time noticing, subjectively, a sense of feeling calmer and more centred. This practical tool engages even the most sceptical client in recognising the physiological impact of breath, thoughts and emotions, and provides coaches with a tangible rationale for inviting clients to work with other experiential and introspective techniques as part of the *Breakthrough Conversations* approach.

Hormones and emotional regulation

Hormones are the chemical substances produced by the body to control and regulate the activity of cells or organs, and many are active in more than one physiological process. One of the powerful ways that hormones influence conversational effectiveness is through their impact on emotional regulation. Paul Gilbert[6] suggests three emotional regulation systems, each using different hormones. The hormones governing the threat and self-protection system include cortisol and adrenaline, essential for picking up on threats and mobilising for action. These hormones are associated with feelings of anger, anxiety and disgust and so a conversation driven primarily by these hormones is unlikely to lead to breakthrough.

A key hormone in the incentive and resource seeking system is dopamine, which motivates us towards achieving goals and satisfying needs, and gives rise to feelings of wanting, pursuing, achieving and consuming. The motivational aspects of dopamine are important in a conversational context, because clients will only engage in developing their conversational skills if they can see a positive purpose or outcome. However, the goal-focused aspects of dopamine may also be linked to striving for outcomes, and conversations that focus purely on tasks may miss the value of attending to other contextual or relational factors that support collaboration. An important hormone for the soothing, caring and contentment system is oxytocin, which is associated with the experience of trust in relationships. Oxytocin supports us to feel safe and can be a key part of developing the sense of calm connection that underpins skilful interactions.

In the next section I draw together these various aspects of neurobiological research to characterise three subjectively experienced and scientifically informed body–brain systems underpinning conversations as a basis for supporting clients to assess and manage their own body–brain states.

Three body–brain systems

In distinguishing three body–brain systems – reactive, habitual, and reflective (RED, AMBER, GREEN) – we provide clients with a diagnostic lens for understanding their own emotional states during conversations, and for attuning to the emotional states of others (Figure 2.1). I link the neurobiological research described above to each of these systems and outline the capacities and limits of each system in terms of conversations. In offering this three-system characterisation I do not wish to imply that our scientific understanding offers a literal mapping from brain structure to behaviour. Instead I view this kind of extrapolation from the science as providing a useful indicative picture for testing against subjective experience.

The RED/reactive system

The RED/reactive system refers to how the body–brain is activated in response to situations that are perceived to be threatening. As discussed above, the reactive, threat system evolved as a survival mechanism in relation to life threats. It is designed to keep us alive. However, in humans in the 21st century this same system is triggered by our perception of psychological threats, and readily arises in conversational contexts. The survival circuitry of the human body–brain includes aspects of all of the four interacting systems described above: the brainstem, the limbic area, the endocrine (hormone) system, the polyvagal system and the changes in the variability of the heartbeat. The limbic area works in concert with the brainstem to create our drives and emotions. It tells us if an experience feels good or bad, and triggers corresponding emotional responses, including our instant sense of liking or not liking someone based on a non-conscious matching with previous experiences.

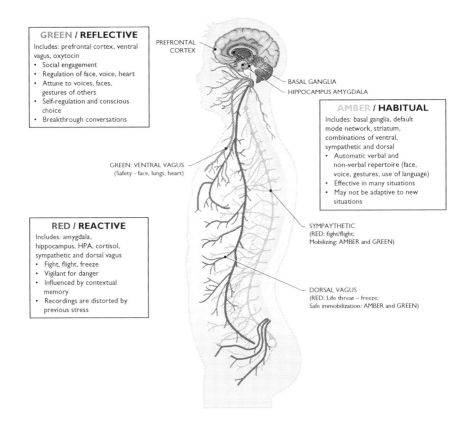

Figure 2.1 Three body–brain Systems Shape Conversations.

The limbic system contains the almond-shaped amygdala, which is important in triggering a fear response. This response activates the hippocampus, which acts like a recording machine, converting moment-to-moment experiences into memories. Scientists characterize the amygdala and hippocampus working together, the amygdala registering a potential threat, and then linking with the memory banks of the hippocampus to determine if the current situation matches with a previous experience of threat. It is the amygdala and hippocampus that might trigger our instant reactivity to a tone of voice, a gesture or a specific set of words, even though we may not consciously connect those behaviours with a previous situation that was threatening.

The amygdala and hippocampus trigger the endocrine system through the HPA (hypothalamus-pituitary-adrenal) stress response. The hypothalamus in the limbic area triggers the pituitary gland to release a hormone, which in turn triggers the adrenal glands above the kidneys to release the stress hormones adrenaline and cortisol into the blood. These hormones mobilise energy by putting the entire metabolic system onto high alert to meet whatever challenge it faces. These reactive responses operate in concert with the polyvagal system, shutting down the social engagement system and triggering sympathetic, flight-flight behaviours or dorsal, freeze behaviours. Vagal tone is reduced, corresponding to irregular changes in heart rhythm, a more irregular breathing pattern, a tightening of the muscles around the eyes and mouth, and reduced tonal modulation of the voice. It is this reactive state that often drives less productive conversations.

The RED system in conversation

In conversation, the reactive system assesses for social threats: indications that we may be undermined in some way. It will trigger, for example, if there is a perceived threat to status, self-esteem, recognition, autonomy, certainty, fairness, goal achievement] or a clash with personal values. The key word is 'perceived'. Each person's valency for being triggered depends on their unique blend of innate tendencies and lifetime experiences. The contextual memory of the hippocampus is key to predicting outcomes from past experience and reacts accordingly.

The RED system is useful in the sense that it signals safety concerns. Interpersonally, it alerts us to a sense of our boundaries being crossed or of being taken advantage of. Reactivity can also communicate personal investment; we don't react about things we don't care about. However, as I describe below, harnessing the benefits of reactivity within conversations, and not letting the reactivity lead to clashes or avoidance, means engaging the reflective body-brain system. In many conversations, reactivity limits conversational effectiveness. It sacrifices a relational approach to solving problems in order to protect the self. It tends to evoke a win-lose dynamic, and so undermines trust and collaboration. Learning to manage the RED system during conversation lies at the heart of the *Breakthrough Conversations* approach.

The AMBER/habit system

Much of human behaviour becomes automated through the development of habits, and this is as true for conversational styles as it is for other repeated and routine aspects of our lives. Neuroscientists trace habit-making behaviours to a part of the brain called the basal ganglia, which also plays a key role in the development of emotions, memories and pattern recognition.[7]

Undertaking new behaviours requires the involvement of the executive functions of the prefrontal cortex, but as soon as a behaviour becomes automatic, activity in the decision-making parts of the brain is reduced. The great evolutionary advantage of habits is that they leave the conscious processing parts of the brain available for handling new challenges and solving problems in fresh ways. In many situations habits are invaluable shortcuts that reduce the need for conscious processing.

Habits are governed by a three-part habit loop, a cue, a routine and a reward. The cue triggers the habit, which can be a mental, emotional or physical routine, and then the reward tells the brain if this loop is worth repeating in the future. For example, in the interpersonal domain, the cue might be seeing someone's face, which triggers a routine of smiling warmly in greeting, and then the reward is seeing the other person smile back in response. The habit of smiling is sustained and useful because it tends to evoke collaboration. Or, the cue might be hearing a critical comment from someone, which triggers the routine of expressing one's views more forcefully, followed by the reward of the other person backing off or moderating their view. In some circumstances this kind of habit may be useful. But, in other circumstances the habit may lead to conflict and a lack of collaboration. The automatic behaviour, unmoderated by the conscious activity of the prefrontal cortex and the social engagement of the ventral vagal, might in fact trigger the fight/flight reactivity of the other person, and this could lead to conflict or impasse. The development challenge presented by habits is that once they are learned and embedded it can be difficult to change them, as most of us know from trying to cut down on our favourite foods or trying to follow a new fitness regime. Many clients in coaching have no, or only partial awareness, of the limitations of their conversational habits. The widespread use of 360° feedback for managers in organisations is one way that clients can learn about the impact of their relational habits that otherwise might remain out of awareness. The coach's role is to highlight which conversational habits are potentially enabling or limiting. Through this awareness, he or she will be able to support the development of new habit loops with more enabling conversational routines.

The AMBER system in conversation

In the conversational domain most of us don't realise how much of our interactive styles are governed by habits encoded into the basal ganglia and its numerous associated neural pathways, electrical and chemical, extending throughout the body–brain. The habit system gives rise to automatic patterns of talking, listening and questioning, and will be accompanied by a rich non-verbal repertoire of facial expressions and gestures, characteristic use of the voice in terms of tone, pace, pitch, cadence and volume, and the use of language will have characteristic patterns of vocabulary, phrasing and sense-making.

The great benefit of the habit system in conversation is that it allows for fast interactions, it frees up the brain for conscious mental processing, and is effective for many types of conversation. However, its limits are that it is not adaptable to new situations because there is little conscious processing to assess if a different interactive style might be more effective. It is also relatively blind to complexity and the emotional dimension of interactions, it may trigger the reactive system in others and it is less likely to support shared creativity.

The GREEN/reflective system

The GREEN/reflective system refers to the matrix of body–brain systems that allow us to engage our capacities for conscious reflection, judgement and decision-making. These include the activity of the prefrontal cortex working in concert with the social engagement of the ventral vagal system, the calming and regulating hormones of the endocrine system, and the reinforcing feedback evoked by heart rate variability coherence. The GREEN system supports *Breakthrough Conversations* by its capacity to modify the AMBER and RED systems. Conscious choice allows clients to take a mental step back and to review the impact of their behaviour, and so provides the pivotal foundation for making more skilful choices. One of the ways in which we support clients to engage the reflective system is to tune into their body sensations. Directing awareness in this way uses the part of the cortex called the insula, which is also key in self-awareness and empathy.[8]

The GREEN system in conversation

When the reflective system is engaged in conversations it slows down interactions, allowing both parties time to attune to a wide array of internal and external stimuli, such as body sensations, feelings, thoughts, facial expressions, tone and pace of the voice, the words being spoken, the nuances of meaning, the purpose of the conversation and the contextual factors driving the conversation. It is by attending to the richness of factors underlying the emerging quality of the conversation that clients gain insight into their tendencies. The reflective system deepens self-awareness and mutual understanding, it reveals habitual and reactive patterns and fosters attunement.

However, it is unrealistic to expect all of our conversations to be underpinned by the dominance of the GREEN system. The need to process experience means that it works more slowly than the habit or reactive systems, and its operation uses up mental resources. It can also seem indulgent to clients who want to focus on tasks and make quick decisions. A further challenge of the GREEN system is that the practices required to develop it are unfamiliar to many clients and coaches. Clients can respond with scepticism, and coaches can feel uncomfortable being sufficiently directive. But, if the scientific rationale for the approach is complemented by techniques that are accessible, clients quickly feel empowered, and are often impressed by their own insights. In the next section I turn to how we support clients to attune to their body–brain systems in conversation, and how these acts of awareness are, in and of themselves, ways of engaging the GREEN system.

Diagnosing body–brain states

Our goal in diagnosing body–brain states is two-fold: one, for clients to attune to their own body–brain states and two, to pick up clues about the body–brain states in others. There are three primary sources of information that we, and our clients, are aiming to attend to: body sensations, non-verbal behaviours and verbal behaviours. Clearly, body sensations occur inside the body and so are only available to subjective awareness. By directing clients to attend to their body sensations and asking them to describe how patterns of sensations are changing, we support them to bring curiosity to this domain of experience. Unlike sensations, non-verbal and verbal behaviours can be observed, whether noticing our own behaviour, or that of others. So, in coaching clients we are also encouraging a noticing of behaviour, non-verbal and verbal, whether one's own, or of others.

I describe the indicative sensations and behaviours, non-verbal and verbal, that signify RED, AMBER and GREEN (*RAG*) body–brain states, and Figure 2.2 provides a summary of these indicators. In my experience clients usually find this figure, together with Figure 2.1. extremely useful, and they can be used with Worksheet 2 at the end of this chapter as a basis for creating their own, personalised summary of their subjective experience of RED, AMBER and GREEN states and the impact these have on their conversational tendencies. I would note that this frame is as useful for coaches in their own self-reflection, as it is for their clients. The more we, as facilitators, can recognise our own body–brain states, the more we are able to access our own GREEN states and so provide a more steady, reflective environment for our clients.

Signifiers of the RED body–brain system

Clients can readily attune to the notion of the RED body–brain system by bringing to mind a challenging relationship or conversation, and then

Developing a breakthrough body–brain 39

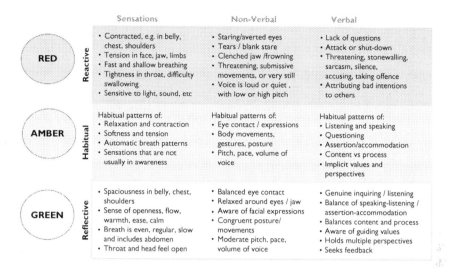

Figure 2.2 Diagnosing RAG body–brain States.

noticing the associated interior body sensations. Also, with the support of the coach, they can notice their characteristic non-verbal or verbal behaviours when in RED.

RED body sensations

Most people are unfamiliar with attending to body sensations, and in particular, interoception,[9] which refers to attending to the body sensations coming from inside the body. In the next chapter I talk about how we can use mindfulness practices to support clients to cultivate this dimension of awareness. At this stage, it is useful to show clients an indicative list of interior sensations, and to ask them to turn their attention internally to see what, if any, resonate with their subjective experience when describing or having a difficult conversation:

- Contracted; tightness in the belly, chest, shoulders, or other parts of the body
- Tension in hands, limbs, face, jaw, mouth, …
- Sensations in the head: pounding, heavy, tight, muddled, whirring,…
- Sensations of breathing: shallow, fast, short, uneven,…
- Sensations in the throat: strangled, blocked, hard to swallow,…
- Sensitivity to light, sound, physical pressure or touch,…

Invited to attune inwards in this way, and with a checklist as a prompt, clients readily identify some of the body signals listed above, and so begin to develop a subjective anchor for recognising the Red body–brain state.

RED non-verbal signals

When observing others, and possibly ourselves, during conversation, there are many non-verbal signals we can attend to, including the eyes, face, body movements, postures, physiology and voice. When a person is in RED, characteristic non-verbal signals include:

- Eyes: staring, frequent blinking, averted eyes, looking down, narrowed eyes, tears
- Face: biting lips, frozen expression, knitted eyebrows, gritted teeth, clenched jaw, frowning, continuous smiling
- Movements: pointing, wagging finger, restlessness, immobility, sharp movements, foot tapping, tapping fingers, bouncing feet, clasped hands or fists, self-hugging, biting fingernails, twirling hair, covering mouth, submissive palms, turning away, shaking head, distracted
- Posture: Slouching, rigid, arms crossed, slumped head, crossing legs, face turned away
- Physiology: Increased heart rate, sweating, fast and shallow breathing, tense eye muscles, tense jaw muscles, gulping, reddened face/neck, hair raising on back of neck, yawning, dry mouth, spittle at corners of mouth, physical tension
- Voice: monotone, faster or slower pace, high or lower pitch, menacing or appeasing tone, loud or soft, reduced prosody/modulation

RED verbal signals

In attending to verbal signals of body–brain states I consider seven categories, questioning, speaking/listening, assertion/accommodation, content/process, interpersonal values, viewpoints and attitude to feedback. Some of the characteristic verbal signals of a RED/reactive body–brain state are as follows:

- Questioning: little or no questioning; questions used as a form of attack or control: e.g. *'how do you expect me to trust you if...?'* or *'so, do you agree that this was a mistake?'*
- Assertion/Accommodation: either a bias towards assertiveness or towards being accommodating; emphasis on areas of disagreement, communicated as global statements: *'you never'*, or *'you always'*. Assertion takes the form of fight behaviours such as blaming, shaming, attack, dismissiveness, undermining humour, cynicism, complaining,

interrupting, and threatening. Accommodation takes the form of flight behaviours in the form of opting out, agreeing, compliance, colluding, approval seeking, appeasing. Disengagement indicates freeze behaviours such as being overly quiet, silent, still, frozen or shutdown.
- Content/Process: focusing exclusively on content and outcomes, with little capacity to step back and to notice the process and the emotional tone
- Interpersonal values: usual personal standards of respect and kindness may be overshadowed by self-protective strategies: point scoring, belittling, dismissing, teasing, bullying,...
- Viewpoints: unable to see things from another's perspective and remaining fixed to one perspective
- Use of feedback: closed to receiving feedback but may deliver critical feedback

Signifiers of the AMBER body–brain system

Inviting clients to attune to their AMBER body–brain-system is more challenging than it is for the RED system because habits vary from person to person much more than reactive tendencies, and because these states are so automatic their characteristic patterns sit outside of awareness. Consequently, the following descriptions of sensations, non-verbal signals and verbal signals emphasise the need to bring an attitude of curiosity to what is most automatic when in conversation:

AMBER body sensations

- Characteristic patterns of tension and relaxation in the body when engaged in routine, non-conflictual conversations
- Some clients will come to see that they routinely hold tension when in conversation, perhaps in the belly, chest or shoulders. This is not so much a consequence of a present moment triggering of the reactive system, but rather an automatic, embedded pattern that they bring to the conversational context.

AMBER non-verbal signals

- Automatic patterns of facial expressions, eye contact, body gestures, postures, physiological signals such as breathing and swallowing, and the use of the voice in terms of pace, pitch, tone volume and rhythm
- It is helpful for clients to compare self-observation with their observation of others in relation to non-verbal signals in order to discern what is similar or different in their characteristic ways of relating, and, subsequently, to consider the impact of these habits on the conversational context.

AMBER verbal signals

- Questioning: automatic bias, often towards too few questions, with insufficient probing, clarifying, and summarising. Conversely the bias can be towards asking too many questions, so that a conversation can feel like an interrogation.
- Speaking/Listening: often an automatic bias towards doing either more speaking or more listening, without awareness of the impact of this on the conversation
- Assertion/Accommodation: automatic bias towards either assertion or accommodation, without awareness of the impact
- Content/Process: automatic bias towards either content or process, without awareness of the impact
- Interpersonal values: may have underpinning guiding interpersonal values (e.g. integrity respect, fairness), but these are implicit and not open to consideration and review
- Viewpoints: unquestioned automatic tendency, perhaps holding a single viewpoint strongly, or routinely brokering between multiple viewpoints, but a lack of adaptability to choose when to be definite and when to be consultative
- Use of feedback: habitual tendencies in relation to giving and receiving feedback, but without conscious reflection in different situations about if, when, with whom, and how feedback can be best used

Signifiers of the GREEN/reflective body–brain system

The GREEN body–brain state is fundamental to *Breakthrough Conversations*. Clients in GREEN can take a mental step back, observe themselves and others, and so be consciously reflective, rather than operating habitually or reactively. By learning to distinguish body–brain states, and by developing techniques for shifting from RED or AMBER states to GREEN states, clients have a powerful tool for engaging in more skilful conversations. One of the great benefits of inviting clients to differentiate body–brain states is that to do so they must use their conscious awareness. To attune to themselves, or to diagnose the state in another person, clients need to engage the discerning faculties of their prefrontal cortex. They need to enlist such cortical structures as their insula to notice body sensations or to empathise with others. In short, they need to use their GREEN body–brain system to notice which of the *RAG* states is most dominant. The act of inquiring evokes the very state we are seeking to foster in the service of *Breakthrough Conversations*.

An outline of some of the body sensations, and non-verbal and verbal behaviours characteristic of the GREEN body–brain system follow:

GREEN body sensations

- Spaciousness in belly, chest, across shoulders, or other parts of the body
- A sense of openness, flow, settledness, calmness, ease, warmth, relaxation
- Body feels steady, grounded, anchored, present
- The ever-changing patterns of sensations can be noticed with curiosity
- Breath is even, regular, slow, and includes abdomen as well as chest
- Head and throat feel free and open

GREEN non-verbal signals

- Eyes: relaxed muscles around the eyes, comfortable eye contact
- Face: expressions are empathic, mirroring the emotional content of communications
- Movements and posture: gestures, head, and body movements and body postures are congruent with the content of interactions whether speaking or listening; such posture choices as sitting forward or sitting back can be used consciously to moderate the intensity of an interaction
- Physiology: breath is even and regular, the facial colour is neutral, the muscles around eyes and jaw are relaxed, the heart rate is regular and coherent
- Voice: the tone, modulation, pace, pitch and rhythm match the content of interactions, and can be consciously used to moderate the body–brain state of others

GREEN verbal signals

- Questioning: Demonstrate curiosity, asking probing questions to deepen understanding, clarifying questions, and summarising back what has been heard
- Speaking/Listening: Aware of the balance of speaking and listening in a conversation, and depending on circumstances, may choose to aim for an equal proportion for each person, taking time to express one's position, and taking time to draw out the position of the other person
- Assertion/Accommodation: Flexible in the use of assertion and accommodation, and can maintain a balance even if the conversation becomes challenging or conflictual
- Content/Process: Able to move between observations about process, e.g. *'we seem to be expressing quite different points of view – shall we take some time to explore each of our perspectives?'*, and content, e.g. *'this is what I think we should do'*

- Interpersonal values: Aware of explicit guiding values for engaging in conversations (e.g. integrity, respect, fairness, equality etc.) and use these consciously to avert reactive tendencies
- Viewpoints: Able to hold and value more than one, potentially opposing, perspectives about an issue. Actively seeks out different perspectives as a basis for seeing different views
- Use of feedback: Actively seeks out feedback from others to enrich awareness, receives feedback that is offered with curiosity, and finds the courage and skill to give feedback to others

By supporting clients to bring attention to their body–brain states, and in particular, to notice how their body–brain states are impacted by different conversational contexts, they increase their interactive awareness. By recognising and distinguishing RED, AMBER and GREEN body–brain states they become observers of their subjective experience, and this observational capacity initiates and strengthens GREEN states. The strengthening of reflection, and the triggering of the social engagement system provides an important foundation for engaging in more productive conversations with others.

I will finish this chapter with a case study. Rather than showing the use of the *RAG* frame by a coach, I will share a case of its use by a manager working with two of her team members. I am including this to emphasise the accessibility of this model and how, with some support, it can be readily assimilated by clients not only for themselves, but also for supporting their colleagues.

Julia, Lucy and Amir: A Team Leader Facilitates Two Team Members

Two of the people in Julia's senior team, Lucy and Amir, had for some time had a distant and strained relationship. Although effective with routine work, non-routine issues caused friction and disruption between them. Lucy would approach challenges with urgency, proactively suggesting bold solutions. Amir took a more measured and pragmatic approach, preferring smaller incremental changes. She felt frustrated with what she saw as his downbeat and sceptical stance, and his tendency to belittle colleagues. He felt frustrated with what he saw as her tendency to dramatise issues, and her failure to deal with performance issues in her own team.

In the past Julia, as team leader, had needed to step in to resolve issues that involved both Lucy's and Amir's area, but as her role expanded and she was required to travel to other geographies, she needed all her team members to be better at resolving their differences themselves. Having experienced the RED, AMBER, GREEN (*RAG*) model in one-to-one coaching, and then sponsoring a *Breakthrough Conversations* workshop with her team, Julia decided to use this frame to explore the relationship between Lucy and Amir. Julia spoke to each of them individually first, preparing them for paired conversations (see Chapter 5), and reminding them of the *RAG* frame. During the workshop they had each completed their own personalised summary *RAG* sheet, based on Figure 2.2. She asked them to look at those summaries and to consider the body–brain systems that governed their interactions, Amir's with Lucy, and Lucy's with Amir. Independently, they acknowledged that they operated in AMBER states for many of the more routine interactions with each other, but that they were triggered into RED states when more challenging issues arose that they needed to address together.

In a paired session with Lucy and Amir, Julia used Figure 2.1 to remind them of the scientific background to the *RAG* body–brain systems, and then asked them each to talk about their personal experience of these states. Lucy's AMBER was characterised by a tendency to talk more than 50 per cent of the time, to use self-deprecating humour, and to look for connections that blended the business-like and warm-heartedness. But when she was triggered into RED, as occurred with Amir, she noticed she became tight in the belly, tended to lean forward, gesticulate more, speak more, interrupt more, and Julia also commented on how Lucy's gaze had a staring intensity as she looked at Amir, trying to get through to him.

Amir, with Julia's support, acknowledged that his AMBER style with Lucy was to be flippant and distracted, with a facial expression that moved between bland and mildly amused, and he discovered that he had almost no awareness of his body sensations. When Amir was more triggered in his RED state, Julia pointed out how he turned his body away from Lucy, looked out of the window, gave no eye contact, and, if he spoke, it was monotonous and elliptical (i.e. hard to follow). Invited to notice his own body sensations, he realised that in a RED state he was numb and shutdown and described himself as having left the room.

Unpacking the way these evolutionarily driven body–brain states manifested with each other was a valuable turning-point for Lucy and Amir. As Lucy made the conscious choice to be reflective, she shifted to a GREEN state: she relaxed in her body, sat back in her chair, stopped gesticulating so much, asked more questions, listened to the answers without interrupting, spoke in a slower, more gentle tone and

> allowed more spaces for silence. Julia also noticed that Lucy's gaze was less intense and the muscles around her eyes and jaw were more relaxed. For Amir, just pointing out that he had been turning away from Lucy led to him turning towards her and meeting her gaze. He noticed that as he moved into GREEN, he listened to Lucy's comments more actively, feeling more curious than defensive. Although still unfamiliar with the idea of describing body sensations, he did notice a broader sense of being open and wanting to find a constructive way forward with Lucy. This and following sessions marked a shift in the relationship between Lucy and Amir. Supported by Julia's facilitation, Lucy and Amir gained invaluable insights into their relational tendencies and found more conscious ways of working collaboratively. I pick up this case again in Chapter 7 to illustrate the use of personality profiles as a further avenue for enhancing mutual understanding and collaboration.

The *RAG* approach to identifying body–brain states has the virtue of identifying relational patterns, without judging them. RED and AMBER states are normalised as intrinsic parts of our human makeup. As occurred with Lucy and Amir, when invited to explore these aspects of personal and interpersonal experience, clients can be supported to engage the curiosity and openness of their GREEN states, and so open the door to fresh understandings of self and others, and how they can relate more skilfully.

Summary

A primary aim in *Breakthrough Conversations* is to support clients to recognise and regulate their emotions. Attending to body–brain states provides a powerful technique for identifying and managing emotions and for enhancing self-awareness. Opening up this terrain of interior subjectivity also paves the way for fostering greater curiosity about the emotional states underpinning the behaviour of others. Drawing on key areas of brain science – differentiations in the key structures of the brain, polyvagal theory, heart rate variability, and an understanding of the hormones associated with different emotional states – I propose a distinction between three body–brain systems: the RED, AMBER and GREEN systems. These systems underpin three characteristic patterns of relating to others, and they shape whether conversations are productive or unproductive. By recognising these different body–brain states, clients can become more self-aware. Using a combination of guided reflection and indicative clues from body sensations, and non-verbal and verbal behaviours, clients can be supported to recognise *RAG* states in themselves and others. The very act of inviting clients to observe and discriminate experiences in terms of the *RAG* categories requires conscious intention, implicitly activating the GREEN/reflective system, and so in itself plays a part in fostering the basis for *Breakthrough Conversations*. In this chapter the focus has been on the development of body–brain awareness. In the next chapter I expand this investigation of awareness beyond the body–brain to other domains of experience that impact conversational effectiveness.

Worksheet 2: Identifying body–brain states

The purpose of this worksheet is to support clients to identify and distinguish their subjective experience of RED, AMBER and GREEN states, as they imagine, or undertake, different kinds of conversation. It can be used in individual sessions, paired sessions, as part of a workshop, or given to clients to review in their own time.

Begin by introducing the three body–brain systems to clients, using diagrams, written descriptions and verbal descriptions, as you prefer. Then explain that learning to recognise one's own body–brain state is invaluable in managing oneself skilfully during conversations, and so this exercise is designed to make a detailed diagnosis of their experience of three body–brain states: RED/reactive, AMBER/habitual and GREEN/reflective. Show clients a copy of Figure 2.2 (possibly also referring to Figure 2.1) and provide a blank template for them to complete during the exercise. Then follow the process as described below.

1. Take a moment now to ground yourself in the present moment, bringing awareness to your posture... the contact your feet are making with the floor... and where your body is in contact with your chair. Become aware of the movement of your breath, perhaps in your belly. (At the outset take as long as is required to support clients to settle into the exercise.)
2. Now bring to mind a recent conversation that was difficult or challenging, and in which you felt quite triggered – in which the RED body–brain system is activated. Bring an image of the person and the situation to mind, and remind yourself about some of the things that were said, and the ways in which you felt most triggered. Holding this difficult conversation in mind, what sensations in your body are associated with this experience of difficulty? In particular be curious about areas of tightness or contraction, perhaps in the belly, chest, or around the muscles in the face. Take your time to tune into your own experience. Now, turn your attention to your behaviour when you are in

this RED state. (Refer to the indicative behaviours in Figure 2.2).

An alternative approach is to ask clients to role play a difficult conversation with the coach playing the other person. The advantage of a role play is that the coach can feed back their own observations about non-verbal and verbal behaviours when clients are in RED.

The client or the coach captures the identified sensations, non-verbal and verbal behaviours on the blank template.

3. Repeat step 2, this time asking clients to bring to mind a warm, trusting and connected conversation to draw out a description of the characteristics of the GREEN body–brain state, and then repeat this step for a routine, everyday, practical conversation, to draw out typical characteristics of the AMBER body–brain state. The AMBER state is often the hardest for clients to recognise because it is so automatic to them, and so coach's need to be prepared to offer their own observations about common behaviours and their impact. (Chapter 7 describes how psychometric instruments and a consideration of attachment patterns can also shed light on indicative, habitual behaviours.) Colleague feedback processes can also be a useful source of information about the perception others have of indicative conversational styles.
4. Invite clients to reflect in their own time on their completed summary of body–brain states adding new characteristics when they observe them. Some clients choose to share their summary with a partner, colleague or friends, and ask for feedback about what others perceive during difficult, routine and flowing conversations.

Notes

1 Siegel, D. (2010). *Mindsight. Transform your brain with the new science of kindness.* Oneworld, p. 52.
2 Porges, S. (2009, February). The polyvagal theory: New insights into adaptive reactions of the autonomic nervous system. *Cleveland Clinic Journal of Medicine*, 76(4, suppl. 2), S86–S90.
3 Levine, P.A. (2010). *In an unspoken voice. How the body releases trauma and restores goodness.* North Atlantic Books, Chapter 5, pp. 73–95.
4 Childre, D., Martin, H. (2000). *The HeartMath solution: The Institute of HeartMath's Revolutionary Program for Engaging the Power of the Heart's Intelligence.* HarperOne.
5 Sakaki, M., Joo Yoo, H., Nga, L., Lee, T.H., Thayer, J.F., Mather, M. (2016, October 1). Heart rate variability is associated with amygdala functional connectivity with MPFC across younger and older adults. *Neuroimage*, 139, 44–52.
6 Gilbert, P. (2010). *Compassion focused therapy: Distinctive features.* Routledge, p. 43.
7 Duhigg, C. (2012). *The power of habit: Why we do what we do in life and business.* Random House.

8 Singer, T., Critchley, H.D., Preuschoff, K. (2009, August). A common role of insula in feelings, empathy and uncertainty. *Trends in Cognitive Sciences*, 13(8), 334–340.
9 Self-regulation is proposed to be dependent on the accuracy with which we interpret and respond to interoceptive information, with greater accuracy leading to enhanced adaptability and self-regulation. Farb, N., Daubenmier, J., Price, C.J., Gard, T., Kerr, C., Dunn, B.D., et al. (2015). Interoception, contemplative practice and health. *Frontiers in Psychology*, 6, 763.

Chapter 3

Awareness is the key to breakthrough

Understanding the nature of awareness and how it can be directed is central to *Breakthrough Conversations*. Awareness gives us the freedom to make choices. Without awareness, conversations will be driven by our habit or reactivity. In the last chapter I introduced the *RAG* (RED, AMBER, GREEN) frame to support clients to bring awareness to different body–brain systems underlying conversations. In this chapter I introduce two further models for enhancing conversational awareness, the *PACES* (*Pause, Actions, Cognitions, Emotions, Sensations*) framework for deconstructing experience, and the *Five-Eyed Model of Conversations*. These models have emerged from my life-long relationship with mindfulness practice, and the desire to provide clients with accessible methods to be more reflective, even though they don't usually practice mindfulness themselves. I begin the chapter with a theoretical discussion about the nature of awareness, drawing on the mindfulness literature. I distinguish awareness from thinking, highlight the importance of being able to take an observer perspective and discuss the role of self-awareness on self-identity. If you are less drawn to these more theoretical considerations, then you may prefer to jump forward to the second half of the chapter, where I introduce the two practical models, the *PACES* framework and the *Five-Eyed Model of Conversations*. I use a case study to illustrate the practical application of these models. Finally, Worksheet 3 at the end of the chapter shows how we can usefully bring together insights emerging from the *RAG* and the *PACES* frameworks thus providing clients with a powerful encapsulation of their conversational tendencies.

What is awareness?

Awareness is the capacity to know. There is an infinite array of things we can know and so awareness is necessarily selective, guided by the focus of attention. In most conversations, awareness is focused on the content of what is being said or heard, but there is potential to attend to a much broader range of inputs. I have already discussed how habitual (AMBER) and reactive (RED) behaviours occur largely outside conscious awareness and so limit conversational adaptability. But, with awareness, provided by the GREEN/reflective body–brain system, there is the possibility to learn, to adapt and to make skilful choices. So, supporting clients to enhance their use of awareness is central.

It is tempting to believe that we are in charge of our awareness, but evidence suggests that, without mental effort, much of the time our minds are running automatic routines. Neuroscience has found that the human brain has a default mode network, a network of interacting brain regions that are most commonly active during passive rest, perhaps when we are daydreaming, remembering the past, imagining the future, recollecting events about one's self, or making social evaluations of things being good or bad.[1] Although research into this default state is still emerging[2] the notion that the mind can be busy with thoughts without our conscious intention fits with our subjective experience. If we pause to notice how our minds are occupied, we might notice ourselves ruminating about something that has happened, rehearsing something we wished we had said, comparing ourselves to others or planning our next holiday. The tendency to ruminate is a contributing factor in stress and depression, and the preoccupation with what others might think about us can make us shy or overbearing. A lack of awareness impacts how we relate to ourselves and to others.

Awareness and thinking are not the same

Thinking is the dominant mental experience for human beings. From the moment we wake up in the morning our minds are busy with thinking, whether it is consciously directed thinking, or the more automatic mental activity associated with the default mode network. The problem with thinking is that most people believe what they think. Thoughts feel like facts. When clients describe their view of colleagues or friends or partners, they believe what they say to be true. *'She is a good team leader'*. *'He is good with numbers'*. *'She is disorganised'*. *'He is dismissive'*. Packed into such statements are a host of perceptual biases: the impact of past experience, personality preferences, cultural assumptions, and so on. If we or our clients believe these judgments to be the truth, conversations are shaped accordingly. Habitual or reactive ways of relating click into operation, driven by automatic thoughts. But if we can take a step back to observe how our thinking is driving our behaviour, then we may make different choices.

In discussing the value of observing thoughts, it is important to draw a distinction between cognitive behavioural approaches that seek to replace limiting thoughts with more enabling thoughts, and a mindful approach that supports a stepping back into the experience of awareness itself. This is in done in order to observe all thoughts from a position of neutral curiosity. Both of these approaches are useful, but clients are usually much more familiar with the idea of doing something, rather than simply observing experience. Fostering our awareness of thoughts, whatever they are, can seem passive in comparison to choosing actively to have more positive thoughts. So, it is useful to distinguish these two modes of relating to thoughts, and to invite clients to experience the power of both. The mindfulness mode brings curiosity, receptivity and spaciousness and, by itself, can give rise to profound shifts in perspective. The cognitive mode helps clients to shift from limiting to enabling thoughts and can help them to reframe challenges and feel more resourced. These mindfulness and cognitive modes are often used in tandem, mindfulness bringing the spaciousness to examine experience with fresh eyes, and the cognitive mode bringing the active choice about what will be a more resourceful way of thinking. The 'being' of mindfulness paves the way for the 'doing' of cognitive choice. But, as I have said already, clients are usually much more familiar with the 'doing' of cognitions and, without our guidance, are unlikely to sustain a mindful inquiry.

My emphasis here is on the value of fostering the mindful step of noticing the experience of thinking itself. The aim is for clients to see that the thoughts and feelings driving their conversational styles are in and of themselves constructed, circumstantial, fluid, and open to change. That is not to say that thinking is unhelpful. Thinking is arguably mankind's greatest tool. We need to have thoughts, and our thoughts and judgments about others are essential for going about our lives. But, to enhance conversational agility, we all need to be able to step back periodically and to question our thoughts. Mindfulness practices provide a powerful method for taking this step back into the experience of awareness itself.

Using mindfulness to notice awareness

Mindfulness is commonly defined as attending to the present moment with an attitude of warmth and curiosity. By turning attention to some aspect of here-and-now experience, such as the sensations of breathing or the experience of sound, the habitual activity of the mind is reduced. Many clients new to the concept of mindfulness believe the aim is to stop having thoughts. This is a misunderstanding. Rather, the aim is to develop a capacity for awareness as a grounded vantage point from which we can observe the arising and passing of thoughts, or, indeed, any other mental phenomena. The aim is to experience the distinction between awareness and the contents of awareness. Thoughts, feelings, sensations, and images are all examples of mental content. If we can observe these mental contents with genuine curiosity, we have a vehicle for seeing how our own mind constructs reality. Without the distinction between awareness and thoughts, we become unconsciously identified with our thoughts.

The collapsing of thinking and identity in Western civilization is captured by Descartes's famous phrase: 'I think, therefore I am'. According to this formulation, thinking gives rise to being. Our existence is our thoughts. However, within contemplative traditions, 'being' is distinct from 'doing'; the 'I am' of phenomenological experiencing is separate from any narrative our minds create. This apparently philosophical distinction has been shown to be underpinned by activity in different parts of the prefrontal cortex (PFC). For example, when subjects without mindfulness training are asked to be aware of whatever arises as it arises – to be momentarily self-aware – there is activation in their narrative circuitry (i.e. the medial prefrontal cortex). In contrast, when subjects with mindfulness training are given the same instruction, there is less activity in their narrative circuitry, and enhanced activity in their experiencing circuitry (i.e. the right lateralised, posterior prefrontal cortex).[3] This research shows that awareness of primary 'bottom-up' experience can be attended to without being dominated by top-down, narratives. The significance of this for conversations is that clients may come to notice, for example, body sensations of tension, and these may be linked with their RED body–brain system and a tendency to respond aggressively. However, observing these sensations, without the intervening dominance of narratives about what the other person has done wrong, gives clients space to interrupt a potentially aggressive reaction. The space of awareness allows them to observe their sensations and any associated feelings and thoughts, and to make conscious choices about the best way to respond.

Mindfulness techniques play a more complex role in supporting conversational agility than simply emphasising bottom-up awareness of body sensations. Mindfulness includes many aspects of prefrontal activity, drawing together bottom-up and top-down processes. These include being non-judgmental and non-reactive, acting with awareness of present sensory experience, using words to label and describe the internal world, and being self-observating.[4] The last of these is particularly central to *Breakthrough Conversations*. Self-observation, the capacity to witness one's own experience, implies observing the self, as the self observes the present moment, or what might be described as awareness of awareness. The key takeaway for our discussion is that awareness is different from the contents of awareness. Supporting clients to understand, and most importantly, to experience this distinction, provides an invaluable foundation for examining their conversational patterns and tendencies. The concept of taking up an 'observer' perspective during conversations is a useful approach for evoking this experience.

Taking an observer perspective

In mindfulness training the idea of taking up an observer perspective in relation to thoughts, feelings, body sensations or indeed any mental phenomena, is illustrated using a range of analogies. In one, the wide-open space of awareness is like the sky, and thoughts are like the clouds passing across the sky. Some thoughts are dark and heavy, whilst others are wispy and fluffy. Sometimes the thoughts so completely fill the sky of awareness that we see no blue. However, we do not mistake the clouds for the sky. We know the sky is always there behind the clouds. In a similar way, awareness is always there behind the thoughts.

As another analogy, awareness is like us sitting in the cinema watching a film, and our thoughts are the images appearing on the screen. When we are immersed in the film our narrative experiences take over and we forget we are sitting in a cinema. But, at any moment we can notice ourselves in our chair as the observer of the film. We are aware of ourselves being aware of the story unfolding on screen. More analogies include thinking of mental phenomena as leaves floating past on the surface of a river, or cars passing along a road. The observer perspective is to imagine ourselves sitting by the side of the river or road while the thoughts, feelings and emotions come into view and then leave, all the while keeping our seat, knowing ourselves to be the observer, and at the same time to observe what is passing through awareness. Many clients find such metaphors helpful, perhaps combined with guided mindfulness practices. Different metaphors work better for different people.

Zooming-in and zooming-out

The capacity for clients to step into an observer perspective is part of cultivating the mental agility to make choices about where they are placing their attention. Introducing a further metaphor, awareness is like the lens of a camera. When taking an observer perspective, we zoom-out with our wide-angle lens, expanding the perceptual field. Zooming-out lets us see the big picture or the broadest context, and from this vantage point we can notice the interrelationships between such aspects as internal and external, personal and interpersonal, rational and emotional, private and public. But we don't only want to be able to zoom-out. We also need to be able to use our attention to zoom-in, to focus in on specific details, perhaps even to switch from a camera to a microscope and to understand things at the most granular level of experience. Ultimately, the aim is to develop the agility both to zoom-out and to zoom-in, and if we are very practiced, perhaps to get a sense of being zoomed out at the same time as being zoomed-in, or at least to be oscillating so quickly between these perspectives that it seems like we have a kind of dual-awareness.

One of the practices used at the outset of many mindfulness trainings is the body-scan, where participants are guided to place their attention on different parts of the body and to notice the sensations that are arising. For example, they are asked to focus on their left foot – to let their attention shine like a spotlight on their left foot – and to notice any patterns of sensation, perhaps coolness or heat, pressure or contact, vibrations or pulsations, and, if there are no sensations, then simply to notice that. After a short period of time concentrating on that part of the body, they are then invited to let go of the focus on the left foot, and move the attention to another part of the body, perhaps to the left knee, and then to repeat the process of being aware of their sensations in that part of the body. This guidance asks participants to use their attention to zoom-in, and then after a while, to let go of that focus, to place their attention somewhere else, and then zoom-in again. Zooming-in like this exercises the muscle of attention, using it like a microscope. Later in the practice participants might be asked to zoom-out and to get an overall sense of the breathing body, or to imagine hovering above their body and seeing themselves from outside. Here the attention is being used to expand the field of awareness, and to take up the observer perspective. Going one step further in the practice, participants might be invited to notice their wider experience of the breathing body, and at the same time, notice that they can choose to bring their attention in close to specific body sensations, moving back and forth between details and the bigger picture, zooming-in and zooming-out, and maybe getting a sense of noticing granular sensations at the same time as noticing the wider experience of the breathing body. We can use mindfulness practices such as these as part of coaching sessions to support clients to view their attention as a muscle that can be exercised, and to begin to view awareness as distinct from the contents of awareness, such as thoughts, feelings and sensations.

An especially powerful target for taking up an observer perspective is oneself, since this can be the basis for profound shifts in self-awareness and self-identity. In my view, conversations that sustain a quality of mindfulness or reflectiveness provide a particularly potent domain for enabling such shifts in identity, and these shifts go hand-in-hand with shifts in conversational skilfulness. (I discuss these shifts in identity and consciousness further in Chapter 8 in relation to vertical development.)

Self-awareness and self-identity

We can think of self-identity as constructed out of 'me-thoughts', narratives about the self that become implicit, unquestioned beliefs. These implicit narratives create a sense of self, and whether those narratives are positive or negative relative to others defines the nature of our self-esteem. Some authors describe this process of creating a self as 'selfing' to capture the implicit construction involved in having a sense of self.[5] Whether clients are interested or not in the deeper implications of an inquiry into the nature of the self, the capacity to see self-narratives as constructions brings paradigm shifts in how clients relate to themselves. For example, a client whose father was distant and hostile noticed how his own way of evaluating himself had a cool, critical quality to it. He used his awareness to observe how a part of his mind, the voice of the internal father, judged his behaviour and achievements, and, with my support, was able to tune in to another part of his mind that could offer a more generous and supportive inner voice. The space of awareness allowed him to observe the interaction between these different me-thoughts, or parts of the mind, and stepping back into the observer position enabled him to see that he could loosen his implicit sense of self and choose how to re-shape it in ways that supported him to be at his best. In coaching we use many techniques – cognitive, emotional and behavioural – to support such changes in perspective, but the additive, paradigm-shifting value of mindfulness-based approaches comes from the distinction between awareness and thoughts. When all mental activity is seen as constructed there is the potential to consider new perspectives, about oneself or others, without being so caught by emotionally driven identifications. When we support clients to discover such new ways of relating to themselves and others their conversational agility is markedly enhanced.

Teaching clients to relate to their thoughts, and themselves, with more agility is an invaluable part of enabling more skilful conversations, and mindfulness techniques are an excellent way of doing this. There are many courses and phone apps available for learning mindfulness skills. The application of mindfulness to the coaching context for coaches and clients is explored by Liz Hall,[6] whilst Chaskalson and McMordie[7] focus specifically on supporting coaches to become more mindful in the service of their coaching presence and effectiveness, and offer an 8-week programme with guided practices. Bringing mindfulness more explicitly into the relational context, Donaldson-Fielder has explored how relational mindfulness can support the development of awareness and insight for coaches and leaders.[8,9] As I said before, my own work as a coach and psychotherapist has benefited greatly, both from my own personal and interpersonal mindfulness practice, and from learning to teach mindfulness, and I routinely encourage coaches or clients to embrace the potential for mindfulness practices to transform their ways of being and relating. The approach I offer here, however, whilst drawing heavily on mindfulness practices and experience, is also based on the recognition that the appetite for mindfulness varies substantially. Even coaches and clients who have attended mindfulness courses or use mindfulness apps report mixed success in terms of maintaining a regular practice. Even if they like the idea of mindfulness, most of them wish they were doing it more, and, at some level feel like they are failing for not making enough time to practice. For this reason, I often use visual, practical models to support guided reflection that do not need to be explicitly labelled as evoking mindfulness.

Practical models for enhancing conversational awareness

Any framework that invites clients to self-observe – 360° feedback, psychometric instruments, reflective worksheets, etc. – can enhance awareness and thus, serve more reflective conversations. The two models that follow,

Awareness is the key to breakthrough 57

the *PACES* framework and the *Five-Eyed Model of Conversations*, are both grounded in the concept of mindfulness, where the capacity to pause is the initiating step for reflective inquiry. However, unlike mindfulness practices, clients are invited to move back and forth between introspection and description, with the facilitator directing attention to specific domains of experience and potentially capturing what clients say on a worksheet. The approach invites clients to describe their inner worlds and allows us to follow their emerging experiences. We come to understand the nuances of their inner processes more accurately and can support them in recognising how these inner patterns impact conversational behaviours.

PACES – deconstructing experience

The *PACES* framework, and the *ACES* worksheet that goes with it, is a practical tool for supporting clients to observe themselves, and to bring new levels of curiosity and precision to what they can notice in different domains of their awareness (see Figure 3.1). I have used this model extensively for 15 years or more, in workshop settings, in one-to-one coaching and in supervising coaches and it has proved to a powerful method for increasing awareness and insight. *PACES* is an acronym for five domains of experience: *Pause, Actions, Cognitions, Emotions* and *Sensations*. We use this

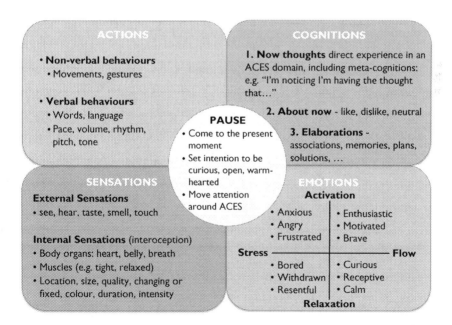

Figure 3.1 The PACES Framework.

frame for directing clients to consider different domains of their experience relative to a specific development goal.

In preparation for using the model, clients are invited to bring to mind a somewhat challenging conversation, either one from the past that did not go well, or one they need to have in the near future that they predict will be challenging. It is worth saying that we do not only deconstruct challenging conversations. Sometimes it is useful to begin with successful conversations, particularly if clients are dispirited or self-critical, as this builds confidence. But, focusing on challenging conversations is useful as it allows us to look at both limiting and enabling conversational tendencies. Clients are asked to describe the circumstances of the conversation, focusing on their goals, and what the outcomes of the conversation was or will be if it does not go well. The difference between goals and outcomes represent the development gap we are seeking to address through more skilful conversation. The following case study illustrates the preparation for using *PACES* with Kulinder.

> Kulinder, a gifted IT professional, had been invited to take on a managerial role several years prior to coaching, and the aim of the coaching was to support him in delegating more, and working more in partnership with other parts of the business. Since becoming a manager his team had expanded rapidly, with increasing investment in technology as the driver of business success, and his department was constantly under pressure to deliver against very stretching timelines. There were inevitable hiccups and delays and Kulinder often found himself struggling to manage the expectations of frustrated colleagues. When pressured by others he would tend to hide behind procedures and detailed explanations of why things were taking longer to complete, but these communications exacerbated rather than mollified his colleagues. He was getting a reputation as a bottleneck to the growth of the business, and some saw his meticulous approach as unhelpfully risk averse.
>
> Looking at his development challenges through a conversational lens, we identified a number of key stakeholders, and one of those we focused on was his relationship with Mike, who headed up a key business division. Mike had been highly critical of Kulinder and his team and felt the management of external development resources was unnecessarily bureaucratic. Mike wanted his own department to bypass Kulinder's department, and to use his budget to commission work directly with external suppliers. Kulinder believed this would be a recipe for confusion and fragmentation of development resources. I suggested to Kulinder that we might explore what happens in his interactions with Mike by using the *PACES* framework. He said he was happy to do that.

Awareness is the key to breakthrough   59

We can take clients through the *PACES* exercise with them sitting in a chair, and us writing their responses onto a blank *ACES* worksheet. However, my preference is to work with them standing up. I place five large, laminated cards onto the floor, each one labelled with the word and description from the *PACES* frame, so in effect we recreate Figure 3.1 on the floor. Then, we can take clients through the exercise asking them to stand on the card relevant to where we are directing their attention. This way of working evokes a more embodied experience, and so supports our emphasis on body sensations and body–brain awareness.

Pause

Clients are invited to begin by standing next to, or on, the *Pause* card, and are guided to take a moment to bring their awareness to the present moment. There are many ways we can do this. I typically ask clients to take a deeper breath or two, to become aware of themselves standing, and after 10 seconds or so, I invite them to bring their awareness to the sensations of standing – to notice how their feet are making contact with the floor. In this way we move their attention from the *Pause*, to *Sensations*, and emphasise that as we go through this practice it may be useful at any point to come back to the *Pause*, and the *Sensations* of being grounded on the floor. Figure 3.2 shows another way of representing the *PACES* model that emphasises the importance of grounding in body sensations. The *Pause* is a mental choice to interrupt the momentum of habit or reactivity – to resist the dominance of *Actions* and *Cognitions* – and to bring the awareness down the body, perhaps to the breath in the lower belly, to sensations in the feet, or to some other part of the body. This focus on local, bodily sensations, can also be expanded, perhaps to encompass the whole body, or to extend

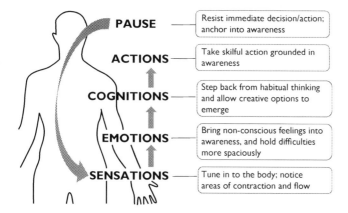

Figure 3.2 Grounding *PACES* with Sensations.

beyond the body to encompass another person. So, we use awareness of body sensations to support the pause, and as a doorway into the observer perspective.

Having paused, we invite clients to bring their goal, often in the form of a challenging conversation, to mind, perhaps visualising the other person and thinking about a conversational issue. We then ask them to say what is in their awareness, listening for whether the client begins with *Actions, Cognitions, Emotions* or *Sensations*, and, wherever their attention goes, ask them to move and stand by, or on, the laminated card for that domain. In working with *PACES*, and in using the complementary *ACES* worksheet to record what the client says, our aim is distinguish limiting and enabling patterns. By deconstructing these limiting and enabling patterns clients are deepening their understanding of their body–brain conversational states, and the interior and exterior shifts they can make to move from RED or AMBER limiting states to GREEN, more enabling states. I work through all domains of a limiting *ACES* pattern first, before then repeating the process for the enabling *ACES* pattern.

> Kulinder stood on the *Pause* card, and with my guidance, closed his eyes and brought his attention to the sensations of his feet on the floor. After a minute or so I invited him to let his awareness move to the sensations of his belly expanding and contracting with the in and outflow of his breathing. I also invited him to notice if there was any tension in his body, and, if so, as best he could to let that go … breathing into and out of that part of the body … and if the tension remained, just to notice that and to meet it with a gentle awareness.
>
> I then asked him to bring to mind a recent conversation with Mike, and I asked him to recall his goals and current outcomes. He said his goal was to work collaboratively and create a sense of working in partnership between their two departments, but he also acknowledged that the outcome of the last conversation was a repetition of previous interactions. Mike had been curt, frustrated by the lack of progress on key projects, and Kulinder had slipped into his habitual style of detailed justifications. To capture Kulinder's experience I began to complete an *ACES* worksheet as shown in Table 3.1, completing the sections for Goals and Outcomes.

Actions

Actions in the *PACES* model refers to what clients say or do, or imagine saying or doing, verbally or non-verbally, during a conversation. Drawing on the distinctions between the non-verbal and verbal behaviours relating to

Awareness is the key to breakthrough 61

Table 3.1 Illustration of a Completed ACES Worksheet

Goals: What are your goals?
To work collaboratively with Mike's team

Outcomes: What are the current outcomes?
Mike is curt and frustrated, and Kulinder finds himself offering detailed justifications

In relation to this intention:	Limiting	Enabling
Actions: What are your behaviours?	I prepare detailed emails about requirements, timelines, and potential delays. I set up meetings by email. I escalate to my manager when there are difficulties	Make time to speak face-to-face – book a meeting room. Have an upbeat, warm demeanour. Take time to set the context. Share experience of other challenging IT projects. Clarify roles
Cognitions: What are your thoughts?	They have unrealistic views about my team's role. Are they stupid? I am keen to be helpful and feel it's unfair when they are so critical. Poor decision-making in the past is being blamed on me and my team	I want to understand the views of others. I can see that they are anxious for these new products to be available. We are on the same side; we are not enemies. I know that we are doing a great job and I need to help them understand that
Emotions: What are your feelings?	Irritated, frustrated, disappointed, anxiety about how I am perceived, disheartened	More optimistic, even excitement; uplifted, happy, alert, relief, some regret for how I have behaved when reactive.
Sensations: What are your sensations?	Tense in shoulders, jaw; tightness in chest; restlessness in arms and legs; frowning brow.	Bouncy, flowing, energetic, steadier, anchored, bright.

Impact: What is the impact of focusing on the Enabling ACES?

I feel a greater sense of resilience to cope with inevitable challenges and frustrations. I want to collaborate more.

Changes: What can you do to foster more of the Enabling ACES pattern?
Remember my goals, especially when there are pressures around priorities and timelines
Confront harsh feedback about, and to, my team members in a respectful, mature way
Use mindfulness practices to support myself to feel grounded and to bring perspective
Avoid escalating to my manager if possible
Set up regular context and priority setting meetings

the RED, AMBER and GREEN body–brain states described in Chapter 2, when clients are describing their Limiting *ACES* we are not surprised to find them using either habitual or reactive behaviours, and when we later ask them to *Pause* again, and to consider what *Actions* would be most enabling, they typically begin to describe behaviours we would associate with the GREEN body–brain system. Our emphasis as coaches is on supporting clients to return to the *Pause* whenever their reactivity narrows awareness, viewing awareness as the essential ingredient for insight, and trusting in the power of being grounded in body and breath to deepen awareness and to bring more skilful capacities to the fore. In some circumstances we may feel the need to seed possible, more enabling behaviours, asking clients if they could imagine adopting a particular tone, pace or expressive style, but, wherever possible, our aim is foster our clients' own discoveries rather than seeking to teach them specific techniques. Examples of the actions I captured for Kulinder are shown in Table 3.1.

Cognitions

I use the word cognition to refer to any mental contents that are concerned with perceiving and interpreting experiences, so it includes such aspects as thoughts, memories, ideas, images, self-identity, plans, proposed solutions and value-statements. Much of what fills our minds are cognitions, and, as I have discussed above, seeing thoughts as mental contents that can be questioned and scrutinised is central to being consciously skilful in our interactions.

Although the *PACES* model invites clients to move attention to different domains of experience, cognitions are always involved in perceiving and naming these experiences, and so we need to distinguish between *Now* thoughts as observations of direct experience, the *About Now* judgements that we make, and the *Elaborations* or narratives that can quickly develop (see Figure 3.1). For example, consider seeing a frown on the face of a friend or colleague. The phenomenological, *Now* observation may be to notice how the person's brow furrows and how the muscles around the eyes tighten. But almost instantaneously, beneath awareness, is an *About Now* response, either of disliking, of feeling neutral, or of liking. Based on the response that is evoked in us, our minds start to build *Elaborations*, narratives about what we have perceived. Perhaps we think the person is angry with us, perhaps we think the person is under pressure to achieve something, or perhaps we think the person is squinting because they have forgotten their glasses. Our minds click into gear, making sense of experiences, and if allowed to run, our minds proliferate narratives, one thought leading to another. And it does not stop there. If we think the person is angry with us, this is likely to trigger an emotional response, perhaps of fear or defensiveness or retaliatory anger, and the emotion will trigger further responses in all of the other elements in the *PACES* frame.

By inviting clients periodically to *Pause* and anchor themselves in the body – standing or sitting, noticing breathing – we support them to come back to the simplicity of awareness, and then to observe again the process of thinking, distinguishing the *Now* phenomena, the judgements that the mind rapidly makes *About Now* phenomena, and then the *Elaborations* that develop. The *Pause* allows clients to interrupt the momentum of their narratives, to see the proliferating array of *Cognitions* as interpretative creations of the mind that can be reviewed and evaluated, rather than simply believed as the truth.

A linguistic approach that can support clients to see their elaborative thoughts as mental objects, rather than truths, is to insert the term: '*I notice I am having the thought that…*'. For example, a client may say: '*I am useless at presentations*'. If we inquire, we will find there is a rich set of experiences and judgements that have led to this statement and unpacking some of this may be very useful. But also useful is simply to see the statement as a thought: '*I notice I am having the thought that I am useless at presentations*'. In this second statement, the term '*I notice …*' emphasises the observer part of the self, the act of awareness, as being distinct from the judgmental thought: '*I am useless at presentation*'. By emphasising the gap between observation and cognitive judgements, clients are more able to soften their judgements, and to bring curiosity to their own tendency to make such judgements. (See Table 3.1 to see the cognitions that emerged in my work with Kulinder.)

Emotions

Emotions have been defined as 'the complex pattern of bodily and mental changes that includes physiological arousal, feelings, cognitive processes, visible expressions, and specific behavioural reactions made in response to a situation perceived as personally significant.[10] Such a definition shows how emotions are linked to all domains of *PACES* patterns and are fundamental to skilful conversations. There are many theories of basic emotions, such as Ekman's six basic emotions of anger, disgust, fear, joy, sadness and surprise,[11] or Plutchik's, which are the same as Ekman's with the addition of acceptance and anticipation.[12] However, in using *PACES* patterns our aim is not to limit the choice to basic emotions, but rather to support clients to investigate subjective experience, and to find language that is personally meaningful. One client may use the word 'aggravated', whereas another may use the word 'peeved' to describe a similar experience. Our role as coach is to encourage curiosity, and importantly, to link any emotional description to its body sensations (as discussed below). Clients vary greatly in their ability to name emotional states, and it can be useful to offer a page of emotion words as prompts.

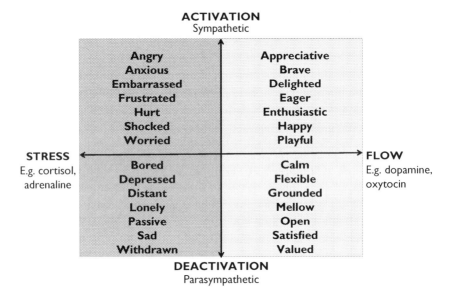

Figure 3.3 Mapping Emotions.

An accessible two-dimensional classification of emotions suggests that all emotions can be distributed according to valence and arousal,[13] where for example in Figure 3.3, valence is described as Stress-Flow, and arousal as Activation-Deactivation.

This model can be readily related to our understanding of the sympathetic (activating) and parasympathetic (deactivating) branches of the autonomic nervous system, and the distinction between RED, stress hormones (e.g. cortisol and adrenaline), and GREEN, flow hormones (e.g. dopamine and oxytocin). Emotions can be placed into each of the resulting four quadrants: on the left-hand side are stress-based emotions: activated emotions like anger and anxiety at the top, and deactivated emotions like bored and depressed at the bottom. On the right-hand side are flow-based emotions: activated emotions like enthusiasm and happiness at the top and deactivated emotions like calmness and grounded at the bottom. This two-dimensional approach is useful because it can be readily connected to subjective experience, and supports clients to distinguish different types of RED, AMBER or GREEN body–brain states. For example: I recall asking one senior executive to describe where his most predominant emotions during a typical day would sit in terms of the four quadrants. He said that he began his day in the bottom right quadrant, feeling curious, receptive and calm, but by the end the day he would be in the top left quadrant feeling anxious, angry and frustrated. This clarity helped us to explore what he could do to find renewal during the day, which in his case included taking a walk by the River Thames at lunchtime to enhance his experience of the GREEN, deactivated, flow emotions like ease and tranquility. (See Table 3.1 to see the Emotions that emerged in my work with Kulinder.)

Sensations

The focus on body sensations and seeing how specific body sensations are associated with specific emotions is often the domain in the *PACES* model that is most surprising to clients. As discussed in Chapter 2, body sensations are the clearest subjective indicator of which of the three body–brain systems is activated, with contracted sensations being associated with RED states, and spacious sensations being associated with GREEN states. Although clients use different words such as tight, strangled, or gripping for contracted states, and flowing, relaxed or centred for spacious states, research shows that the relationship between emotions and the areas of the body that feel most activated or deactivated is fairly consistent across different people.[14] The advantage of bringing attention to sensations is that they are steadier than thoughts, which typically proliferate very rapidly. As for emotions, it can be helpful to offer clients a page of indicative sensation words, both as prompts, and to emphasise the distinction between sensations and emotions. The indicative list below groups sensation words into broad categories:

- **Contracted:** Tense, Tight, Constricted, Clenched, Knotted, Wooden, Congested, Dull, Dense, Frozen, Icy, Disconnected, Thick, Blocked, Heavy, Drained, Suffocated, Cold, Dry, Numb, Disconnected, Closed, Dark, Hollow, Empty, Bloated, Brittle, Damp, Dark, Deflated
- **Expanded:** Calm, Energized, Smooth, Streaming, Relaxed, Open, Light
- Spacious: Airy, Releasing, Expansive, Flowing, Floating, Fluid
- **Heat:** Hot, Warm, Full, Sweaty, Clammy, Cold, Cool
- **Tender:** Sensitive, Bruised, Achy, Fragile, Delicate, Frail, Feeble
- **Movement:** Shaky: Throbbing, Pounding, Fluttery, Shivery, Queasy, Wobbly, Bubbly
- **Dizzy:** Spinning, Spacey, Breathless, Faint, Nauseous, Whirring, Scattered
- **Jittery:** Prickly, Electric, Tingling, Nervy, Twitchy, Burning, Radiating, Buzzy, Itchy

In working with *PACES*, the coach's goal is to support clients to deconstruct their internal experiences and to explore how they relate to behaviour. As clients become more curious about the linkages between each of the *ACES* domains, their curiosity and self-observation is markedly enhanced, and these qualities are foundational for approaching conversations with fresh eyes.

Completing an *ACES* Worksheet for Kulinder

Having begun by being guided to pause and to become centred, and to consider what happened with Mike when the interactions remained stuck and unproductive, I then invited Kulinder to tell me what he was noticing as he thought about these conversations. I guided him to speak about the *Actions, Cognitions, Emotions* and *Sensations* that were all part of his limiting interactive style with Mike. As he talked about each domain, I asked him to step onto the card corresponding to that domain, so that he was moving his body and staying attuned to the ongoing sense of the connection between the four domains of the *ACES* pattern. As he spoke, I captured what he was saying on the *ACES* worksheet (Table 3.1).

Having completed each of the *ACES* domains for the limiting scenario, I then asked Kulinder to pause again, to become anchored once again in his sense of his breathing body, and then to bring to mind an image of himself having a successful conversation with Mike. I encouraged him to get a rich picture in his mind's eye of success, drawing on memories of other successful conversations with other colleagues, and attuning to a sense of himself as resourceful and effective. I then repeated the process of getting him to step onto each of the *ACES* cards, this time capturing his enabling *ACES* pattern. Kulinder found it very useful to deconstruct his experience in this way, and to identify how he could shift to a more resourceful, GREEN, enabling state. I completed the *ACES* worksheet with him by asking, first, what the impact was of focusing on the enabling *ACES* pattern, and second, by asking him to say what he could do to foster more of the enabling *ACES* pattern.

The value of the *PACES* frame and the corresponding *ACES* worksheet is the detailed deconstruction of inner experiences and a recognition of how these inner experiences impact external behaviours. A complementary frame the *Five-Eyed Model of Conversations* opens up our inquiry to external and systemic factors.

The *Five-Eyed Model* of Conversations

The *Five-Eyed Model of Conversations* provides a big picture view of what is happening in a conversation. We might think of this model as the more overarching model in that it contains the five elements of the *PACES* framework. I use them separately and usually start with the *PACES* frame to encourage an emphasis on personal agency and self-awareness. Systemic factors are just as important as interior mindsets, and they are of course inextricably linked, but if we start with the bigger picture there is a danger of clients attributing development blocks almost entirely to external factors, and so failing to take ownership for what they can personally change.

When we think of a conversation, we might at first glance think of it like a tennis match, with words being batted back and forth in a two-way exchange like a tennis ball. We speak, the other person listens. They speak, we listen. The tennis ball is the content of the conversation. This metaphor certainly captures part of the conversational dynamic, but in the *Breakthrough Conversations* approach we invite clients to consider further aspects, summarised in the *Five-Eyed Model of Conversations* (Figure 3.4).

The *Five-Eyes* refer to the five vantage points for observing a conversation, the *Observer Perspective* that becomes available with a mindful pause, the *Context* of a conversation, the *Me* view of the conversation, the *You* view of the conversation, and the *We* view. Supporting clients to step back or to zoom-out in relation to key conversations allows them to see these different viewpoints, and supporting them to zoom-in allows them to deconstruct elements of their experience in more detail. As discussed above, it is this capacity to bring curiosity to the multiple factors driving conversations and to shift perspective between them that yields the potential for new insights and conversational breakthrough.

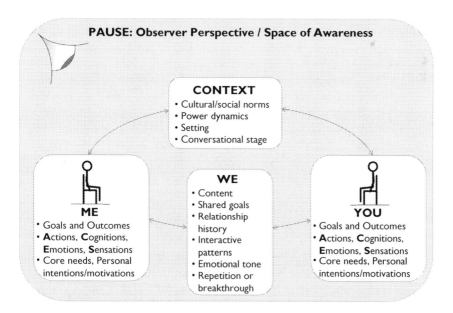

Figure 3.4 The *Five-Eyed Model* of Conversations.

Observer perspective

I have already talked about the ability to take an *Observer Perspective* as one of the potential benefits of mindfulness practice, and here we apply the observer vantage point to conversations. It is initially the coach who holds the *Observer Perspective*, noticing where clients place their attention as they speak about, or engage in, conversations, actively inviting them to move their attention between some or all of the areas already described. However, in the *Breakthrough Conversations* approach a central goal is for clients to step into the *Observer Perspective* themselves. If we ask clients to consider the domains of *Context*, *Me*, *We* and *You*, they are in effect taking up an observer position in order to step back mentally and explore each of those domains. However, in drawing attention to the *Observer Perspective* we are doing more than inviting clients to observe the other four domains. We are supporting them to notice their own act of observing. By experiencing this witnessing perspective, clients begin to cultivate a part of the mind that notices what is arising without being overly identified with the arising contents.

Presented with the Five-Eyed Model of Conversations, I invited Kulinder to imagine himself seeing a recent conversation with Mike from the Observer Perspective. 'Take some time now to take a pause ... perhaps noticing how you are feeling in your body ... noticing bodily sensations ... noticing the flow of your breath ... etc'. After spending some time supporting Kulinder's capacity to become present to his experience through attuning to here-and-now body sensations, I invited him to '... allow your awareness to expand to encompass a wider sense of yourself in relation to all the factors impacting your conversation with Mike ... and perhaps getting a sense of yourself as the observer ... letting your awareness move around between the Context of the conversation ... your personal, Me view of the conversation, your imaginings of Mike's You view of the conversation ... and your sense of what is being co-created between you, or the We view of the conversation. And knowing that at any moment you can pause, anchoring awareness in the breath ... or perhaps the sensations of your feet on the floor ... and then, opening out your awareness again and noticing once again yourself as the observer of experience ... letting yourself be in the Observer Perspective ... attuned to the part of your mind that can witness yourself and Mike talking to each other, whilst you are watching from a distance ... as if you are getting a helicopter view of everything that is occurring between you'.

Kulinder found it very helpful to be guided into the Observer Perspective, where he noticed he felt less agitated and recognised that he could look at what was happening between Mike and himself more dispassionately.

When clients can truly inhabit the observer position, albeit only briefly, they often experience a sense of spaciousness or calmness. The disidentification from the contents of awareness gives them the freedom to examine their own reactivity with a quality of dispassionate curiosity. Finding ways to facilitate such shifts in perspective is a key part of the coach's repertoire. In my experience many clients and coaches try to make this shift through mental agility, and indeed my descriptions here draw on cognitive capacities. However, the power of the *Observer Perspective* lies in embodied, experiential knowing, and so it is important that conceptual models are balanced with guided, experiential inquiry. (I discuss introducing clients to mindful inquiry as part of *Managing Emotional States* in Chapter 6.)

Context

Context is concerned with the systemic factors that influence a conversation. I group these into four aspects: *cultural and social norms*, *power dynamics*, *setting*, and *conversational stage*. The cultural and social norms refer to the shared expectations and rules that guide how people behave in the conversational context. These norms are learned and reinforced from our earliest social experiences with parents, siblings and wider communities through to all of the subsequent contacts with parents, friends, teachers and colleagues. Directness versus being more indirect, harmony versus challenge, a focus on task versus relationship, and being more individualistic versus more collectivist, are examples of how norms can differ across cultures, organisations, communities, families and individuals. In coaching, our intention is not to judge these norms, but rather to bring into awareness their potential impact on the conversational dynamic. If the organisational culture is one that is dismissive of emotional vulnerability, then we may wish to highlight this and invite curiosity about the impact of such a mindset on trust and collaboration. In a client pair, if one client has learned to be conversationally direct whilst another's expectation is for a more subtle and reserved interaction, then our aim as a coach is to support clients to see that different cultural assumptions are influencing their ways of approaching conversations, and to decide together what this means for them in terms of having optimally productive conversations. Our curiosity about social and cultural norms also needs to take into account the question of power.

Power dynamics often underly conversations. If we are facilitating a conversation between a manager and his or her direct report, then the power relation may mean the direct report is more cautious about speaking openly or being critical. Power dynamics also play out in relation to many social and cultural factors, such as race, class, gender, religion, education, language, politics and disability. If not explicitly brought into awareness, implicit bias is bound to exist in many of these areas because it derives from our conditioning. Once again, our goal is not so much to judge these biases – that leads to shame and defensiveness. Our aim is to invite clients to bring curiosity to their implicit ways of making sense of their relationships with others, and to embrace the idea that having biases is inevitable. By bringing such biases into awareness and talking about how these biases are influencing their conversational styles, clients are freed up to make more conscious choices about how to relate to others with greater awareness and humility. (The ways in which we can bring the impact of *social and cultural conditioning* more into awareness is explored further in Chapter 7.)

The setting is concerned with the practical environment in which a conversation takes place: sitting or standing or walking, inside or outside, in an open plan area or in private space, sitting face-to-face or at an angle, with or without a desk or table, in person or by video call or by phone, the potential for interruptions or privacy, the choice of room, the time of day, the use of note-taking or video recording. The questions of setting are elements we would usually want to consider in advance of coaching, but, when clients reflect on a conversation they have had, or one they wish to undertake, noticing the importance of setting allows them to plan how to create the optimal conditions for a constructive conversation.

The fourth aspect of context is to invite clients to assess their conversations as occurring as part of an evolving process, and to recognise that different capabilities will be required at different stages of a conversation. The *Map of Breakthrough Conversations* (see Chapter 4) provides one such framework. An overarching process map such as this normalises what is occurring at different stages so, for example, the reactivity characteristic of Stage 2: *Managing Emotional States* is understood and even expected.

> Considering the *Context* of the conversation with Mike, Kulinder was aware that the conversational norms of his department were different from those of Mike's. His background in IT was based on logical reasoning. Rationality dominated discussion of issues, and it was rare for conversations to become personal. In contrast, in Mike's department the sales and marketing focus brought a more extraverted and direct conversational style, and when problems arose, being vocally critical of other people and departments was a relatively common response. Kulinder also spoke personally about the culture at home when he was growing up, where there was a strong emphasis on harmony and courtesy, even if that meant not saying exactly what you mean. In contrast, for Mike, his upbringing was characterised by a more direct and confrontative style, where blunt humour or sarcasm might be used to deliver a tough message. Noticing these contrasting norms supported both Kulinder and Mike to explore what shared norms would support them to have more productive conversations.

Mike acknowledged that it would be useful if he could restrain his tendency for making barbed comments, whilst Kulinder agreed to be more open in naming his frustrations.

There was also an important power dynamic between Kulinder and Mike's departments, because IT was viewed as a service function that, from Mike's point of view could be outsourced. Kulinder felt that Mike's area, together with other client-facing functions, did not treat IT with mutual respect. This dynamic meant that Kulinder could feel on the backfoot from the outset of conversations with Mike, and this could lead to Kulinder feeling he had to justify events, rather than enter into an equal discussion of how to address challenges. Once again, naming these implicit dynamics gave Kulinder and Mike the opportunity to explore mutually constructive ways of addressing issues.

In terms of setting, most meetings with Mike were part of larger committee meetings, and so in the past all one-to-one meetings occurred as a snatched few minutes at the end of a larger meeting, or a few minutes in the corridor or in an open-plan area. Prior to coaching, Kulinder had never set up a dedicated one-to-one meeting with Mike, either in a meeting room or by going out for a coffee or a walk together. One of the outcomes of the paired coaching was for Mike and Kulinder to have regular monthly meetings.

Using the *Map of Breakthrough Conversations*, Kulinder and Mike recognised that they usually got stuck at Stage 2, with Mike dominating discussions and making sure that his view prevailed, with Kulinder doing his best to present the resource challenges facing IT. The visual representation of a pathway for more productive conversations supported them to invest time in unpacking their conversational tendencies in more detail.

Me and you

A further focus of attention for clients can be on themselves or others, whether imagining, recalling, or having a conversation. As discussed in Chapter 1 and explored further in Chapter 5, we need to understand the goals of a conversation from each person's perspective, and also the view of the current outcomes of conversations. Usually there is a shortfall between the goals and the outcomes, otherwise clients would not choose this conversation as something to explore in coaching. If we have already used the *PACES* frame, then we may have already explored certain key goals and outcomes, but this focus may draw out a richer array of goals, as was the case for Kulinder.

> As Kulinder reflected on a recent conversation with Mike, I asked what the goals of the conversation were from his perspective and what the current outcomes were. There were a number of goals. At the level of organisational success, he wanted to understand which technology developments would have the most significant commercial impact. At the level of his relationship with Mike, he wanted things to be more collaborative rather than combative. For himself he wanted others to recognise how difficult the technology challenges were. And for Mike, he wanted him to feel that he could trust Kulinder to deliver results.

We

When we ask clients to recall or imagine a conversation, they usually begin by talking about the content of an interaction in the *We* category, typically describing background information, the issues being addressed, and the views and ideas being exchanged. Allowing time for the voicing of content is an important part of clients feeling heard, as well as enabling the coach to gather information. But, as we shall see, the repetition of well-rehearsed narratives, especially if conversations have become difficult, tends to fuel a conversational impasse. Being willing to interrupt clients immersed in content and inviting them to place their attention on others aspect of experience is key to enhancing awareness and the possibility of more skilful interactions. Within the *We* area, as we shall see in later chapters, the inquiry can be expanded to include such aspects as shared goals, the shared history of the relationship and previous conversations, patterns of interaction, emotional tone and noticing if the conversation is leading to repetition or breakthrough.

> In the *We* domain Kulinder thought that both he and Mike had a shared goal of wanting to find a way of developing the IT infrastructure that would rapidly support the commercial success of new product innovations. But they both tended to get caught into content conversations and differ on what they each thought was the best technical solution. Interactively, Mike would tend to dominate, and his emotional tone would quickly become elevated (RED body–brain reaction). In contrast Kulinder would usually maintain a steady emotional tone, although sometimes he would be silenced by the strength of the opinions being expressed by Mike (also a RED body–brain reaction). Kulinder could see that interactions with Mike, either by email or in brief post-meeting exchanges, were often unproductive and repetitive, and he was keen to find a way of striking a more positive note.

The *PACES* frame and the *Five-Eyed Model of Conversations* are usually introduced in Stage 2 of the *Breakthrough Conversations* process, supporting clients to investigate the interior and exterior factors impacting conversational effectiveness, but we may refer back to these tools at any point in our work to support clients to be more reflective about the factors shaping their interactions.

Summary

Enhancing awareness lies at the heart of the *Breakthrough Conversations* approach. The human mind has evolved to run automatically much of the time, drawing on habitual routines and default mode circuitry, and in these circumstances mental activity is not under conscious control. Thoughts flow rapidly from one to another, so much so that awareness and thoughts seem subjectively synonymous. Drawing out the distinction between awareness and thinking, mindfulness practices provide one method for creating space to experience phenomena without mental activity being so dominated by narrative circuitry. Clients can hone their awareness 'muscle', learning methods for taking up an *Observer Perspective*, zooming-in and zooming-out with their attention, and learning to disidentify from thoughts by viewing self-identity as constructed from me-thoughts and self-narratives. I have developed two linked models for deconstructing conversational experience, the *PACES* frame and the *Five-Eyed Model of Conversations*. The *PACES* frame, and the corresponding *ACES* worksheet, supports clients to deconstruct limiting and enabling experiences in terms of the domains of *Pause, Actions, Cognitions, Emotions* and *Sensations*. Capturing the results of these explorations on an *ACES* worksheet provides an explicit record of how certain conversational tendencies manifest, and empowers clients to make conscious choices about how to be more skilful. The *Five-Eyed Model of Conversations* supports clients to view their interactions in a wider context, and to acknowledge the array of systemic, historical and interpersonal factors that contribute to conversational outcomes.

Worksheet 3: Deconstructing body–brain states using *PACES*

Worksheets showing the *Five-Eyed Model of Conversations*, the *PACES* framework, the *ACES* worksheet, the emotions map, and the sensations checklist can all be useful tools at different times for supporting clients in raising their awareness in the context of conversations. A further worksheet invites clients to connect their diagnosis of *RAG* body–brain state, discussed in Chapter 2, with the deconstruction of experience provided by the *PACES* framework (Table 3.2). Guiding clients through directed conversation to populate the cells of this worksheet provides a rich picture of how the

Table 3.2 RAG States in Terms of ACES Patterns

PAUSE
What Do I Notice Right Now? Am I RED, AMBER or GREEN?

Body Brain State	RED (Reactive)	AMBER (Habit)	GREEN (Reflective)
Actions	• Fight, flight, freeze • Compliance, defiance, silence, violence	• Habits of relating and doing • Habitual tone, pace, pitch of voice, language	• Conscious of body, breath, sensations • Actions arising from awareness of thoughts, emotions and sensations • Conscious listening and speaking
Cognitions	• Ruminating thoughts • Limiting beliefs • Past/future focus • Historical complaints	• Habits of thinking • Thinking driven by implicit assumptions	• Conscious intentions • Noticing own thinking process
Emotions	• Reactive feelings may not be in awareness • Fear, anxiety, anger, helplessness, …	• Habits of feelings • Feelings often out of awareness	• Awareness of emotions • Attuned to vulnerability • Self-compassion • Appreciation • Empathy • Joy …
Sensations	• Tension in belly, chest, throat, head • Shallow or faster breathing • Temperature changes …	• Habits of sensation (may not be in awareness) • Habitual breathing patterns, posture, places of tension/ease	• Regular, even breath through belly/heart • Conscious of sensations and able to 'soften, soothe and allow'

body–brain states typically manifest in terms of *Actions, Cognitions, Emotions, and Sensations*, and so provides a powerful basis for ongoing self-observation.

Notes

1 Buckner, R.L., Andrews-Hanna, J.R., Schacter, D.L. (2008). The brain's default network: Anatomy, function, and relevance to disease. *Annals of the New York Academy of Sciences*, 1124, 1–38.
2 Li, W., Mai, X., Liu, C. (2014, February 24). The default mode network and social understanding of others: What do brain connectivity studies tell us. *Frontiers in Human Neuroscience*, 8, 74.

3 Farb, N.A.S., Segal, Z.V., Mayberg, H., Bean, J., McKeon, D., Fatima, Z., Anderson, A.K. (2007, December). Attending to the present: Mindfulness meditation reveals distinct neural modes of self-reference. *Social Cognitive and Affective Neuroscience*, 2(4), 313–322.
4 Baer, R.A., Smith, G.T., Hopkins, J., Krietemeyer, J., Toney, L. (2006, March). Using self-report assessment methods to explore facets of mindfulness. *Assessment*, 13(1), 27–45.
5 Hanson, R., Medius, R. (2009). *Buddha's brain: The practical neuroscience of happiness, love and wisdom*. New Harbinger.
6 Hall, L. (2013). *Mindful coaching. How mindfulness can transform coaching practice*. Kogan Page.
7 Chaskalson, M., McMordie, M. (2018). *Mindfulness for coaches: An experiential guide*. Routledge.
8 Donaldson-Fielder, E. (2020). An anchored connection. *Coaching at Work*, 15(3), 35–38.
9 Donaldson-Fielder, E. (2020). Developing leadership. *Coaching at Work*, 15(4), 44–48.
10 Gerrig, J.R., Zimbardo, P.G., Campbell, A.J., Cumming, S.R., Wilkes, F.J. (2015). *Psychology of life*. Pearson Higher Education.
11 Ekman, P. (1992). An argument for basic emotions. *Cognition & Emotion*, 6(3–4), 169–200.
12 Plutchik, R. (1980). *Emotion: A psychoevolutionary synthesis*. Harpercollins College Division.
13 Ressel, J. (1980). A circumplex model of affect. *Journal of Personality and Social Psychology*, 39, 1161–1178.
14 Nummenmaa, L., Glerean, E., Hari, R., Hietanen, J.K. (2014, January 14). Bodily maps of emotions. *Proceedings of the National Academy of Sciences of the United States of America*, 111(2) 646–651.

Chapter 4

A map of breakthrough conversations

In this chapter I offer a *Map of Breakthrough Conversations* that describes five archetypal stages, together with the capacities required to move effectively through each of the stages. To put this map into context, I begin by briefly summarising a number of conversational models and the evidence for their impact on conversational effectiveness. I highlight that, although many of these models have similar elements, the *Breakthrough Conversations* approach is distinctive in its emphasis on embodied, personal and relational awareness as the foundation of mutual connection and creativity. I begin by considering four groups of models deriving from different fields of inquiry: negotiation, conflict, couple therapy and mindfulness.

Negotiation

One of the earlier areas of research into effective conversations was in the field of labour-management negotiations. Walton and McKersie[1] introduced the term 'integrative bargaining' to emphasise the importance of mutuality in negotiations: mutual agreement about the problem, mutual exchange of information, and mutual trust and search for the best alternative. The emphasis on mutual gains in negotiation was developed further by the Harvard Negotiation Project and published in the book *Getting to Yes*.[2] In this approach negotiators are encouraged to listen to each other, treat each other fairly and jointly explore options to increase value. Key guidelines include: separate the people from the problem, focus on interests rather than positions to understand what is motivating each party, learn to manage emotions, and express appreciation for the other party's perspective. These guidelines are designed to support collaborative inquiry, so that each negotiator is able to stand both in their own shoes and the shoes of the other, and so find new solutions that marry the needs of both parties.

Conflict

A further group of approaches, with some overlap to negotiation, focus on how to be more effective in undertaking potentially conflictual conversations.

DOI: 10.4324/9781003054542-4

The book *Difficult Conversations,*[3] also from the Harvard Negotiation Project, views all challenging conversations as having three deeper conversations: the 'What Happened?' conversation is concerned with disagreement about the facts; the 'Feelings' conversation is concerned with recognising how underlying difficult emotions, such as feeling hurt, can be expressed as angry judgments about others; the 'Identity' conversation is concerned with how, in difficult conversations, people can feel threatened around their competence, likeability or worthiness. In this approach discussants are encouraged to consider the psychological as well as the practical factors impacting how they converse as a basis for being better able to listen to each other, and being more open to expressing underlying needs and feelings.

In *Crucial Conversations*[4] the need to see each other's point of view in making decisions is described as 'filling the pool of shared meaning'. Viewing mutual respect and shared purpose as creating the conditions for safety, people are encouraged to express what matters to them, owning how their viewpoints are influenced by their own stories and experiences, listening to others, and from the shared meaning that emerges, take decisions and follow through with unity and conviction.

Non-violent communication (NVC)[5] is a further approach designed to support constructive dialogue. NVC holds that most conflicts arise from miscommunication about human needs, where rather than understanding and expressing what people really need, they use coercive or manipulative language that induces fear, guilt or shame in others. NVC practitioners are invited to focus on four components of conversation: the 'observations' of what they are seeing and hearing, the 'feelings' they have free of thoughts and narratives, the core 'needs' they are seeking to get met, and the 'requests' that they can make around getting their needs met. Emphasis is placed on the specific use of language and the ability to make skilful requests that are empathic, compassionate and nurturing of the interests of both parties.

Couple therapy

There are many approaches from the world of psychotherapy for supporting couples to resolve differences and to transform conflict into an opportunity to grow and heal. I will outline two approaches that have become widely established and used throughout the world: Imago Relationship Therapy (IRT) and Emotionally Focused Therapy for Couples (EFT).

In IRT[6] there are four underpinning principles: becoming present to one's partner, learning a new way to talk that emphasises equality, safety and connection, replacing judgement with curiosity, and infusing the relationship with positive feelings. These principles are supported by a three-stage approach to listening and reflecting the words and feelings of a partner: mirroring, validating and empathising. By using these skills partners feel more understood by the other, and through an ongoing switching of speaker and listener roles, shared meaning and trust is fostered. Research shows that individuals in treatment experience significant increases in marital satisfaction, but evidence for the long-term effectiveness of this approach is not clear.[7]

In EFT[8] the approach to healing relational stress and strengthening the bonds that couples have with each other is grounded in the neuroscience of attachment theory. Attachment views human beings as innately relational, social and wired for intimate bonding with others. In their closest relationships people implicitly look for safety, acceptance, empathy and connection. If those relational needs are not met, self-protective strategies, often learned early in life in relation to parents, come to the fore, typically in the form of pursuit or withdrawal. The protective strategies used by each partner mutually reinforce each other creating an emotionally escalated negative cycle, the pursuer reacting to withdrawal with more pursuit, the withdrawer reacting to pursuit with more withdrawal. The healing process in EFT occurs in three stages: assessment and cycle de-escalation, changing interaction patterns and creating new bonds, and consolidation and integration. By supporting clients to recognise and step out of their negative cycle, and to experience and name the vulnerable feelings associated with their attachment needs, they are able to establish relational safety, trust and connection. Unusual in the field of psychotherapy, EFT has undergone rigorous research validation demonstrating both its long-term effectiveness in enabling relationship recovery, and discerning the specific interventions that contribute to treatment success.[9]

Mindfulness

Although widely taught as a personal technique for managing stress and for fostering positive emotions towards self and others, the individual focus of mindfulness has also been applied to the interpersonal domain to support people to be more grounded and aware as they listen and speak with others. In Insight Dialogue[10] the purpose is not focused on developing relationships, but rather on using relational contemplations to encourage a direct and intimate inquiry into the human experience. Sitting opposite each other in mindful practice, pairs are invited to follow a series of six guidelines as they consider contemplations about such topics as the self, ethics, and views and judgements about others. The six guidelines are: Pause, to step out of habitual thoughts and reactions; Relax to calm the body and mind; Open, to extend mindfulness from the internal to the external; Attune to Emergence, to enter the relational moment without an agenda; Listen Deeply, to discover what is emerging within and between; and Speak the Truth; to voice one's subjective experience. In order to engage fully with this experience practitioners are expected to have an established individual mindfulness practice, so they can bring themselves to the relational field with a fair degree of awareness and steadiness. Importantly, the relational field is viewed as one that can accelerate the development of awareness, compassion and insight, and the practical application of relational mindfulness[11] is an important underpinning for *Breakthrough Conversations*.

The potential value of mindfulness for coaches and psychotherapists is linked to the concept of therapeutic presence. Towards the end of his life, Carl Rogers, an influential founder of humanistic psychotherapy, stated that he had become more aware of his use of 'self' within the therapeutic environment and that when he was intensely focused on his client, his presence alone instigated the healing process.[12] In this use of the term, presence refers to much more than simply attending to the present moment, but is more broadly defined as "…having one's whole self in the moment on a multiplicity of levels, physically, emotionally, cognitively and spiritually."[13] In line with this notion of presence, the 8-week Mindfulness-Based Stress Reduction (MBSR) programmes, originally developed by Jon Kabat-Zinn,[14] includes a mindful listening practice where participants are invited to attend to their whole field of awareness whilst listening to another person speak: i.e. body sensations, emotions, reactions and interpretations. So, although not applied to full conversation, this practice can be seen as developing a quality of personal and relational presence. Taking mindfulness a step further, it has been used as the foundation for dialogue in personal or workplace relationships, and one author suggests five keys to mindful communication[15]: establishing presence, listening with encouragement, speaking with gentleness, showing unconditional friendliness, and responding playfully.

Research evidence

Although there are plentiful anecdotal reports of the effectiveness of these models in different circumstances, the research evidence for most is sparse or absent. For example, one reviewer notes that there is no quantitative evidence that suggests the effectiveness of 'Getting to Yes' over other models of negotiation, such as positional bargaining,[16] but acknowledges that the approach is often helpful. The same might be said for the conflict models. There are some studies suggesting the effectiveness of non-violent communication in reducing violence and increasing empathy,[17] although the singular impact of the NVC approach is clouded by a lack of relevant outcome measures, and in some studies the combining of NVC with other interventions such as mindfulness.

The one approach to conversations, amongst those discussed above, that has been thoroughly researched over more than two decades is EFT. A meta-analysis of nine studies identified as randomised control trials showed that EFT is an effective treatment for couple distress, both in facilitating change during treatment and in maintaining improvements following treatment.[18] Mindfulness has also been shown to have a positive impact on relationships; in one study, it reduces cortisol levels thus the speed of recovery from couple conflict increases,[19] and in another study, mindfulness reduces stress, depression and anxiety in parents of preschoolers and children with disabilities.[20] These studies suggest that the positive impact of mindfulness on interactions occurs as a result of enhancing individual self-regulation and empathy.

Turning to the *Breakthrough Conversations* approach, like most of the models discussed, it has emerged from the practical honing of ideas whilst working with clients, rather than from academic research, and, although there are many case studies illustrating positive results, there are no controlled research studies to demonstrate its efficacy. Having said that, two of the most distinctive aspects of this model stem from a combination of EFT and mindfulness, the two approaches most underpinned by rigorous research.

The *Breakthrough Conversations* approach in context

At one time or other I have used all of the models described above, and in my experience all of them are useful in the right circumstances, each with distinctive strengths. Taken together they highlight many critical elements for an effective approach to conversations:

- creating a sense of safety
- establishing a mutual sense of purpose
- cultivating presence, respect, curiosity, empathy and appreciation
- distinguishing fact from feelings, people from problems, intent from interpretations, experiences from narratives about those experiences
- balancing speaking and listening by each person in relation to problems, ideas and solutions
- recognising, experiencing, and naming underlying fears and relational needs
- making skilful requests in relation to core needs

The *Breakthrough Conversations* model seeks to include all of these elements, but draws particularly on mindfulness and EFT, with a distinctive emphasis on embodied awareness as the pivotal foundation for skilful conversations, and on recognising how understanding emotions, communicated most tangibly through body states, is a key doorway to empathy and connection. Other elements included in the *Breakthrough Conversations* approach but not so evident in the models described above are: the psychoeducation around the neurophysiology of conversational states, the explicit benefit of moving between working with individuals and pairs, the offering of techniques for supporting awareness without expecting clients to be mindfulness practitioners, the role of personality and culture as well as early attachments on conversational availability, and the notion of vertical development as a promoter and product of skilful conversations.

A Map of Breakthrough Conversations

Having sketched the broad territory of conversational models and approaches, I now turn to describe the *Map of Breakthrough Conversations*.

A Map of Breakthrough Conversations

There are two aspects to the *Map of Breakthrough Conversations*, the sequence of five stages that conversations pass through, and the key capabilities required to navigate each stage successfully, as shown in Figure 4.1. The successive stages are shown as looping and overlapping to indicate the fluidity of real conversations, which necessarily move back and forth between stages, but the overall trajectory is towards greater levels of awareness and collaboration. Key capabilities are aligned to each of the stages, and build on each other, so that capabilities developed at an earlier stage can be utilised and combined with other capabilities at later stages. These capabilities are exactly the same as the ladder of capabilities for facilitating change (Figure 1.2) required by coaches using this approach. Coaches need to be able to 'walk the talk' in order to be effective in guiding clients through the process.

This map captures the essential components of *Breakthrough Conversations*, whether that is one-to-one conversations between a coach and client, or the facilitation of paired conversations between two clients. Each of the stages is described below together with an outline of the capabilities required at each stage.

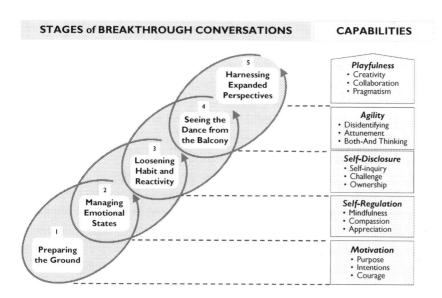

Figure 4.1 A Map of Breakthrough Conversations – Stages and Capabilities.

Stage 1: Preparing the ground

In the first stage we begin by introducing the idea of a conversational lens as a powerful and practical way of exploring and realising change. Our goal at this stage is primarily to engage the intrinsic motivation of clients, and we do this by clarifying the purpose of the work and exploring how we might construct purpose in terms of conversation. Inviting clients to envision successful outcomes also supports motivation. A further source of motivation comes from sparking the aspiration of clients to consider the character habits required of them to be their best selves. I introduce the *Character Compass* as a framework for drawing out client intentions regarding the character habits they wish to develop through more skilful conversations. Practical considerations are also explored at this first stage, such as the regularity of meetings, confidentiality, and the gathering of feedback. We can also share with clients an overview of the five-stage process and explore the possibility of having paired as well as individual sessions.

Stage 1 Capability: Motivation

At the first stage the key capability is the *motivation* for change. We foster motivation by considering three elements, *purpose*, *intentions* and *courage*. *Purpose* motivates through the identification of external goals, and *intentions* motivate through the identification of desirable inner qualities. *Courage* is the third element of motivation, because it is required to overcome the fear of discomfort that is inevitable when we seek development.

Stage 2: Managing emotional states

In Stage 2 the focus is on supporting clients to observe, name and manage their emotional states. We can offer an outline of the neurophysiology of body-brain states as preparation for using mindful inquiry to lead them into experiencing RED, AMBER and GREEN (*RAG*) body-brain states. A further model, the *PACES* frame, is introduced for deconstructing experience into five elements: *Pause, Actions, Cognitions, Emotions* and *Sensations* and further reinforces the capacity to observe experience. These models applied in one-to-one sessions provide the basis for introducing the *9-Minute Form* for managing emotions during conversations and can be most powerfully used as part of paired coaching sessions.

Stage 2 Capability: Self-regulation

Self-regulation is the key capability we are seeking to develop in supporting clients in *Managing Emotional States*. Three elements of self-regulation are discussed: *mindfulness, compassion* and *appreciation*. *Mindfulness* is initiated by the pause, and the intention to observe emerging experience. *Compassion*, and self-compassion, provide a skilful way of meeting difficult emotions that arise as clients consider certain challenging conversations. *Appreciation* fosters a positive mindset and counteracts the mammalian negativity bias intrinsic to the human brain.

Stage 3: Loosening habit and reactivity

In Stage 3 we support clients to unpack their habits and reactive tendencies during conversations by examining four factors: *core needs, personality, attachment styles* and *cultural and social conditioning*. Uncovering *core needs* helps clients to understand their reactive tendencies. *Personality* preferences indicate how innate preferences tend to manifest in habitual and reactive forms. *Attachment patterns* shows how relational tendencies developed early in childhood tend to persist into adulthood. Explorations of *cultural and social biases* indicate how conditioning can shape expectations and styles of communication. Bringing these different facets of habit and reactivity into view deepens self-awareness and provides the basis for disclosing personal biases to others.

Stage 3 Capability: Self-disclosure

Self-disclosure about personal tendencies and biases when conversing with others supports connection and trust, and so is an important capability for *Breakthrough Conversations*. I think of the capability of *self-disclosure* as containing three elements: *self-inquiry, challenge* and *ownership*. *Self-inquiry* is a motivational state of interest and openness directed towards oneself as introspection. *Challenge* is concerned with supporting clients to find the blend of safety and courage necessary to face shortcomings or mistakes that they might usually avoid or deny, and self-compassion may also be useful here. *Ownership* is concerned with taking responsibility for one's actions, where necessary admitting mistakes. When clients, in paired sessions, take ownership for their biases and tendencies in conversation, this often heralds a shift in shared openness and a deepening of the potential for collaborative working.

Stage 4: Seeing the dance from the balcony

At the fourth stage of the *Breakthrough Conversations* process the grounding and conversational awareness developed in the earlier stages support a fundamental shift in sense making. It is at this stage that clients can truly step back from their habitual identifications and view the many factors feeding into a conversation from a larger perspective. *Seeing the Dance from the Balcony*[21] is a metaphor for being able to rise above the immediacy of the conversational dance and to bring more of the elements impacting the conversation into view. I discuss how these shifts of perspective can be understood in terms of vertical development – the idea that the development of mental and emotional agility continues throughout adulthood and moves through distinct stages. Clients can be supported to see their conversations from a larger perspective, in particular by understanding the dance of underlying emotions and needs driving their habitual or reactive behaviours, and so moving towards more reflective (GREEN) conversational cycles.

Stage 4 Capability: Agility

The key capability at Stage 4 is to develop mental and emotional *agility*, which allows clients to shift perspective and to embrace the complexity of moving between different viewpoints. With agility they can zoom in to the details whilst sustaining a view of the bigger picture, and they can attend to the emotional as well as the practical content of conversations. Three factors that contribute to mental and emotional agility are *disidentifying*, *attunement* and *both-and thinking*. *Disidentifying* allows clients to observe their thoughts and beliefs, about themselves, about others or about the issues being discussed, without becoming overly attached or identified with them. Like mindfulness, it implies a dispassionate observing of thoughts and feelings, and so clients are less likely to be pulled into habitual or reactive communication styles. *Attunement* enables clients to empathise with the thoughts and feelings of others, standing in their shoes and seeing the world from their viewpoint. *Both-and thinking* enables clients to harness the different perspectives, motivations, concerns and hopes of self and others, and this paves the way for the fifth stage in the *Breakthrough Conversations* process.

Stage 5: Harnessing expanded perspectives

The opening up of the perspectives achieved in Stage 4 naturally flows into Stage 5, where there is the possibility of true collaboration and co-creation. This stage is the great prize of all of the reflective depth and awareness developed at earlier stages. We support clients to make use of the *Pause* to recognise and strengthen positive cycles of interaction. The capacity to sustain ambiguities and uncertainties is the basis in some situations for creative breakthroughs, and in other situations for coming to accept compromises and finding effective accommodations. Finally, we support clients to translate new ideas or solutions into practical next steps.

Stage 5 Capability: Playfulness

In this last stage we are aiming to foster *playfulness*, the capability to explore and experiment with others without fear of judgement or other threatening consequences. I think of *playfulness* as having three elements: *creativity*, *collaboration* and *pragmatism*. *Creativity* refers to the generation of fresh, adaptive ways of thinking or solving problems. A key stage in the creative process is 'incubation'; the ability to sustain the tension of uncertainty in order to allow new possibilities to emerge. *Collaboration* refers to the need for the new ideas in *Breakthrough Conversations* to arise from shared exploration and a mutual suspending of judgement, so that solutions are genuinely the product of interaction. *Pragmatism* refers to the need for solutions to be achievable and realistic, so that good ideas can be translated into shared action plans for which both parties feel a sense of ownership and commitment.

Summary

A review of a number of models of conversation from the areas of negotiation, conflict, couple therapy and mindfulness show both some of the common elements across many models, as well as certain features distinctive to specific models. A number of conditions and qualities that foster skilful conversations include mutual safety, purpose, respect, presence, curiosity, empathy and appreciation. Further key factors include distinguishing intent and interpretation, and naming underlying fears and needs. The *Breakthrough Conversations* approach draws on all of these useful approaches, bringing particular emphasis to the role of embodied awareness as a method for fostering self-regulation, for distinguishing body-brain states (RED-AMBER-GREEN), and for observing one's own reactive tendencies in order to make more skilful, conscious choices. The *Map of Breakthrough Conversations* moves through five stages, each with an associated key capability. Stage 1 is *Preparing the Ground* and the key capability is *motivation*. Stage 2 is *Managing Emotional States* and the key capability is *self-regulation*. Stage 3 is *Loosening Habit and Reactivity* and the key capability is *self-disclosure*. Stage 4 is *Seeing the Dance from the Balcony* and the key capability is *agility*. Stage 5 is *Harnessing Expanded Perspectives* and the key capability is *playfulness*. Having considered an overview of the five stages of this map, the following chapters look at each of these stages in detail.

Worksheet 4: Recognising conversational stages and capabilities

The purpose of this worksheet is to support clients to step back from key conversations, and to deepen their understanding about two things: one; what happens at different stages of the conversational process, and two; to reflect on the degree to which they make use of key capabilities at each of the stages.

Ask clients to bring to mind two conversations, one that was positive, fun or creative, and one that was more challenging, stuck or difficult.

1. Ask clients to look at the *Map of Breakthrough conversations*. Briefly describe each stage and ask clients to consider:
   a. To what extent did each of the conversations you identified move through each of the five stages?
   b. Which stages feel most familiar or comfortable for you, and which stages feel most unfamiliar or uncomfortable?
   c. What stages did the positive conversation move through?
   d. What happened in each stage in the difficult conversation?

2. Describe the key capabilities linked with each stage of the conversations map. Explore with clients:
   a. Which capabilities do you consider to be strengths and which do you consider to be development areas?
   b. Invite clients to give examples of conversations that demonstrate the use of key capabilities, or conversations where they would like to enhance their use of key capabilities.

Notes

1 Walton, R.E., McKersie, R.B. (1965). *A behavioural theory of labor negotiations.* McGraw Hill.
2 Fisher, R., Ury, W. (1981). *Getting to yes: Negotiating agreement without giving in.* Penguin Group.
3 Stone, D., Patton, B., Heen, S. (1999). *Difficult conversations: How to discuss what matters most.* Viking Penguin.
4 Patterson, K., Grenny, J., McMillan, R., Switzler, A. (2001). *Crucial conversations: Tools for talking when stakes are high.* McGraw Hill.
5 Rosenberg, M. (2003). *Nonviolent communicaton: A language of life.* Puddledancer Press.
6 Hendrix, H. (2005). *Getting the love you want: A guide for couples.* Simon and Schuster.
7 Gehlert, N.C. (2017). Randomized controlled trial of imago relationship therapy: Exploring statistical and clinical significance. *Faculty Bibliography*, 12, 188–209.
8 Johnson, S. (1996). *The practice of emotionally focused couple therapy.* Routledge.
9 Johnson, S., Hunsley, J., Greenberg, L., Schindler, D. (1999). Emotionally focused couples therapy: Status and challenges (A meta-analysis). *Journal of Clinical Psychology: Science and Practice*, 6(1), 67–79.
10 Kramer, G. (2007). *Insight dialogue: The interpersonal path to freedom.* Shambhala Publications.
11 Donaldson-Fielder, E. (2020). Mindfulness: A magical shift. *Coaching at Work*, 15(2), 44–48.
12 Baldwin, M. (2013). Interview with Carl Rogers on the use of self in therapy. In M. Baldwin (Ed.), *The use of self in therapy* (3rd ed., pp. 28–35). Routledge.

13 Geller, S.M., Greenberg, L.S. (2012). *Therapeutic presence: A mindful approach to effective therapy.* American Psychological Association, p. 7.
14 Kabat-Zinn, J. (1991). *Full catastrophe living.* Delta.
15 Gillis Chapman, S. (2012). *The five keys to mindful communication: Using deep listening and mindful speech to strengthen relationships, heal conflicts, and accomplish your goals.* Shambhala Publications.
16 White, J.J. (1984). The pros and cons of getting to yes. *Journal of Legal Education*, 34(1), 115–124.
17 Riemer, D. (2009). Creating sanctuary: Reducing violence in a maximum security forensic psychiatric hospital unit. *On the Edge*, 13(3), 7–10.
Suarez, A., Lee, D.Y., Rowe, C., Gomez, A.A., Murowchick, E., Linn, P.L. (2014). Freedom project: Nonviolent communication and mindfulness training in prison. *SAGE Open*, 4, 10.
18 Beasley, C.C., Ager, R. (2019, January). Emotionally focused couples therapy: A systematic review of its effectiveness over the past 19 years. *Journal of Evidence-Informed Social Work*, 3, 1–16.
19 Laurent, H.K., Hertz, R., Nelson, B., Laurent, S. (2016). Mindfulness during romantic conflict moderates the impact of negative partner behaviors on cortisol responses. *Hormones and Behavior*, 79, 45–51.
20 Corthorn, C., Milicic, N. (2016). Mindfulness and parenting: A correctional study of non-meditating mothers of preschool children. *Journal of Child and Family Studies*, 25, 1672–1683.
Dykens, E.M., Fisher, M.H., Taylor, J.L., Lambert, W., Miodrag, N. (2014). Reducing distress in mothers of children with autism and other disabilities: A randomised trial. *Pediatrics*, 134(2), 454–463.
21 This term is an adaptation of a phrase coined by Ronald Heifetz and Marty Linsky for helping leaders to get perspective: They describe operating in and above the fray as "…getting off the dance floor and going to the balcony," in, Heifetz, R., Linsky, M. (2002, June). A survival guide for leaders. *Harvard Business Review*, 80(6), 65–74.

Chapter 5

Preparing the ground

When we begin to work with clients our first task in Stage 1 is to *Prepare the Ground* for the coaching journey. I think of the primary capability we are seeking to engage at the outset of coaching as *motivation*, specifically the intrinsic motivation of clients. If clients are having conversations with us because a manager or partner told them to, then they are unlikely to approach the work with the degree of commitment required for real change to occur. They will be resistant from the outset. Even if clients do feel motivated to change, they may still have confusion about what they want to change, or have doubts about their capacity to change. So, at the initial stages of our work, we need to support clients to organise their hopes and intentions in ways that spark their intrinsic motivation and their courage. What do they most want from the work? What will success look like? What kind of support do they imagine will be most conducive to their development? What are their fears, and what will make the journey safe enough to confront their fears?

In this chapter I describe how we engage the *motivation* of clients by focusing on three elements, *purpose*, *intentions* and *courage*. I begin by introducing the notion of a conversational lens and the usefulness of anchoring the purpose and vision of our work in terms of specific conversational outcomes. I then consider a further key aspect for engaging intrinsic motivation: the cultivation of character. I use the concept of character as a way of defining the intentions clients have for being their 'best selves', and so viewing the conversational domain as a practical opportunity for developing specific character habits. I introduce the *Character Compass* as a frame for supporting clients to assess their conversational character habits, for identifying those habits that are most aligned to their intentions, and specifically exploring the character habit of *courage*. Finally, I discuss practical considerations and consider how we engage client reflectiveness from the outset.

Introducing a conversational lens

I was originally trained in psychoanalysis, but it was the solution-focused therapy approach that taught me the importance of understanding client challenges in behavioural terms. If a client said they were depressed, rather than asking the question: *What is making you depressed*, or *Why are you depressed*, I was taught to consider an evocatively different question: *Can you tell me how you do depression?* Clients would then describe themselves as staying in bed until midday, keeping the curtains drawn, not bothering to have a shower, and perhaps listening to music that had a depressive theme. The idea of this line of inquiry is to consider the smallest behavioural change they could make that would represent a non-depressive way of behaving. I was impressed by the effectiveness of this approach. It seemed to plant a seed of hope and opened the door to clients being more committed to therapy, and subsequently allowed for a deeper investigation of their psychology. Bringing this behavioural emphasis to *Breakthrough Conversations*, our goal is to consider how a presenting development challenge might be constructed as a conversational development challenge.

For example, a manager stated that one of his coaching goals was to learn how to be more efficient in managing the high workloads in his department. He said he needed to be more efficient in managing his time, and he talked about the need to recruit a better calibre of staff. When I asked him to tell me more about key team members it became clear that he was frustrated with several of them for not showing the commitment he would expect. But when I ask him if he had made his expectations clear it turns out he had not. He felt awkward being demanding, preferring for them to intuit what he considered to be real commitment, but then got resentful when they didn't operate to his standards. Although the coaching went on to consider his fear of conflict and the origins of this in his life, our work was constructed behaviourally around the challenge of having more direct conversations about his expectations. More effective team member conversations became the target for change, and learning how to have more assertive conversations became the doorway into exploring his self-identity. The conversational focus shifted the purpose from being about managing workloads to being about relational courage.

Constructing purpose in terms of conversation

Whether clients say they want to be better at presentations, to develop more confidence, to motivate team members, to influence stakeholders or to collaborate more with a partner or colleague, any of these development goals can be explored in terms of the specific behavioural conversations that are experienced as challenging. One way of introducing the conversational lens to clients is to describe the four purposes of conversation (Figure 1.1) and to invite them to identify enabling and limiting conversations that occur in each domain (Worksheet 1). Each of these domains provides opportunities for self-inquiry and for experimenting with new ways of relating. Within these broader categories of purpose, our inquiry into what is happening in one or two specific relationships allows us to shape specific conversational goals. The following case study shows how I worked with Doug to convert his initial concern about stress and overwhelm into the challenge of having more direct and transparent conversations with a specific colleague, Frasier.

> An initial session with Doug began with him talking about how a rapid growth in the demand for their services was causing stress and overwhelm for the whole of the core team. When I asked him to talk about how his relationship with key colleagues was helping or hindering him in addressing these challenges, he spoke about Frasier, a man he had brought in to update organisational processes. Doug wanted to speak positively about Frasier, but he reluctantly acknowledged that he was disappointed with his contribution, and in particular, his capacity to step back from the details and to see the bigger picture. I asked Doug if he had given feedback to Frasier about his perceptions and expectations. He said that he had. Not accepting that at face value, but wanting to understand the texture of Doug's conversational approach, I asked him to give me a flavour of what he had said to Frasier, perhaps even imagining that I was Frasier. What became immediately apparent was how difficult Doug found it to speak directly about what he wanted. He began with broad general comments, veered off into elaborate digressions, and failed to land any direct statement about his expectations and concerns. When I reflected these observations back to Doug, he said he did not want to be ungrateful for all the work that Frasier was doing, but also acknowledged that he did not like conflict. As we explored this dynamic further it seemed that Doug's lack of clarity and his unwillingness to be direct with others was a key obstacle to addressing the organisation's emerging challenges. I began to construct the development challenge as helping Doug to have more direct and transparent conversations with Frasier and other key colleagues. At first glance this construction can seem behavioural and transactional, but, as I have emphasised already, this kind of practical goal is a window into a much deeper unpacking of self-awareness, self-regulation, beliefs and relational attunement, and it is this journey of awareness that ultimately yields enduring shifts in conversational skilfulness.

In my experience clients are relieved by the translation of broadly defined concerns into practical, conversational challenges. If a client is frustrated by decision-makers showing a sustained lack of investment in technology, the development challenge becomes one of knowing how to have more effective, influential conversations with decision-makers. If a client does not feel listened to in meetings, the development challenge becomes one of knowing how to communicate specific ideas in specific meetings with presence and impact. If two departments are at loggerheads about shared responsibilities, the development challenge becomes one of orchestrating effective conversations between the two team leaders. Conversations offer an engaging behavioural anchor for constellating profound psychological change.

Four specific conversational goals

Once we have supported clients to frame their development goals in terms of a number of specific conversations; either that they will enact with us but undertake outside the coaching space, or that they will undertake as part of paired sessions with us, it is useful to ask them to distinguish four goals for a conversation:

- What do I want for myself?
- What do I want for the other person?
- What do I want for the relationship?
- What do I want for the organisation or wider group?

Clients are often surprised to realise that a conversation can have multiple goals. I continue the case study with Doug and Frasier to illustrate this multifaceted exploration of goals.

> Using the case illustration introduced above, Doug considered each of these questions in relation to Frasier. He found it easiest to start with the fourth question first: what do I want for the organisation? He said he wanted the core team to feel as if the systems and processes were working well, that their roles were clearly defined, and that they felt as though they were being supported to be at their best. Asked about what he wanted for himself, he said he wanted to feel able to provide clear direction, and not to be diverted by new ideas or his fear of conflict. For Frasier, he wanted to be able to communicate in ways that helped Frasier be successful and to have confidence in taking charge within his own area. For the relationship, he wanted to maintain a strong sense of care and trust, and to establish a quality of ease and light-heartedness that used to be part of their relationship.

Drawing out these goals with clients helps to engage their motivation for having constructive conversations and to find the courage to explore what it would take to have conversations in new ways. A further, linked aspect of fostering motivation is to invite clients to envision a picture of success. A vision opens clients to their hopes, optimism and constructive intentions, and so fuels their motivation. Many clients considering the prospect of a conversation readily imagine difficulties, and if they pause to notice their feelings and bodily sensations, they discover anxiety, fear, together with tightening in the body, perhaps in the belly, chest or throat. In terms of body-brain awareness, we could say that the very thought of a conversation evokes a RED state. Shifting focus to imagining positive outcomes opens up a sense of possibility and is associated with GREEN states.

We can simply ask clients: what would a successful conversation look like? However, this question, without an invitation to a reflective pause, will be answered from a purely cognitive perspective. So, we might use guided inquiry, to support a deeper and more embodied reflection. I typically ask clients to take a moment to pause, anchoring awareness in the sensations of body and breath, to notice what is present for them, and then when they are settled, to bring to mind the issue they need to have a conversation about, and to get a picture in their mind of how things would be if the conversation was optimally successful.

> In the case illustration introduced above about Doug having a more direct conversation with Frasier, Doug welcomed the opportunity to be guided in a brief visualisation of a successful conversation and its outcome. With my guidance he closed his eyes, brought his awareness to the sensations of his body in contact with the floor, and the chair, and then settled for a couple of minutes with the sensations of the flow of his breathing. I then asked him to think about Frasier and himself having constructive conversations, and letting a picture emerge in his mind's eye of how they would look together if they managed to do that. His picture of success was seeing himself and Frasier smiling and laughing together, celebrating a sense of alignment around how to tackle some of the organisational challenges they faced. I encouraged Doug to notice how it felt in his body as he savoured this positive vision. He described a sense of bodily ease and relaxed breathing, and he noticed that his brow was less furrowed with worry. In terms of body-brain state, he was describing a GREEN state, readily evoked by his vision of success. This motivating picture reinforced Doug's strong need to treat Frasier fairly and to be able to have the conversation in a way that communicated his sense of care and warmth for Frasier as a friend and colleague.

In terms of engaging the motivation of clients, I have so far spoken about identifying the purpose of the work, translating broader purpose into more specific, behavioural, conversational goals, and also the potential value of envisioning a successful outcome for conversations. A further important aspect of intrinsic motivation is to invite clients to consider their character habits and the potential to use conversations as a place to cultivate being one's best self.

Character habits and personal intentions

Many clients are motivated by the idea of being their best selves. This is why people make New Year's resolutions; they have an intrinsic desire to be 'better' in some aspect of their lives such as their health, their education, their time-management, their compassion or their work-life balance. In coaching we can harness these intrinsic motivations by linking character habits to specific coaching goals. Some coaches like to explore values with their clients, offering a list of values and descriptors and taking clients through a process to discern their top five values. I personally prefer to distinguish between values and character habits. Values refer to a collection of guiding principles that are deemed to be correct and desirable in life, especially regarding personal conduct such as honesty, integrity and kindness. These may be powerfully motivating ideas, but I think many people are conflicted or woolly about their values. They want to be honest, but they also know they sometimes lie to avoid difficult conversations. They want to show integrity but know they can be opportunistic in some situations. Values are desirable external standards, but most of us know that we sometimes fail to live up to our own standards, and in these circumstances, values become more a source of conflict or denial than a source of motivation.

In contrast, I think of character habits as qualities or values enacted through behaviour.

When we hear a speech about someone's achievements, they are often described in terms of strengths of character, the qualities expressed through their actions. Character implies that certain moral principles have been internalised and integrated into who they are, as evidenced by how they conduct themselves. In a person's character there is an integration of self that brings together thoughts, feelings, and actions into harmony, resulting in someone who walks the talk of his or her belief system. Conversations, as the primary channel for relational behaviour, reveal the status of our character habits, and, if we are seeking to develop ourselves, they are a powerful domain for strengthening positive character habits.

The Character Compass

There are many models suggesting sets of positive character habits drawn from moral and religious traditions across all cultures, and researchers have sought to classify groups of character strengths into an overarching model.[1,2] Although useful, I have found these models that list multiple dimensions a little unwieldy, perhaps because I prefer something I can visualise, and if possible, experience in some way in my body. It was this desire to create a framework of character habits, both for myself and for my clients, that led to the development of the *Character Compass* (Figure 5.1).

The core idea is to envisage character as an actual moral compass, so that we use character to guide our behaviour in life and in our conversations. I will first describe the basis for the vertical and horizontal axes of this compass. The vertical dimension expresses the opposing energies of, at the lower end of the dimension, *Grounded* in the character habits of *integrity*, *self-regulation* and *responsibility*, and at the upper end, reaching towards the *Seeking* character habits of *courage*, *intention* and *vitality*. This *Grounded-Seeking* dimension resembles those characterised in other models for

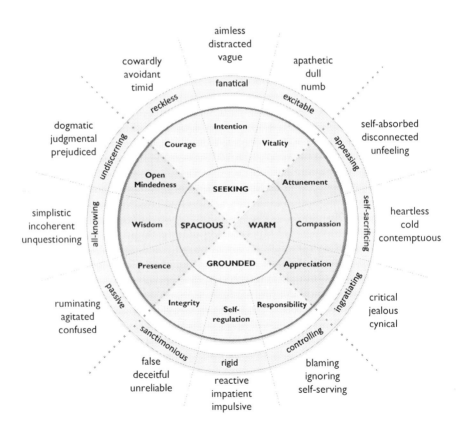

Figure 5.1 The *Character Compass*.

mapping change, where the opposing ends of the spectrum are transactional and transformational, practice and vision, sensation and intuition, and data and ideas.[3] I like to imagine this as an embodied dimension, like we might in a yoga or tai chi class, with our feet *Grounded* on the floor, rising via the body to the *Seeking* tendencies of the mind with its capacity to set intentions and imagine new futures. Just standing, we can imagine ourselves *Grounded* in our *integrity*, *self-regulation* and *responsibility* in our feet, and at the same time feel ourselves reaching up through our *Seeking* aspirations – *courage*, *intentions* and *vitality* – lifting from the shoulders and head.

The horizontal dimension expresses the opposing energies of, on the left, *Spaciousness*, which includes *presence*, *wisdom* and *open-mindedness*, and on the right, *Warmth*, which includes *attunement*, *compassion* and *appreciation*. This *Spacious-Warm* dimension draws on the balance of wisdom and compassion described in Buddhist psychology, which uses the metaphor of the two wings of a bird for these complementary qualities. Like the *Grounded-Seeking* dimension, we can also think of this *Spacious-Warm* dimension as an embodied experience, with each of our arms outstretched representing the balance of spaciousness and warmth in the expression of our character habits. So, at its simplest level, the *Character Compass* has just two dimensions, *Grounded-Seeking* and *Spacious-Warm*, giving rise to the four cardinal directions of character. At this level, we can invite clients to consider how they wish to approach conversations, holding in mind the balance of these four energies.

Some clients will readily name their tendency to approach most conversations with a bias towards *Seeking*. They have bold ideas about what they want to achieve and have the courage to express them, but they may not show the grounded integrity and self-regulation for getting buy-in to their ideas. Or some clients recognise a tendency to approach most conversations with a bias towards Warmth, with a strong emphasis on attunement and appreciation, but without the balancing sense of discernment that comes with the *Spacious* quality of wisdom. Supporting clients to consider the four cardinal directions of character can provide an easily remembered frame for connecting to core character habits, and, as we shall see, reminding oneself of one's best intentions during conversations.

Twelve-character habits

Some clients choose to look more closely at their character habits, and in this case we can provide them with a more detailed account of the *Character Compass*. As shown in Figure 5.1, each of the four cardinal directions at the centre of the compass is divided into three indicative character qualities, making a total of 12-character qualities. The *Grounded* habits – *integrity*, *self-regulation* and *responsibility* – are concerned with providing emotional steadiness and moral clarity in our conversations. The *Spacious* habits –

open-mindedness, wisdom and *presence* – are concerned with bringing perspective, equanimity and insight to our conversations. The *Warm* habits – *attunement, compassion* and *appreciation* – are concerned with bringing kindness, positivity and emotional intelligence to our conversations. The *Seeking* habits – *courage, intention* and *vitality* – are concerned with bringing direction, energy and boldness to our conversations.

A further concept I have borrowed from Buddhism is the idea of near and far enemies. In the ring directly outside the 12-character habits are terms to describe 'near enemies', where the character qualities are taken to an extreme and distorted. For example, having *integrity* is a positive character habit, but if it is taken to an extreme it becomes a near enemy of being *sanctimonious* or *holier than thou*. In the outer ring are the 'far enemies', the behaviours that stand in opposition to the character habits. For example, the far enemy for *integrity* is being *false* or *deceitful*. A more detailed description of the terms for the character habits, near enemies and far enemies for each of the cardinal directions is shown in Table 5.1.

Sharing these descriptors by character habit allows clients to find the words that resonate most strongly for them and provides the basis for creating a personalised *Character Compass*. I share a copy of Figure 5.1 and Table 5.1 with clients and ask them to underline words in red, amber or green to indicate which are most characteristic or habitual (their AMBER state), which near or far enemies are most evident when they are triggered (RED state), and which are the qualities they most want to develop or build on in being most skilful in their conversations (GREEN state). I get them to use this traffic light distinction, even though I don't usually introduce *RAG* body-brain states until Stage 2 in the *Breakthrough Conversations* process where we are focused on *Managing Emotional States*. At this stage our focus is on sparking motivation and reflection on skilful or less skilful behavioural habits. Some clients have used this frame as the basis for a 360° feedback exercise with colleagues, inviting them to note which items are most characteristic and which arise when the person being assessed is being more reactive.

When we have gathered this information, I prepare a personalised *Character Compass* for clients, based on this analysis, as a visual reminder of their personal intentions for use before engaging in conversations, or for reflecting afterwards about how a conversation went. Some clients choose to put this on the wall by their desk or to share it with a partner. In working with the *Character Compass*, I encourage clients to add their own words or to illustrate the cardinal directions and qualities with their own real-life examples, so that it becomes a personal, practical tool that readily makes sense to them.

Combining character qualities

Just as primary colours can be blended to create a myriad of other colours and shades, we can think of the *Character Compass* as providing

Table 5.1 Character Compass: Qualities and Terms

Seeking	Similar Terms	Near Enemy	Far Enemy
Courage	Bravery, boldness, risk taking, challenge, assertiveness, confidence, conviction	Reckless, devil-may-care, foolhardy, rash, defiant, red mist	Timid, avoidant, cowardly, surrendering, indecisive, doubting
Intention	Purpose, hope, focus, optimism, future-orientation, ambition, vision, strategy	Fanatical, obsessive, narrow-minded, zealous, stubborn	Aimless, distracted vague, lost, pessimistic, negative, hopeless, near-sighted
Vitality	Desire, energy, joy, motivation, drive, passion, inspiration, enthusiasm	Hyperactive, restless, overzealous, excitable	Dull, numb, bored, apathetic, gloomy
Grounded	*Similar Terms*	*Near Enemy*	*Far Enemy*
Integrity	Sincerity, honesty, authenticity, humility, respectful, treating others as we would wish to be treated, moral, loyal, trustworthy	Holier than thou, sanctimonious, aloof, harsh candour	False, deceitful, unreliable, disrespectful, dishonest, gossiping
Self-Regulation	Resilience, discipline, stability, prudence, persistence, determination, tolerance, patience, restraint, non-reactivity	Rigid, inflexible, repressed, pig-headed, set in one's ways	Reactive, impatient, impulsive, impetuous, unpredictable
Responsibility	Ownership, admitting one's mistakes, justice, citizenship, fairness, duty, service	Controlling, it's all my fault, over-protective, rescuing	Blaming, complaining, self-serving, blind to own mistakes, ignoring
Spacious	*Similar Terms*	*Near Enemy*	*Far Enemy*
Open mindedness	Curiosity, challenging own biases, valuing different perspectives, receptivity	Anything goes, undiscerning, indifferent, sycophantic	Dogmatic, prejudiced, judgmental, inflexible
Wisdom	Discernment, balance, insight objectivity, creativity, humour, perspective, playfulness, big picture	All-knowing, sceptical, bombastic, overly logical	Simplistic, misguided, incoherent, overly literal, unquestion

(Continued)

98 Preparing the ground

Table 5.1 (Continued)

Seeking	Similar Terms	Near Enemy	Far Enemy
Presence	Mindfulness, acceptance, allowing, equanimity, being, stillness, calmness	Passive, laissez-faire, uninvolved, indifferent, bystanding	Ruminating, agitated, confused, scattered, obsessive, overly vigilant
Warm Attunement	*Similar Terms* Empathy, emotional intelligence, psychological mindedness, mentalising	*Near Enemy* Merging, compliant appeasing, submissive, manipulative, meek	*Far Enemy* Self-absorbed, disconnected, unfeeling, incurious, distant
Compassion	Kindness, love, forgiveness, goodwill, generosity, affection, self-compassion	Self-sacrificing, spoiling others, compassion, fatigue	Cold, harsh, contemptuous, merciless, heartless
Appreciation	Wonder, gratitude, excellence, joy, positivity, celebration	Ingratiating, unctuous, sugary, overblown	Critical, jealous, undermining, self-critical

a set of primary character qualities and habits, and these are often blended to give rise to other qualities. For example, *attunement* with *wisdom* provides the discernment to have boundaries, and to prevent the arising of merger or co-dependency. The self-discipline in *Self-Regulation*, without the tempering aspects of self-compassion (*compassion*) can lead to self-harshness and self-criticism (far enemies of *appreciation*). Being controlling, which can manifest as a near enemy of the quality of *Responsibility*, is often a way of managing fear by denying vulnerability, which is linked to a lack of empathy (*attunement* and *compassion*) towards oneself. Learning to trust others is a key challenge for many clients, and we might ask them which character habits they would need to draw on in developing their trust for others. One client said that for him trusting others is a combination of the discernment in *wisdom*, the risk-taking in *courage*, the humility in *integrity* and the emotional intelligence in *attunement*. He explained this by noting that he needs the discernment to decide who was trustworthy, the risk-taking to let a person learn from their own mistakes, the humility to not assume that he could always do things better than others and the emotional intelligence to understand how others want to be given the opportunity to develop and to take on more responsibility. Having identified these four-character habits he went through each member of his team to decide how he could stretch his own capacity to trust, whilst being wise and prudent, and we used coaching sessions to reflect on how his conversations could support these positive intentions.

Self-awareness is a central capacity in *Breakthrough Conversations* and so is required for bringing attention to any of the character qualities, but we can also ask clients to consider which qualities will foster their self-awareness the most. Clients often point towards a blend of *open-mindedness* to bring curiosity and self-inquiry, *courage* to challenge themselves and *responsibility* to be willing to own their vulnerabilities or mistakes. (These qualities, *self-inquiry*, *challenge* and *ownership*, are also those identified as constituting the capability for s*elf-disclosure* required at Stage 3 of the *Breakthrough Conversations* process). Confidence and self-belief are further qualities that many clients are looking to develop. The primary character quality in confidence is *courage*, but this needs to be blended with other qualities, such as empathy (*attunement*) if confidence is not to become blind conviction and omnipotence. For others, confidence develops by combining *courage* with the discernment of *wisdom*, so that they recognise their own competence and self-efficacy. Also, for many clients the key to developing confidence is to have an antidote to their inner self-critic, and so the quality of *courage* needs to be combined with self-kindness and self-compassion (*compassion/appreciation*).

The *Character Compass* and the 12-character habits provide a basis for a rich exploration of motivating intentions. How we use such a frame needs to be driven by the preferences of clients. Some clients find it most useful to target just one 'far enemy', such as a tendency to ruminate about problems and mistakes, and so focus on the development of *presence* as the antidote. Others identify three or four key qualities they wish to develop. And some find it more useful to work with the four cardinal directions – *Grounded*, *Seeking*, *Spacious*, *Warm* – and to set the intention of balancing these as they relate to others. One client likened the balancing of the four cardinal directions to surfing, the *Grounded-Seeking* dimension allowing him to be firmly connected to his surfboard through his feet, whilst allowing his knees and body and head to respond flexibly to the rise and fall of the waves, and the *Spacious-Warm* dimension was his arms supporting him to maintain his balance, to thrill in the spaciousness of being with the elements, and delighting in his appreciation of his aliveness. The following case study with Rana provides a detailed illustration of the use of the *Character Compass* in relation to key conversations.

Illustration using the *Character Compass*

When I was briefed about offering coaching to Rana I was told that he was one of the most able members of the team, with a valuable breadth that spanned technical knowledge and an ability to think

100 Preparing the ground

creatively with clients about how new solutions could be tailored to their needs. His credibility in forming client relationships was highly valued. These qualities had led to him becoming more influential within the organisation, but internally his challenging interpersonal style was causing waves with certain departments and senior colleagues. Feedback from his team also showed that he did not make sufficient time for managing his team because he was most motivated by addressing his own business challenges and was quickly bored by the administrative parts of his role. The goal of coaching was twofold: to support him in developing a more flexible influence style with other key business functions, and to develop his team management skills. We agreed that coaching would combine individual sessions with some paired sessions with key stakeholders, as well as one or more team development sessions.

When I asked Rana about his motivation, both for his work and for engaging in a piece of development through coaching, he was very upbeat; describing how stimulated he was by his work challenges, and by the prospect of using coaching to be more effective in his role. He acknowledged his ambition to take on more responsibility, and to have the remit to shape the direction of his role, but recognised that his people management skills needed to develop. He said that he often found himself at odds with colleagues who seemed mired in process and slow decision-making, and he was quick to call out issues, even with senior colleagues. We explored his habitual ways of relating, and how he would behave if he was triggered. He said that he was most aggravated by the difficulty in getting others to look at the world the way he did, and, when he met resistance or what he perceived to be a lack of engagement, he acknowledged that he would quickly become reactive. This was particularly evident in relation to senior colleagues, and he agreed that he could seem like a trade-union shop steward, determined to challenge 'management' for what he saw as their poor decisions and lack of care for junior members of staff.

Using the *Character Compass* and the list of descriptors he identified his RED behaviours such as being *stubbornly challenging*, *dogmatic*, *critical* and *complaining*. He could also feel self-righteous at these times and so believed that his harsh candour was part of operating with integrity. These RED states were in contrast to his more habitual (AMBER) style, when he would typically be *optimistic*, *driving* things forward with a balance of *discernment* and *creativity*, and inspiring others with his *determination* and *generosity* in supporting others to solve difficult problems. Each of these italicised descriptors is shown in Rana's personalised *Character Compass* in Figure 5.2. Getting Rana to be more reflective, I invited Rana to identify the character qualities he felt he most wanted to develop for

Preparing the ground 101

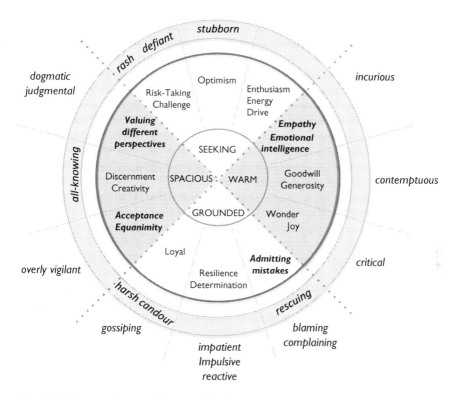

Figure 5.2 Character Compass Summary for Rana.

relating to others more effectively, and these descriptors are shown in bold.

For descriptive purposes we can think of the compass as having three rings outside the central circle showing the four cardinal directions. The words that are not in bold in the first ring represent those that are Rana's habitual strengths, such as resilience, loyalty, energy and optimism. (In a colour print of the compass these could be shown in amber). The words in the shaded, second ring represent Rana's 'near enemies' that might occur habitually but more often occurred when he was triggered into reactivity, when he might typically be stubborn, rash and rescuing of others. In the third, outer ring, are Rana's 'far enemies' in terms of character, when he might seem to others as contemptuous, blaming or gossiping. The key part of this approach for engaging motivation concerns setting character habit intentions, and as I mentioned already, these are the words shown in bold in the first ring. Rana said there were four areas he most needed to cultivate as he approached his conversations with others.

> First, he felt he needed to connect with a sense of *acceptance* that he could not control everything, and to develop his *equanimity* so that he would not be overinvested in specific outcomes. He also recognised that he could be overly vigilant and hypersensitive to the notion of injustice, and so wanted to use his awareness to notice rather than react to these tendencies. Second, he saw that he needed to develop his *empathy* and *emotional intelligence* to counteract his tendency to be task-focused and relatively incurious about others. Third, he acknowledged that he wanted to take ownership for his errors of judgement by *admitting mistakes*. Fourth, he wanted to step back from being dogmatic and prescriptive with others, and to cultivate open-mindedness by *valuing different perspectives*.
>
> In sessions that corresponded to later stages in the *Breakthrough Conversations* process Rana engaged in paired sessions with two of his colleagues and for each of these sessions he used his personalised *Character Compass* as a tool for setting his intentions in advance of the meetings. The *Character Compass* supported him to find a more spacious and inquiring way of relating to his colleagues. He found himself listening more attentively and asking more questions so he could deepen his understanding of their positions. When he noticed himself becoming triggered he could pause, using some of the skills I discuss in the next chapter to manage emotional states in order to bring himself back to a more GREEN state. He saw the *Character Compass* as helping him to find his way amidst the emotional complexity of conversation, and it contributed to him engaging in a number of *Breakthrough Conversations*.

Recognising fears and the need for courage

The primary reason for working with the *Character Compass* is to identify character habits that clients are intrinsically motivated to cultivate in themselves. But, as I have described, the *Character Compass* also includes descriptions of near and far enemies, and so it does also provide an opportunity for clients to identify areas of reactivity. Given that we are seeking to engage the motivation of clients at this stage I do not usually dwell on reactivity – there is plenty of opportunity to do this more insightfully at later stages when we have introduced clients to the techniques for managing body-brain states. However, the one area of reactivity that it is useful to address more directly in this first stage is potential fears about what the coaching conversations will evoke. It is natural for clients to feel anxious about an approach that encourages self-examination and potentially moves towards paired conversations to address conversational tendencies. We can normalise such fears as part and parcel of all development, and so a natural part of seeking to develop oneself through new conversational behaviours.

To move foward in the face of fear requires *courage* (one element of the cardinal direction of *Seeking*), and relational courage is key to collaboration and more agile forms of leadership. We can explicitly ask clients to talk about any concerns they have about coaching, and, as I describe below, invite them to reflect on their reactions. In this way we seed the idea at the outset that emotional responses are always present and that in this coaching approach we are especially interested in bringing these responses into view. In addition, we can reassure clients that we will move at an appropriate pace that supports them to expand their windows of emotional tolerance, and that such expanded awareness and resilience are themselves central outcomes of development.

Practical considerations

So far in this chapter I have focused on the importance of motivation as paving the way for developing clients through a conversational lens. By clarifying purpose, envisioning success, setting specific goals and identifying investment in the development of character habits, we encourage clients to find their intrinsic motivation and courage. Initial sessions will also necessarily need to cover practical considerations: the regularity of meetings, the potential gathering of feedback through interviews or questionnaires, the use of psychometric instruments, the inclusion of three-way review meetings with managers, and the use of online or face-to-face meetings. Some clients also like to have an overarching view of the journey they are being invited to take with us, and so I will show the *Map of Breakthrough Conversations* (Figure 4.1) and briefly describe the stages. However, I would caution against being overly detailed in such accounts of the approach. Some cognitive understanding is useful for clients, but it can also serve as a diversion from beginning to talk about what is most important for clients.

Introducing paired sessions

A further important practical consideration is the question of whether the work will involve facilitated pair conversations as well as one-to-one sessions. Sometimes the reason clients choose us is because they know we offer paired coaching combined with one-to-one work, and so the blending of individual and paired sessions is part of the contract from the outset. However, if it is the sponsor rather than the coachees who are asking for paired sessions, then we need to approach the notion of paired work more cautiously. Sponsors sometimes decide that mediation will be the solution to difficulties between two people, without the buy-in of the people involved. This is a recipe for resistance. In such circumstances I prefer to meet with the individuals involved for one or more sessions, develop my own diagnosis of what is happening in the relationship, and then if appropriate, explore with those clients individually if they are open to the idea of being coached as a pair. When we have time to build trust and safety in one-to-one sessions, clients often become open to paired work that they would previously have rejected. In some cases I work with clients one-to-one for a while before the notion of paired work surfaces naturally from the conversational focus of our work. In terms of contracting with coaching purchasers, I usually propose a block of coaching that includes the possibility of being extended to include paired work. So, a typical contract might contain six individual sessions plus three paired sessions, with one or more individual sessions for the other member of the pair. Or, another popular approach is a nine-session coaching package: three individual sessions for each individual, plus three paired sessions. I have another client who has opted for a six-session package, consisting of two individual sessions for each member of a pair, plus two paired sessions. Yet another useful approach has been to introduce the concept of *Breakthrough Conversations* in a workshop setting to groups of people, and then to include follow-up paired coaching for participants after the workshop. The workshop setting has the benefit of normalising the challenge of being conversationally skilful and encourages a more open attitude to being facilitated in pairs. The approach can also be extended to small group or team settings where we typically facilitate clients in a blend of pairs, trios, quartets and larger groupings.

Engaging client reflectiveness

Central to this whole conversational approach is the importance of the client's capacity for reflection, supported by skills to observe and manage body-brain states. I focus explicitly on *Managing Emotional States* in Stage 2 of the process once I have engaged the client's motivation for change. Nevertheless, it is important to instil a quality of reflectiveness into the conversational dynamic during this first stage. We can do this quite naturally and seamlessly through the mode and style of our inquiry. For example, we might ask:

1. *What is your experience?* To this question, clients will tell us about something that they are interested in or concerned about. And then we can ask:
2. *What do you notice about yourself as you describe this experience?*

This second question is amazingly powerful. It invites clients to become observers to the emotional and embodied experience emerging from them in relation to a specific topic or challenge. Sometimes clients won't notice that we have asked such a radically different question and continue with the narrative about the experience. If this happens, we can gently acknowledge the momentum of their storytelling, and invite them again to see what it is like to pause and to bring their attention to how they are relating to the experience. We might ask them to describe their feelings, or we might ask them to bring attention to their body sensations. Again, this is unfamiliar territory to most clients so we might be explicit about this:

> One of my goals in working with you is to support your self-awareness. A good way of doing that is to bring your attention away from our thoughts and to let it move down into the sensations of the body. So, if you do that now ... letting go of the details of the specific experience you have been describing and bringing your attention down into your experience of your body, what sensations do you notice? ... Are there areas of tightness or spaciousness? ... Is there warmth or coolness? ... What do you notice? ... Is this experience pleasant, unpleasant or neutral? ... What feelings does it evoke? ... What images or thoughts arise as you notice these experiences?

We deepen this inquiry by distinguishing thoughts, feelings, bodily sensations and behaviours – a potential forerunner of using the more structured *PACES* framework in Stage 2. Our aim is to evoke reflective awareness, in relation to positive as well as difficult experiences. So, we might ask clients to think about situations where they cope with challenges more resourcefully, and then to notice how they relate to these experiences. What body sensations arise when they are feeling positive? What are the emotions? When invited to reflect like this, clients typically shift to a positive (GREEN) state, sitting more attentively, relaxing their shoulders, smiling, and speaking in a more upbeat or relaxed way. When this occurs, we again invite clients to pause and to notice this shift in state, reinforcing their capacity to observe their own emotional states and how readily they can change. The following case illustrates the reinforcement of reflective awareness at the early stages of a coaching relationship.

> In her second coaching session Jess talked about having to negotiate a contract with a client and commented on her tendency to be overly compliant. I invited her to tell me about the specifics of the conversation with the person she was negotiating with. As she spoke about this, I noticed that she tended to look down at her hands, to sit very still, and that her voice had a somewhat monotone quality about it. I asked her to take a moment to pause and to observe how she was feeling as she spoke to me about this situation. She said that she was feeling frustration with herself because this compliant tendency was familiar to her and it annoyed her. I acknowledged what she said and invited her to consider the body sensations that went with what she had been telling me. She said that she felt tension in her belly and, staying with that for a while, she noticed a knot or

> lump in her throat. I asked her to take a moment to dwell with these sensations and to see what else came into her awareness. She noticed a heaviness in her chest and then the prickle of tears behind her eyes. I asked her what feelings she would associate with these sensations. She said it was sadness. I asked her to take some time with these feelings, and then asked her what she thought the sadness was about. She said she felt sad because she found it hard to be as assertive as she wanted to be in negotiations. I then asked her to take some time to notice how it felt, having recognised this sadness and its link to her desire to be more assertive. I could see there was something lighter in her now – her way of sitting, in her eyes, in the relaxation of the muscles around her mouth. She said that she felt strangely calm and even excited about the possibility of approaching this kind of situation in a different way.

This case study illustrates how guided reflectiveness can readily evoke shifts in emotional state. It may take clients longer to establish the ease of reflection exhibited by Jess, but most clients will respond very positively to our guidance to evoke more reflective awareness and doing this from the outset of our work prepares the ground for more structured inquiry at later stages.

Summary

The initial stages of the *Breakthrough Conversations* approach are concerned with evoking the motivation of clients to engage in the reflection and self-inquiry necessary for making shifts in how they relate to others. We evoke intrinsic motivation by inviting clients to talk about what they want to achieve through coaching. As we explore the purpose of the work, we also consider the degree to which coaching goals can be framed in conversational terms. So, broader purposes such as being more confident, being more influential, motivating others, or getting teams to collaborate better, are formulated more specifically in terms of particular conversational challenges. These conversational challenges can be further explored by considering them in terms of the different goals clients have for themselves, for others, for the relationship and for the wider group or organisation. This process of honing a sense of purpose and goals strengthens intrinsic motivation because clients feel empowered by seeing a pathway to change that lies within their scope of control. Developing a vision or picture of success can also reinforce motivation. A further strengthening of motivation can be fostered by exploring character habits and supporting clients to consider how they can use the conversational domain as a place to be one's best self. The *Character Compass* is a frame for capturing the four cardinal directions of character:

Grounded, Seeking, Spacious and *Warm*, and these, together with an expanded set of 12-character habits, provide a basis for identifying strengths and gaps in character habits and for prioritising specific habits that clients wish to develop in conversational contexts. The analysis of character also draws out areas of reactivity, and at this stage we bring specific attention to the importance of *courage* in making optimal use of the coaching journey. The initial sessions also need to cover a number of practical aspects of coaching, such as the methods for gathering feedback or other data and the use of paired sessions as well as one-to-one sessions. The first stage of this approach also begins to evoke reflectiveness through the nature of our inquiry, and the invitation for clients to notice their embodied, emotional responses to experience.

Worksheet 5: Checklist of areas for exploration during Stage 1: preparing the ground

The purpose of this checklist is to summarise the range of areas that might be covered during Stage 1: *Preparing the Ground.*

1. The four purposes of conversations (see Worksheet 1).
2. Identifying purpose, constructing purpose in terms of conversational goals, and creating a vision of success.
3. The *Character Compass* as a basis for exploring how conversations can be used to cultivate character habits of being one's best self.
4. Exploring the quality of *courage* for meeting fear evoked by the prospect of experimenting with new conversational techniques.
5. Practical considerations, such as time and regularity of meetings, confidentiality, the use of three-way meetings with a sponsor/manager, the gathering of feedback from colleagues and the potential use of psychometrics.
6. Discuss the potential use of paired sessions with one or more colleagues, combined with one-to-one sessions, as a way of accelerating development.

Notes

1 Peterson, C., Seligman, M.E.P. (2004). *Character strengths and virtues: A handbook and classification.* American Psychological Association.
2 Clifton, D. (2020). *Now, discover your strengths.* Gallup Press.
3 Farey, P. (1993). Mapping change. *Management Education and Development,* 24(4), 442–458.

Chapter 6
Managing emotional states

Emotions underly all human behaviour. Whether we are aware of it or not, emotional states expressed through the activity of our body-brain systems shape how we behave and, in the interpersonal domain, how we relate to others. In facilitating the development of our relationships with others, I have come to see the managing of emotional states as a foundational step. When clients learn to observe and regulate their emotions, their capacity for skilful interactions increases. The value of emotional regulation has led to the rise in popularity of many useful practices such as mindfulness, journaling and yoga, as well as the numerous forms of exercise that can contribute to steadier emotional states. In addition to the value of these various approaches, I view the conversational context as a further potential domain for fostering emotional regulation. Indeed, in my experience the interpersonal realm can be especially powerful for accelerating personal shifts in awareness that many people have not achieved through solitary approaches. In this chapter I describe how we can support clients to recognise and manage their emotional states as a basis for conversing more skilfully. The techniques we introduce at this stage are a resource that we use throughout our work with clients.

I think of the *self-regulation* in Stage 2 of the *Breakthrough Conversations* journey as containing three complementary qualities: *mindfulness*, *compassion* and *appreciation*. We can think of this trio as an emotional management toolkit working together to support clients and coaches to be at their best. *Mindfulness* provides the essential steadiness to see what is arising, within and between. *Compassion* is the quality that best meets emotional difficulty, whether for one's own through self-compassion, or for others through compassion for others. *Appreciation* fosters a positive mindset, counteracting tendencies for negativity, and celebrating the qualities, behaviours and ideas of self and others that build trust and creativity. In this chapter I discuss how we can support clients to develop these qualities in conversation; both in a one-to-one context and in the context of facilitated paired conversations. I begin by describing the application of techniques introduced in Chapters 2 and 3 – *RAG* body-brain states, *PACES* and the

DOI: 10.4324/9781003054542-6

Five-Eyed Model of Conversations. I then turn to the challenge of bringing emotional regulation more actively into the interpersonal sphere and introduce the *9-Minute Form* as a specific technique for fostering emotional regulation whilst engaging in conversations. I end the chapter considering the formal practices in *mindfulness, compassion* and *appreciation* that can increase the capacity for emotional regulation.

Establishing a space for mindful, embodied inquiry

From the outset of our work with clients we adopt a stance of reflective curiosity, and at the first stage of *Breakthrough Conversations* this fosters intrinsic motivation by giving clients the space to clarify their sense of purpose and their desire to use conversations as a domain to be their best self. At this second stage we build more explicitly on the role of reflectiveness, in particular offering structured approaches for tuning in to body sensations and emotions. These techniques are important because without them our conversations with clients are likely to be governed by habitual narratives. When we ask questions most clients respond fairly quickly, offering a stream of thoughts and associations. There is much that we can glean from these responses, but these immediate responses are usually the product of their habitual ways of thinking. They tell us how they usually make sense of their world and their place within it. We need to listen and to hear these accounts, but if we let them continue for an extended amount of time, we are in danger of simply allowing these habitual narratives to be reinforced. One of my observations from supervising coaches is that the understandable emphasis on the importance of listening can result in conversations that give a lot of space for clients to rehearse their old stories about themselves and others. Rehearsing narratives in this way is not a basis for change. In the approach I am proposing, we want to complement our listening with a willingness to interrupt clients and to guide them into ways of observing their own story-making tendencies. We can do this by first supporting them to observe and manage their emotional states.

Awareness of RAG body-brain states

I usually introduce embodied inquiry in the context of the *RAG* (RED, AMBER, GREEN) frame for diagnosing body-brain states. I outline the neuroscience of conversational effectiveness (see Chapter 2) and show the diagram of the three body-brain states (Figure 2.1). I then suggest that I guide clients in a short practice to evoke an embodied experience of these different states. This practice may seem familiar to clients who have previously learned such techniques and they are typically willing to undertake the practice. Other clients who are less familiar may be reluctant or distract us by talking so much that we don't feel able to interrupt them and to guide the practice. In these circumstances I confront what is happening head-on. I ask how they feel about being led in a reflective practice and I support and encourage them to take time to articulate their reactions. Perhaps they are sceptical or impatient. I acknowledge and validate their emotions, and seek to place them in the context of body-brain awareness, pointing out that these reactions will have a physiological basis in the body, and inviting clients to see if they can notice sensations that go with these reactions. So, in a different way, we foster reflectiveness, even if clients do not wish, at that point, to make use of a formal technique.

The two stages to mindful inquiry

In mindful inquiry the first step is to establish a pause in mental activity, and second, to use the backdrop of steadiness provided by the pause to inquire into a specific aspect of experience. The aim of the pause is to calm the mind – or the body-brain – enough to be able to see clearly what is occurring in awareness. We need mental 'stability' to achieve mental 'clarity'. I often use a metaphor to describe this to clients. Imagine the mind, or the body-brain, as an expanse of water. If the mind is like a choppy sea full of white-crested waves we won't even notice if we chuck a brick into the water. It will be swallowed by the waves. But if the mind is like a still lake or pond, then if we drop a feather onto the surface, we will be able to see and feel the ripples that are created.

So, throughout our work with clients we can think of using the two stages of mindful inquiry, first inviting them to pause and attune to their here and now bodily experience, and then second, to notice what insights, images or impulses arise as we drop pebbles of inquiry into their pool of stilled awareness. Initially we might introduce this more formally, asking clients to put down their pen, to sit with both feet on the ground, and so on, following the traditional ways of preparing to be mindful. But, as the approach becomes more familiar, we can simply guide clients to take a moment to pause and to tune into the body, and to see what is arising in relation to the issue we are seeking to address. Ultimately what we are aiming for is a fluid, ever-present capacity to pause, and to bring awareness to here-and now embodied experience. The more we, as coaches, can do this with clients, the more we are modelling the use of this capacity in any moment of conversation.

Here is a possible way of initially introducing mindful inquiry:

Stage one: Stabilising the mind/pausing into body sensations

- *'I would like to give you an experience attuning to these different body-brain states. We will begin by bringing attention to specific body* sensations. Directing our attention in this way shifts our body-brain circuitry away from its habitual thinking patterns towards here-and-now experience. Then we can look closely at what arises within the body and the mind as we consider specific questions or issues that we are choosing to explore'.

- *'So, take a moment now to pause. Become aware of your body in the chair ... your feet on the floor ... the sensations of breathing'.* (We can extend this part of the practice as much as feels appropriate for the individual. We are aiming for spaciousness and allowing time for clients to settle.)
- *'As we do this, we might think in the back our minds that bringing attention to body sensations is a useful way of switching body-brain system. With this, we can tune in to where body sensations are strongest, bringing our awareness like a spotlight to specific body sensations and noticing what is happening moment to moment in this part of the body. Sooner or later the mind will be pulled back into our thoughts ... that's fine, that is what minds are partly designed to do. But when we notice that, we can gently bring our attention back to the body sensations. The mind might keep running away, like a curious toddler or puppy. So each time it does, we smile to ourselves and gently escort the mind back to our chosen focus of attention, and as we continue to do this, we might notice any tension in the body and see if that might soften and relax ... or we might just allow those sensations to be as they are at this moment'.*

Stage two: Bringing curiosity and clarity / inquiring into emerging experience

- *'And now, having paused, you might notice how you feel right now. What sensations are most in awareness? What emotions are most to the fore? What thoughts are passing through your mind?* (It might be useful to share one or more of the metaphors for awareness mentioned in Chapter 3). I sometimes invite clients to speak about their experience out loud, even if they keep their eyes closed.
- *'Thinking in terms of the RED, AMBER, GREEN model of body-brain state, which body brain state feels most to the fore right now?'* (Here we might encourage clients to consider the blend of experience. For example, *'I notice a part of me that is feeling more relaxed and grounded by taking a pause, so the GREEN state is present, but I am also aware of this stirring sensation in my belly that I associate with anxiety, and this suggests also the RED body-brain state'.)*
- At this point we may choose to guide clients to explore the impact of imagining different situations on their body-brain state. Worksheet 2 describes how we can ask clients to consider three conversational

contexts: one that evokes reactivity, such as frustration or anger, one that evokes habitual feelings, such as an ordinary conversation with a friend, and one that evokes delight and ease, such as chatting playfully with a child. The aim is to create opportunities for clients to have an embodied experience of their different body-brain states, RED, AMBER and GREEN.

- As we take clients through this process, we can write down what they report and what we witness in the RED, AMBER and GREEN states, and begin to complete a summary of their subjective experience of RAG body-brain states, as illustrated in Figure 2.2.

This experiential exercise does two things: first, it establishes the distinction between RED, AMBER and GREEN as a useful shorthand for understanding emotional states. Second, it introduces the practical value of embodied inquiry as an approach for interrupting the dominance of reactive or habitual thinking patterns, and provides a technique that we can make ongoing use of in our work.

Body-brain awareness supports emotional regulation

In my experience clients are often impressed by how readily they can assess their body-brain states and they become curious about what it will take to evoke their GREEN state. Rather than answer this question directly, I typically ask them to consider the situations that are most likely to evoke their reflectiveness or their reactivity. Once again, our aim is to foster their reflective curiosity. In this way we can reinforce the potential to pause and notice emotional states. What clients quickly discover is that the act of pausing and bringing curiosity to their body-brain states evokes, at least in part, a GREEN state. It is their conscious, reflective, GREEN state of awareness that allows them to observe themselves and to attune to body sensations, even if the body sensations that they pick up are ones that they associate with a RED or AMBER state. Translating this distinction into ordinary language, it is like noticing that we have body sensations and feelings of anger towards someone (RED body-brain state), whilst the part of us that is doing the noticing is curious and calm (GREEN body-brain state). Our GREEN capacity for awareness can observe our RED anger as the contents of awareness, without being identified with the anger. If we don't fix our identity around the concept of anger, then the RED anger is a wave of emotion passing through the body-brain system, and the act of observing this with openness and curiosity sustains our GREEN state as a container for the passing RED state. Here is an example of this dual awareness from my work with Stuart (this case study is elaborated in more detail later in the chapter).

Stuart: Using *RAG* to distinguish the process of awareness and its contents

I used the mindful inquiry technique in a one-to-one session with Stuart to introduce him to the *RAG* frame, and I captured how his body sensations and non-verbal behaviours shifted as he considered challenging, routine and flowing conversations. He reported typical responses: contracted body sensations and withdrawn non-verbal behaviours in the RED state through to open, flowing and expressive sensations and non-verbal behaviours in the GREEN state. The coaching plan was for the individual sessions to be followed by a number of paired sessions between Stuart and Mick, and so then I asked Stuart to imagine having a conversation with Mick about a currently contentious issue. I asked him to pause, to attune to his body-brain state, holding in his mind's eye a picture of Mick and the conversation he needed to have. As he did this, I asked him to notice his body sensations, taking time to explore areas of tension and areas of ease, and to be curious about the feelings that he associated with these sensations. Then, using Figure 2.2, I asked him to describe his body brain state. He said it was curious to discover that he was experiencing the GREEN and RED states simultaneously. He said that he was in a RED state, in the sense that as he thought about Mick's behaviour towards him he felt really annoyed, experienced as tension in the belly, pressure in his head, and an exasperated desire to throw his hands up in the air and turn his back on Mick. But he noted that as he observed this, and based on our prior conversations about the nature of awareness, he was also aware of a part of himself that was examining this experience with openness and curiosity, and this part seemed like a GREEN state that was looking at his RED reaction with gentle humour. It was as though the voice of his GREEN state was saying: *why are you getting so worked up about this?*

I reinforced Stuart's important observation. Our GREEN state can observe our RED or AMBER states, and this act of observation is itself a valuable reinforcement of our GREEN capacities.

In the language of neuroscience, we might say the executive functions of the prefrontal cortex can observe the reactivity arising from the amygdala and hippocampus in the limbic region. Or, using the language of the polyvagal system, we might say the activity of the social engagement system can observe the reactivity of the sympathetic nervous system. Or, using the language of hormones, we might say the presence of oxytocin and dopamine can support an awareness of the reactivity arising from the release of cortisol and adrenalin. The key point is that the act of observing and reflecting on experience reinforces the potential for a GREEN body-brain state, even if what is being simultaneously observed in the body is a RED or AMBER body-brain state. It is this cultivation of GREEN states that underpins the potential for more skilful conversations.

Deconstructing states using *PACES*

In Chapter 3 I introduced the *PACES* framework (Figure 3.1) for deconstructing limiting and enabling conversational tendencies into *Actions, Cognitions, Emotions and Sensations*. I usually begin to make use of this approach when clients have identified a specific situation that is challenging. Once they have outlined the situation they want to address, I ask them if they would like to use a structured approach for looking more deeply at what is happening for them in this situation. They are usually open to this invitation, and so I take out my *PACES* cards and place them on the floor or use a printout of the *PACES* framework. I briefly describe the framework and then, using the cards on the floor, invite them to stand up and move to the Pause card. In supervising coaches, I have noticed that some are reluctant to get their clients out of their chairs. They intuit some discomfort or embarrassment in the coachee and so choose to do use the *PACES* frame sitting down. I mention this because I want to encourage coaches to get their clients out of their chairs. The act of standing up and moving around evokes a much more powerful experience of embodied awareness, and if we are confident in our use of the tool, it enhances the trust between coach and client. (Chapter 3 has a detailed account of using *PACES*).

In terms of developing emotional regulation, the *Pause* represents the anchor for our investigation and a place to step back to if emotions are too triggering. As clients talk about a challenging situation it is likely that their emotions will be aroused. We want this to happen so that clients can develop the capacity to be with reactive emotions without automatically reacting behaviourally. It is only when emotions are present that they can be experienced and integrated. In my experience the use of the *PACES* frame serves as a container for emotional investigation that rarely evokes overwhelming emotions, but if that does occur, we can invite clients to move back to the *Pause* and to anchor themselves again in the sensations of standing and breathing. We may also choose to invite them to bring a different situation to mind that readily evokes more positive feelings. Once they are more emotionally regulated, we can then explore if they are willing to return to examining the situation that was evoking their emotional overwhelm.

A more common difficulty for clients is their tendency to be overly rational. When we ask them to move to the *Emotions* domain and to describe what feelings are being evoked, they continue to describe their thoughts – they stay in the *Cognitions* domain. So, we may need to offer a lot of guidance and encouragement to get them to explore their emotions. Rather than going directly for emotions, I usually invite clients to move to the *Sensations* domain. I ask them to notice what is happening in the belly, in the chest, in the throat, in the head, and I offer examples of the kinds of sensations they might be experiencing. These directions help clients see what we are asking them to do. It is as though we are legitimising curiosity about areas of experience that they don't usually pay much attention to. Even when we do this it is important to encourage clients to go slowly so they have time to tune in to their embodied sensations. I will typically ask them to take their time, to let their awareness drop down into the body, to dwell there for a while, and then see what they are noticing. We support the idea that *'the slower you go, the more you know'*. When they have identified some body sensations, I ask them to then move to the *Emotions* domain and to consider what words they would use to describe the emotions that go with these sensations. Once again, I encourage clients to go slowly and to dwell with what is arising. They may report a specific emotion, like frustration, and we need to acknowledge and validate that. *'So, you are aware there is frustration about this, and this links to sensations of tension in your belly. How is it for you to just stay with the frustration for a moment, giving it some space, and to see what else arises?'*. This invitation may yield other emotions such as sadness or hopelessness. Guiding clients in this way is intended to give space and light to the full array of emotional experience, and at the same time for clients to notice that they can remain curious and calm in the face of these emotions. They experience themselves as emotionally regulated in the face of difficult emotions.

We can link the use of *PACES* with the diagnosis of *RAG* body-brain states (see Table 3.2) and we usually find that limiting *ACES* patterns are associated with RED or AMBER states. Enabling *ACES* patterns may be associated with some aspect of GREEN states in the sense that there is more reflective awareness, but the prospect of trying to have a more constructive conversation might also evoke an underlying RED anxiety. The importance of the Pause in the *PACES* frame is that it represents the conscious choice to step into a place of mindful observation, and so we might think of the Pause as an anchor for GREEN body-brain states. When clients have completed the full *PACES* exercise, exploring both limiting and enabling patterns, and with us having captured their discoveries on an *ACES* worksheet, they usually seem visibly relieved and relaxed. The process enables them to step back from challenging experiences, to engage their capacity for emotional regulation, and to make concrete plans about how to approach situations more skilfully.

The *PACES* frame supports clients to zoom-in to the details of their personal experience, deconstructing subjective states and providing an observational stance. A complementary frame that also begins with the *Pause* to support observation is the *Five-Eyed Model of Conversations*. As discussed in Chapter 3, this model encourages clients to zoom-out and to explore the broad range of external parameters impacting a conversation. This model is very useful for exploring contextual factors, especially cultural or social norms and power dynamics, and clients typically think about these aspects from a cognitive, rational perspective. However, if we perceive that there are strong emotions associated with this larger perspective, then I return to the *PACES* frame to deconstruct these emotions more fully in relation to the full *ACES* pattern. In brief, The *Five-Eyed Model of Conversations* supports observational agility, but it is the *PACES* frame that fosters emotional regulation.

Emotional regulation during conversations

Being able to manage emotions is an invaluable skill for any of us, and so the techniques I have discussed so far can contribute significantly to any form of development. However, in the *Breakthrough Conversations* approach we are seeking to bring emotional regulation into the conversational context. The key technique I use for extending personal awareness into the interpersonal domain is called the *9-Minute Form*, which I will describe in detail below. First, I will describe a preparatory interpersonal mindfulness practice that is adapted from a practice I first experienced during Insight Dialogue[1] retreats, and which I have subsequently used in workshops and coaching sessions. In this practice two people sit opposite each other and are guided to settle into a mindful state, usually with their eyes closed or their gaze lowered. The aim of the practice is for clients to observe their *ACES* reactions to sitting opposite another person, and to build their relational, emotional regulation. The practice guides them to shift their focus back and forth between their internal experience and their relational experience, and gradually get a sense of how it feels to hold both oneself and the other person in awareness at the same time. Figure 6.1 suggests graphically how we might experience our awareness as expanding ripples flowing from the breath in the belly, outwards to encompass the whole of our own bodies, and eventually, the body and presence of another person.

Here are some suggested guidelines for this practice:

- Start by using the Stabilising the Mind guidelines discussed above
- *'Having taken some time to settle, notice now how you are feeling internally ... perhaps noticing specific local sensations in different parts of your body ... and then, allowing your awareness to expand to encompass the wider field of awareness of your whole body ... holding the whole of your body in awareness ... perhaps noticing the energy in the body ... and allowing your awareness to move right out to the skin ... perhaps to move a bit beyond the skin'.*

Managing emotional states   117

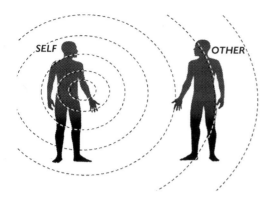

Figure 6.1 Opening from Interior to Relational Presence.

- *'And now, keeping your gaze lowered, let your awareness include what is on the floor or desk in front of you ... taking a moment to adjust to including this expansion of awareness to the external world ... and slowly, gradually allowing your gaze to lift ... so that you are beginning to see my (if a one-to-one session)/the other person's (if a paired session) hands and body... and then gradually my/their upper body ... and then my/their face'.*
- *'Notice how it is to be expanding awareness to include another person ... perhaps holding eye contact for a few moments, or for as long as it feels comfortable ... but then allowing yourself to lower the gaze again, or to close your eyes again when you choose. Taking your time to allow your awareness to move back to the interior experience ... to be aware of your breathing body ... and then, once again, in your own time, to gradually open your awareness once again to the exterior ... letting me/the other person be in awareness'.*
- *'And now, let your awareness move back and forth between yourself and your awareness of another... noticing any changes in your body sensations ... in your breathing ... in how it feels to be attending to your interior ... and then to be attending to the exterior... and then seeing if you can let your attention be balanced between the interior and the exterior ... holding both yourself and another person in your awareness ... and whenever you choose, let your attention move back to the interior. And then, when you are ready, gradually open your eyes again ... once again playing with this experience of moving your attention between the interior, and the exterior, and then both'.*

This practice reveals to clients the unspoken power of the relational field. When we invite them to speak about their experience during this practice, they often report surprise at how much is evoked by opening the eyes and looking at another person. Perhaps there is tension in the body, a change in breathing, a sense of embarrassment, self-judgement, judgement of the other person, a sense of scepticism about the purpose or value of the exercise, discomfort, anxiety, excitement, warm-heartedness, and so on. The relational field has a powerful impact on the body-brain system, before anything has even been said, and this practice enables clients to become more aware of this impact.

If we are doing this practice in a one-to-one session, then we can either invite the client to open their awareness to ourselves, or, we might invite them to open their awareness to a colleague whom they are imagining in their mind's eye. Both of these are useful. The advantage of using oneself is the intensity of the here-and-now experience with the client. The advantage of clients doing this practice in relation to an imagined colleague is that it invites them to notice how their body-brain system reacts to this colleague and this can be a helpful preparation for a paired conversation. A further practice that I have developed, building on techniques from Imago Relationship Therapy and Insight Dialogue, is the *9-Minute Form*. We can introduce the *9-Minute Form* in one-to-one sessions, but it is most impactful when used as part of paired sessions.

The 9-Minute Form

The *9-Minute Form* is designed to support clients to regulate their emotional states during conversations. By slowing down the interactive process clients have the opportunity to sustain a personal, embodied presence whilst interacting interpersonally. It combines the *RAG* diagnosis of body-brain states with a structured process of speaking, listening and reflecting back. I usually introduce this approach when clients raise a relational challenge they are facing. Having understood the issue I might ask them to imagine what they would say to the other person, either enacting this with the person in their mind's eye, or if they find it helpful, imagining me to be the other person. I notice the nature of their communication with a particular curiosity about their *RAG* body-brain state, its impact on my own body-brain state, and how I imagine I would want to respond if I was the other person. In this first run through of the conversation there is no emphasis on emotional regulation. We are in effect getting a baseline picture of how they would communicate. I then introduce the *9-Minute Form*, describing the five time-chunks as follows:

1. **Pause (1 minute)** – both clients (or an individual client if it is a one-to-one session) are invited to take a mindful pause, to think about the conversation that is about to take place, and to tune into the body-brain state that is evoked by the prospect of this conversation. Prior to embarking on the *9-Minute Form* clients are reminded about the three

body-brain systems (Figure 2.1) and the summary pages for diagnosing *RAG* body-brain states (Figure 2.2 and Table 3.2) and are invited to use this as a lens for inquiring into their current state.

2. **Share *RAG* rating (1 minute)** – each person is invited to describe their current body-brain state, referring specifically to their body sensations and emotions. For example, **GREEN**: Centred, focused, calm, optimistic, openness in chest and belly; **AMBER**: mind quite active with the topic to be discussed, aware of habitual thoughts, feeling a bit impatient with the need to go through this process, some tightness in belly; **RED**: feeling quite agitated and irritated, impatient to be getting on with other work, aware of having low expectations about the value of this process, tight in belly and breath is shallow and feeling restless. (In the first couple of rounds it may take more than a minute for both clients to identify their *RAG* states. However, the assignment of 1 minute to this stage emphasises that we are not aiming for any discussion of the topic in question, but only an account of the subjective body-brain state in relation to the prospect of having the conversation.)

3. **Speaker-listener roles (4 minutes)** – agree who will be the first speaker and who will be the first listener, pointing out that in the next round these roles will be switched. The speaker shares her or his viewpoint on the agreed topic; the listener is told that at the end of the 4 minutes she or he will have 2 minutes to reflect back key content and observations of what the speaker has shared, but without any interpretations or questions.

4. **Listener reflects content and observations (2 minutes)** – the listener offers a brief paraphrase or summary of what she or he has heard.

5. **Speaker confirms or qualifies (1 minute)** – the speaker offers feedback to the listener, confirming the parts of the reflection that resonate, but also has the opportunity to qualify or restate what was communicated. Clients sometimes gain deeper insight into what they were seeking to express when they hear the reflection of the listener. If this is brief, the qualification can occur within one round of the *9-Minute Form*. However, if the reflection has triggered greater clarity about something the speaker wishes to communicate, then it may be the pair agree for the first speaker to speak again in the next round. However, this step does not occur without a return to the beginning of the *9-Minute Form*, starting with the Pause and the reporting of *RAG* body-brain state, so that embodied reflective awareness is sustained as the inquiry into the topic is deepened.

At the outset it is helpful for the coach to manage the timings, using the timer on a mobile phone or some other device so that an alarm sounds at the end of each phase. The structure supports clients to feel safe, and to trust the process to support them to be reflective and to resist becoming overly triggered. Once clients have followed the *9-Minute Form* for two or three rounds and have a sense of the process we can be more flexible with timings, allowing speakers to be more elaborative. However, if one or both clients are triggered into reactivity, then it is helpful to adhere to the *9-Minute Form* and support them to observe rather than to react to their RED body-brain state.

When clients follow this process in a one-to-one session with us, they are usually surprised by the improved quality of their communication. The slow, reflective process means that they choose their words more carefully, their tone is more moderate, their messages are more nuanced and there is more ownership of their biases. The pause and reflection evoke a more skilful communication, without any direct focus on their communication skills. We are, in effect, inviting clients to access the natural skilfulness that arises when they are more emotionally regulated. Although the interaction is one-sided in a one-to-one session because I don't usually take up the role of being the speaker, it does nevertheless show clients the power of a having a slower and more structured interaction. I do reflect back to clients the areas of their communication that I found most effective as well as aspects that I experienced as potentially triggering. I also encourage clients to notice how it is to communicate with an ongoing sense of their body-brain state. This one-to-one experience, usually conducted with each member of the pair individually, prepares both clients for a paired conversation. In the paired session I remind them both of the *RAG* frame and the *9-Minute Form*, and we agree a topic that both clients want to address – this has often been identified already during the one-to-one sessions. The following case involves my work with Stuart, the client mentioned above, and his colleague, Mick. In line with my comments about making use of the *PACES* frame, if we use this *9-Minute Form* with clarity and confidence, we can readily evoke significant shifts in relational experience and connection.

Mick and Stuart

Mick was one of a number of senior colleagues contributing to the shaping of product development strategy, with a focus on where to invest to best meet the changing needs of clients. He was invited to receive coaching because, although a promising leader, colleagues experienced him as overly forceful and didactic in his leadership style. He was viewed as strategically insightful and very thoughtful about the welfare and development of his team members, and most people acknowledged the important contribution he was making to the business. However, he was seen as having an excess of conviction. When discussing issues with colleagues he was described as being a poor listener, as only paying lip service to others' ideas, and as being intransigent when challenged by others. In an initial three-way meeting with his boss he was told that moderating this aspect of his management style would enhance his already positive career potential.

As part of an initial series of one-to-one sessions I shared with Mick rich verbatim feedback from colleagues, highlighting strengths and development areas. Mick was interested in the feedback and was open to exploring it in detail, but I had a sense that he was not really allowing it to sink in. At some level I felt he was humouring me, letting me inquire into specific comments, but then diluting their significance with caveats and obfuscations. After a few sessions I felt he was going through the motions of coaching in the same way that his colleagues felt he was going through the motions of consulting with them. I decided that a useful step would be to introduce some paired conversations with one of his colleagues, Stuart, with whom the relationship had become strained.

Mick and Stuart had worked together for many years and both were considered to be influential figures within the company. However, their different views about important strategic issues had become widely known. They were sometimes seen in heated debate, and they sent conflicting messages to the rest of the organisation about priorities and decisions. In recent months their clashes had reduced as a result of them avoiding each other, but this was not sustainable for an organisation that needed to rally around a coherent message.

After one individual session with Stuart to prepare him for the paired sessions, I met with Mick and Stuart together. I began by asking them how they felt about having a paired session. Stuart was delighted to have the opportunity to speak with Mick in a more structured way. He was aware that his relationship with Mick was one of the biggest frustrations in his role, and he was eager to find a way to work more constructively. In contrast, Mick said he felt disappointed that they couldn't resolve their differences on their own. He said he thought they had a good working relationship and it was a pity that they needed to go through this process. Expressions of reluctance or scepticism by one or other client within a pair are not uncommon, and it is important to validate and understand these feelings, rather than to argue with them. I could see that Mick was being slightly reactive to the idea of paired coaching, and I imagined that his RED body-brain system was activated. I acknowledged his feeling that he would like his relationships to flow without need for coaching, and while asking him to take a moment to explore this feeling, I invited him to turn his attention inwards and to notice what body sensations were arising with this feeling of disappointment. With some encouragement he noted that he felt a reduction in the sense of energy in his body, manifesting as a slight heaviness in his shoulders, and a feeling that he wanted to slump into his chair. But having said that, he suddenly sat forward and said he wanted to be constructive and wanted to make good use of the session. Holding a reflective stance, rather than rushing to the next step, I pointed out to Mick that I could hear him describe two different feelings about participating in the session, one was a sense of disappointment that paired sessions were necessary, and another was a positive determination to move forward constructively. By bringing this internal conflict into awareness I was aiming to give Mick permission to be ambivalent about paired coaching, and to show that the full complexity of his experience was welcome in the process.

I then reminded Mick and Stuart of the three body-brain systems and the *RAG* frame for diagnosing body-brain states, and also described the stages of the *9-Minute Form*. I said that the form may at first seem slow, but I encouraged them to try it for a few rounds and then to decide if it was useful. They agreed to do this. In the first session we used the form to explore their shared sense of purpose and to get an initial impression of how they perceived each other. But it was in the second paired session that the richness of the interaction evoked by the *9-Minute Form* gained deeper traction. They agreed to explore some decisions that had been taken in the past week, where Stuart felt as if he had not been fully consulted.

During the 1-minute *RAG* rating, Stuart noted that as he thought about the events of the past week, he was in what he described as the 'RED zone'. He knew that he felt triggered and wanted to talk more about this. In contrast, Mick said he was feeling fairly relaxed about the prospect of this conversation, perhaps a blend of GREEN and AMBER. It was agreed that Stuart would take the first 4-minute speaker-role. He unpacked the various elements of his RED state. He noted that he was triggered by a sense of decisions being taken by Mick and other colleagues without his involvement. He said he felt as though his views did not count and that he was being railroaded by Mick. When this happened, his reaction was to withdraw from Mick and to become an observer rather than a participant. In the 2-minute reflection of what he had heard Stuart say, Mick began to justify his behaviour, but with my support he restricted himself to stating what he had seen and heard Stuart say. In the final minute of the *9-Minute Form* Stuart qualified and emphasised his experience that he felt that his views did not matter, and that this was consistent with a number of other experiences over the preceding months.

In the next round of the *9-Minute Form*, Mick went on to describe all the logical reasons why he and other colleagues had made the decisions they had, emphasising that he had no intention to railroad Stuart, but rather, he simply felt this was the most timely way of moving things forward.

In the next round, Stuart said that this explanation was evoking exactly the same feelings of frustration that he had experienced earlier in the week. I decided to pause the *9-Minute Form* at this stage and to inquire with Stuart to draw out what he wanted from Mick for him to feel more included. Stuart said he experienced Mick as making assertions or statements of fact, rather than inviting Stuart to give his view. I offered an empathic conjecture about his core needs (see Chapter 7), that Stuart wanted to experience Mick as genuinely caring about his point of view. He agreed strongly with this point, saying that he did not want to hear more and more logical explanations from Mick about why his decision was a good one, but rather for Mick to attribute sufficient value to Stuart's experience that he wouldn't consider making such a decision without hearing Stuart's views first.

When we returned to the *9-Minute Form* and I invited Mick to talk about his experience, he explored his sense of pressure to make decisions and to move forward. Using the initial 1-minute pause, he connected with his own RED state, associated with often feeling impatient with the pace of decision-making in the organisation, but realised that his impatience was usually expressed as him offering an endless stream of justifications for his viewpoint, and making little space for others to speak or for truly listening to what they had to say. His strength in his own convictions was closing others down, and in Stuart's case, leading to an unhelpful avoidance of contact.

In the next round Stuart talked about his need to feel respected by Mick if they were to collaborate. Then, in the next round Mick acknowledged that he could see how his desire for closure was sending the wrong message to Stuart. He said that he did respect Stuart, and that he realised he needed to make more time to listen. He also acknowledged that developing his empathy and being open to the views of others was a key developmental challenge for him.

The breakthrough for Mick came from a more profound depth of listening as Stuart expressed his frustrations. It was as if he was hearing about his impact on Stuart, and by extrapolation on others, for the first time. The intensity and slower pace of the conversations using the *9-Minute Form* allowed him to see the result of his impenetrable certainty. He talked about his surprise, and how this impact was completely at odds with his intentions. He acknowledged the need to make time to listen genuinely to Stuart and other colleagues, to empathise with their perspectives and he even generalised these insights more broadly, describing how he was learning to listen more to his wife. Stuart also gained some important insights. He learned how important it was for him to notice and voice his personal experience. In the past he had either argued about strategy from a position of logic, or he had given up and avoided contact. Now he saw

124 Managing emotional states

> that a more productive pathway was to speak directly to Mick about his relational experience: to tell him as calmly as possible when he was feeling railroaded and sidelined. (I return to this case in Chapter 8.)

Formal practices to deepen emotional regulation

The techniques I have described for managing emotional states are practical tools that support clients to be more aware and reflective and do not require clients to be mindfulness practitioners. However, personal mindfulness practices can deepen the capacity for emotional regulation and if coaches or clients are open to making use of such practices, I encourage them to do that. It is not my intention to describe these practices in detail here because there are already many mindfulness resources available through books, apps and online, but I will indicate three primary groups of practices that I consider to be particularly useful. These three groups align to the trio of mindfulness, compassion and appreciation that I have described as core to self-regulation.

Mindfulness

Mindfulness is the underpinning capacity in self-regulation, with compassion and appreciation as specific applications of mindfulness. For clients who want a more precise definition of mindfulness, we can offer the following list of nine distinguishable aspects of mindfulness[2]: (1) *observing/ attending to experiences*, (2) *acting with awareness*, (3) *non-judgement/accepting of experiences*, (4) *self-acceptance*, (5) *willingness and readiness to expose oneself to experiences/non-avoidance*, (6) *non-reactivity to experience*, (7) *non-identification with own experiences*, (8) *insightful understanding*, (9) *labelling, describing experiences*. This list shows that mindfulness aligns with the *Spacious* cardinal direction in the *Character Compass* (see Chapter 5), with its emphasis on *presence*, *wisdom* and *open-mindedness*. There are a wide range of traditional mindfulness practices that enhance these aspects, such as those that focus on mindfulness of breathing, body sensations, emotions, thoughts or a combination of some or all of these. Other practices shift from these *ACES* domains to a more expanded awareness of all phenomena arising and disappearing from awareness, sometimes described as open presence. Guided practices available through mindfulness websites and apps or experienced during mindfulness courses are the best way of learning these, and I encourage coaches and clients to explore these resources to see what works best for them. Some coaches may choose to create their own recordings of guided practices, as I have, and to make those available to clients digitally. I do also sometimes lead short mindfulness practices for coaches and clients at the beginning of sessions if they are open to that approach. I don't see this as essential to using the *Breakthrough Conversations* approach, but it can foster a mode of reflectiveness from the outset.

Whilst mindfulness fosters spaciousness as one of the four cardinal directions in the *Character Compass,* as the definition above shows, it does not include the balancing direction of *Warmth*, characterised by such qualities as *compassion* and *appreciation*, and so it is important to consider practices that foster these qualities.

Compassion

Compassion, and in particular self-compassion, are important complementary practices because what mindful inquiry reveals may be uncomfortable. We may discover difficult emotions such as anger, frustration, self-doubt, hurt, fear or sadness. We may also become aware of unpleasant bodily sensations such as aches and pains, butterflies in the stomach or nausea. Our habitual response to such experiences might include denying them or blocking them out, or perhaps becoming critical of self or others. The tendency to react harshly towards oneself, berating oneself for being weak or flawed is particularly common. So, having brought these experiences into awareness we, and our clients, need to have a strategy for meeting them that supports skilful conversations. Compassion is an attitude of body, heart and mind that has been shown to enhance positive emotions in response to adverse situations[3], and so enables clients to approach conversations with kindness. Again, there are many resources available for experiencing compassion practices and I encourage coaches and clients to find what resonates best for them. My own practices have been greatly enhanced through experiencing and learning to teach mindful self-compassion[4], and one of the practices I guide most often with coaches and clients to meet moments of difficulty is the Self-Compassion Break.[5] In terms of capabilities necessary for supporting clients to engage in *Breakthrough Conversations*, compassion is an essential part of *Managing Emotional States* (see Figure 1.2) and so even if we choose not to introduce more formal practices to clients, our own mode of relating to their difficulties needs to find a balance between spacious inquiry and heartfelt warmth.

Appreciation

There is a well-researched human tendency to give more weight to negative experiences than to positive ones, and this negativity bias[6] has a significant impact on how people perceive themselves and others. Our evolutionary heritage means that our brains are wired to perceive threats in the form of our RED body-brain circuitry, and are less sensitive to valuing good experiences. This is neatly captured in the phrase: *the mind is Velcro for negative experiences and Teflon for positive ones*[7]. Appreciation has been shown to counteract the negativity bias, and to have a positive impact on relationships and conversations. From a mindfulness perspective, opportunities for appreciation are available at any moment simply by turning attention towards things for which we feel grateful, such as the access to food, water, warmth and clothing, the sight of a flower or tree or cloud, the smile on a child's face or the wag of a dogs tail – all the many things in our lives that we might take for granted can be held in awareness and appreciated, and in so doing we are wiring our brains towards positivity. Mindfulness trainings typically include informal practices focused on appreciating the small delights in our lives, the taste of a piece of fruit, the scent of a flower and the sound of birdsong. One of the most widely used appreciation practices for relationships is the cultivation of loving kindness, and these practices are associated with increases in the positive bonding hormone oxytocin.[8] I share information about such practices with clients as part of describing the neuroscience of body-brain states, and as for other practices, encourage clients to explore resources to find those that resonate best. It can be surprising what clients will respond to. I recall the chairman of a major multinational business, someone I might have assumed would be sceptical of such ideas, especially enjoying the loving-kindness practice and the embodied sense of warmth and openness it evoked for him.

Summary

Managing Emotional States is a core aspect of *Breakthrough Conversations*, since it is through self-regulation of emotions that clients are more able to speak and listen consciously and skilfully. *Mindfulness*, and the application of mindfulness to foster the character habits of *compassion* and *appreciation*, are the qualities that underpin the capacity to manage emotional states. Practical techniques are introduced to clients for cultivating these qualities. Through guided inquiry, clients are invited to attune to their body-brain states by paying attention to body sensations and behaviours, verbal and non-verbal, to be able to distinguish RED, AMBER and GREEN (*RAG*) body brain states. These different states are linked with corresponding behavioural tendencies during conversations, and the need to foster GREEN states in order to have more skilful conversations. GREEN body-brain states, supported by the social engagement systems and activity in the prefrontal cortex, enable us to observe reactive or habitual impulses arising from RED or AMBER body-brain circuits without letting them drive our behaviour, and it is this process that represents emotional regulation. A further framework, *PACES*, enables clients to deconstruct their approach to specific conversations into the four experiential domains of *Actions, Cognitions, Emotions, and Sensations*, and to identify how to move from limiting to enabling patterns of interaction. One further technique is introduced, the *9-Minute Form*, specifically for supporting clients to sustain emotional regulation during conversations. These interactive techniques can be usefully supported by formal mindfulness practices, and clients are encouraged to experiment with a range of widely available resources.

Worksheet 6: The 9-Minute Form

This purpose of this worksheet is to outline the *9-Minute Form;* a structured approach for deepening personal and interpersonal awareness during conversations. It can be useful to provide this worksheet with copies of Figure 2.1 (three body-brain systems), Figure 2.2 and Table 3.2 (the summary pages for diagnosing *RAG* body-brain states). These visual tools can provide a reassuring conceptual anchor for clients as they explore their subjective states.

- Clients agree on the purpose of the conversation or the topic to be discussed.
- 9 minutes per cycle: 1 minute, 1 minute, 4 minutes, 2 minutes, 1 minute. The timings will be managed by the coach.
- **1 minute: Pause** – introspective check-in with respect to topic/relationship.
- **1 minute: *RAG* rating:** each person shares briefly: *My level of safety/ energy/presence/other parameter… Is RED/AMBER/GREEN.*
- **4 minutes: Speaker-Listener roles:** Agree speaker and listener roles.

Speaker addresses topic.

- **2 minutes: Listener reflection:** Listener reflects back key content and observations of speaker:

    What I heard you say was…
    What I noticed in your movements, expression was…
    No commentary or inquiry.

- **1 minute: Speaker response:** Speaker confirms accuracy of reflection, qualifies the meaning, or makes brief additions
- Begin next cycle, usually switching roles.

Notes

1 Kramer, G. (2007). *Insight dialogue: The interpersonal path to freedom.* Shambhala Publications.

2 Bergomi, C., Tschacher, W., Kupper, Z. (2013). The assessment of mindfulness with self-report measures: Existing scales and open issues. *Mindfulness*, 4, 191–202.
3 Klimecki, O.M., Leiberg, S., Lamm, C., Singer, T. (2013). Functional neural plasticity and associated changes in positive affect after compassion training. *Cerebral Cortex*, 23, 1552–1561.
4 Neff, K., Germer, C. (2018). *The mindful self-compassion workbook: A proven way to accept yourself, build inner strength, and thrive.* The Guildford Press.
5 Neff, K. (2011). *Self compassion. Stop beating yourself up and leave insecurity behind.* Yellow Kite.
6 Rozin, P., Royzman, E.B. (2001). Negativity bias, negativity dominance, and contagion. *Personality and Social Psychology Review*, 5(4), 296–320.
  Peeters, G. (1971). The positive-negative asymmetry: On cognitive consistency and positivity bias. *European Journal of Social Psychology*, 1(4), 455–474.
  Lewicka, M., Czapinski, J., Peeters, G. (1992). Positive-negative asymmetry or "when the heart needs a reason." *European Journal of Social Psychology*, 22(5), 425–434.
7 Hanson, R., Medius, R. (2009). *Buddha's brain: The practical neuroscience of happiness, love, and wisdom.* New Harbinger.
8 Fredrickson, B.L. (2013). *Love 2.0. How our supreme emotion affects everything we feel, think do, and become.* Hudson Street Press.

Chapter 7

Loosening habit and reactivity

When clients engage in conversations in Stage 2 of the *Breakthrough Conversations* process, they have the opportunity to notice their interactive habits and reactions and to see how these can limit the potential for productive conversations. However, recognising these tendencies does not mean they can be instantly changed. Conversational tendencies develop through decades of life experience and are sustained through non-conscious physiological and psychological patterns. If we are to loosen habit and reactivity, we need to explore how these patterns were formed and to bring the basis of non-conscious biases more into awareness. So, if *Managing Emotional States* in Stage 2 asks the question: *what is your experience*, *Loosening Habit and* Reactivity in Stage 3 asks: *why do you tend to behave the way you to*? By understanding the origins of behaviour and being able to own and name these potentially limiting tendencies, clients create conditions for more collaborative conversations. The goal of this stage is not that clients become perfectly skilful communicators in the sense of using all the right words and gestures. Rather, the goal is for them to decide if it would be helpful to name to others the potential ways in which their communications might be habitually or reactively unskilful. By offering these self-disclosures they create conditions for mutual openness, authenticity and collaboration.

In this chapter I begin by discussing the capability of *self-disclosure* and three contributing elements, *self-inquiry*, *challenge* and *ownership*. These are the qualities we are seeking to foster as we engage clients in looking at their own tendencies. I then explore how we can support clients to unpack four factors driving their conversational tendencies: core needs, personality, attachment patterns and cultural and social conditioning.

Self-disclosure

Self-disclosure serves conversational effectiveness because openness tends to evoke openness from others. Rather than approaching conversations with a façade of completeness, we can engage others with a more realistic sense of our strengths and gaps. This is not to suggest that we should be self-

130 Loosening habit and reactivity

deprecating or present ourselves with false humility. The aim is to approach conversations with self-awareness; owning our biases so that the impact of these can be consciously managed, both by ourselves, and in the interaction with others. I see the capability of *self-disclosure* as containing three elements, *self-inquiry*, *challenge*, and *ownership*. *Self-inquiry* brings curiosity to our inner experiences. The examination of body-brain states already opens up the terrain of self-inquiry, and at this third stage this investigation is taken further. As we begin to explore more deeply it is inevitable that we will discover not only positive qualities, but other aspects that are limiting, and so we need to be willing to *challenge* ourselves. The momentum of *self-inquiry* and *challenge* allows us to take *ownership* for the ways in which our conversational patterns have been shaped, how they can limit our effectiveness, and from this place of awareness we can decide if and how we might disclose these tendencies to others. With the cultivation of these qualities in mind, I turn to exploring four factors driving conversational tendencies.

Identifying core relational needs

A number of relational models emphasise that all human interactions are shaped by underlying interpersonal needs, but these needs often remain out of awareness. Habitual or reactive behaviour occurs when these needs are not being met. For example, if someone ignores us, we might feel upset or angry because our need to be seen has not been met. If someone humiliates us, we react because our need for respect has been cut across. Supporting clients to tune into their core relational needs provides a deep underpinning for their motivation to engage in skilful conversations, as well as helping them to make sense of their reactivity.

Non-Violent Communication suggests a long list of possible human needs,[1] and some clients may find it helpful to use such lists to consider their own core needs. Emotionally Focused Therapy[2] also views unmet relational needs as underpinning relational distress, and the aim is to support clients to express these needs alongside their fear of them not being met. My own preference is to simplify the approach to identifying core relational needs by drawing on FIRO theory, developed by Will Schutz.[3] FIRO is an acronym for Fundamental Interpersonal Relations Orientation. This model postulates that all behaviour is derived from three basic dimensions: inclusion, control and openness, which are driven by our beliefs and feelings about ourselves. These, in turn, are linked to our sense of significance, competence and likeability in our interpersonal interactions. For the purpose of helping clients to identify their core relational needs, the three basic dimensions of feelings suggest three sets of core relational needs (see Table 7.1).

We want to feel significant, which goes with a relational need to feel seen and to belong. We want to feel competent, which goes with the relational

Table 7.1 Core Relational Needs

People Want to Feel:	Underlying Fear of Being:	Core Relational Needs
Significant	Ignored/Dismissed	To be: seen, heard, recognised, accepted, understood. To belong.
Competent	Humiliated/A failure	To be: respected, appreciated, valued. To have: safety, fairness.
Likeable	Rejected/Avoided	To be: connected, loved, close, trusted. To collaborate, play, co-create

need to be respected, and to be treated fairly. We want to feel likeable, which goes with the relational need to be connected and trusted. Holding these three relational needs in mind provides a very accessible lens for inquiring into what is driving behaviour.

> I recall a client, Jeremy, describing himself getting into an argument with his wife while driving home after a social event organised with some of her friends. He told her he was annoyed with how long they had stayed and that he was frustrated with the lack of interesting conversation. His wife was upset by his anger and his negativity. She felt that he was not supporting her initiative to expand their social contacts, and that he was not recognising how often she had attended social functions in order to support him in his career. We unpacked the feelings associated with this interaction and I invited him to be curious about what his needs were in that situation. Initially he spoke about his frustration and impatience, but, encouraging him to anchor himself in his body and to be curious about his body sensations, he became aware of the sensation of wanting to curl into a ball and for his head and shoulders to drop. I asked him what feelings he associated with these sensations. He said he felt like he wanted to make himself small, to hide, and with some further probing and suggestions from me, he said he felt ashamed. Linking this to the core needs identified by Schutz, he acknowledged that when he was mixing with people away from his workplace, and where his seniority and expertise were not important, he could feel very uncomfortable. He felt like a fish out of water at the social event organised by his wife, where much of the conversation was about the different interests of her friends and colleagues, and he had found it difficult to participate. His social discomfort led to him looking to his wife for support, but she had been distracted with her own conversations and had not realised he was struggling. He realised that without the cover of executive competence he felt unseen and ignored. His anger with his

> wife on the journey home was a tragic expression of an unmet need: that he felt lost and alone at the party and that he needed her support in an unfamiliar social context. He later reported to me that he had spoken to his wife about our conversation and told her how difficult he had found the social event. She met his self-disclosure with empathy, and she went on to tell him how lovely it was for him to say how much he needed her support.

In working to uncover core relational needs it is important to go slowly, moving through the layers of emotions from the harder, secondary emotions of anger and frustration to the softer, primary emotions of fear and hurt associated with needs not being met (see Chapter 8 for a detailed discussion of primary and secondary emotions and core needs). Then, when clients recognise the underlying core need there is often a sense of relief at the realisation. Sometimes clients may dismiss such needs as signs of weakness, so it is important for us to acknowledge them firmly and compassionately, and to emphasise that they are part of our evolutionary heritage (see the discussion of attachment patterns below). When clients do recognise and own these relational needs, they are more able to make conscious requests for getting their needs met, without becoming reactive. So, for example, a manager who is fearful of failure, may say to his team members: *'whatever the news, good or bad, please tell me, because the one thing I hate is surprises. If I have warning, there is more chance we can address issues before they escalate'*. Or a colleague might say: *'I know I work best when I feel like there is a friendly team climate and we have the opportunity to get to know each other as people, as well as in our business roles'*. By disclosing our needs we let others see what matters to us, and we make it more likely that they will show us what matters to them.

Personality

Personality is another key factor that influences how people converse. Whilst environmental factors play a significant role in our relational and interactive conditioning, personality theory seeks to shed light on aspects of human experience that are shaped, at least in part, by genetics. In practice we are always a blend of nature and nurture, and research suggests that about half of the variance in personality is attributable to a person's genetics rather than the effects of environment.[4,5,6] Applying this understanding to the conversational context, personality plays an important role in shaping certain habitual and reactive tendencies. Supporting clients to understand their personality enables them to bring curiosity to their behavioural patterns and to see how their conversational styles are, in part, influenced by natural biases.

Personality research differentiates people's characteristic ways of thinking, feeling and behaving in terms of dimensions of personality, and one of the most widespread theories is based on the 'Big Five' dimensions.[7,8] These five factors are captured by the acronym, OCEAN, referring to Openness to experience, Conscientiousness, Extraversion, Agreeableness and Neuroticism. Each of these factors represents a continuum. Individuals can fall anywhere on the continuum for each factor, and the positioning remains relatively stable throughout most of an individual's life. We can think of personality as revealing tendencies in terms of both habit and re-activity. An extraverted person may have the habit of being expressive and social. But, that habit may in some circumstances be overextended and so manifest as reactivity in the form of being overbearing and socially needy. Or, an introverted person may have the habit of being thoughtful and measured, but that habit, if overextended, may manifest as being withdrawn and aloof. Table 7.2 combines descriptors for habit and reactivity for low and high scores on each of these dimensions. We can invite clients to self-assess against these dimensions, and/or ask their colleagues to give feedback about their perception of our clients against these dimensions, and there are also many psychometrics available that provide structured and validated analyses. Such assessments provide the basis for a rich inquiry into the conversational biases of self and others.

Understanding personality differences has been popular in organisational settings for many years for enabling people to explore how to play to their strengths, manage the gaps in their profiles, and to better understand how to work effectively with colleagues. In the *Breakthrough Conversations* approach we bring particular emphasis to how these biases manifest during conversation. For example, clients who score high on conscientiousness may approach conversations with a bias towards structure and order, setting an agenda for meetings with clear time boundaries, keeping minutes, discussing issues according to an agreed sequence, and bringing a conversation back to the objectives if there are digressions. In contrast, clients who score low on conscientiousness may approach conversations with a bias towards flex-ibility, allowing the conversation to flow into unplanned areas, getting excited about new possible avenues, and being more relaxed if conversations extend beyond a planned timeframe.

Clients can readily identify themselves, not necessarily as an extreme, but never-the-less with some bias towards one end or the other of each dimension, and they can see how this plays out in their conversations with others. In individual sessions it is useful to invite clients to consider the impact of their profile on their conversations with a range of key relationships. In paired sessions, a comparing of profiles, perhaps supported by the structure of the *9-Minute Form*, often brings profiles alive, enabling clients to explore

Table 7.2 Habit and Reactivity for the Big Five Factors of Personality (with MBTI labels)

Big Five Factor	Habit	Reactivity
Openness to experience Low Score – Sensing	Practical, factual, cautious, detailed, present-focused	Resistant to change, cynical, oversimplifying, narrow-minded
High Score – Intuitive	Imaginative, conceptual, enjoys ideas, future-focused, radical	Unrealistic, impractical, vague, overcomplicating, indecisive
Conscientiousness Low Score – Perceiving	Open-minded, flexible, emergent spontaneous, easy-going	Unreliable, disorganised, rash, unfocused, mollycoddling
High Score – Judging	Systematic, organised, reliable, structured, purposeful, orderly	Inflexible, obsessive, rule-bound, driven, bureaucratic, rigid
Extraversion Low Score – introversion	Quiet, measured, thoughtful, listening, observant, boundaried	Withdrawn, passive, stonewalling, detached, insular, isolated
High Score – Extraversion	Outgoing, initiating, taking charge expressive, influencing, assertive	Overbearing, controlling, long-winded, poor listening, dominating
Agreeableness Low Score – Thinking	Logical, tough-minded, objective competitive, challenging,	Provocative, ruthless, suspicious, cold, antagonistic, quarrelsome
High Score – Feeling	Empathising, diplomatic, trusting, humble, supportive, forgiving	Compliant, appeasing, avoids conflict, backs down, self-effacing
Neuroticism Low Score	Content, confident, stable, optimistic, composed	Self-important, foolhardy, indifferent, arrogant, impervious
High Score	Vigilant, passionate, stress sensitive, self-appraising	Self-doubting, intense, anxious, volatile, fear of failure, nervous

the lived-experience of their biases through conversation, whilst noticing that this conversation is itself being shaped by their respective biases. The inquiry into personality raises awareness of patterns of habit and reactivity, and enables clients to manage their interactions more consciously, playing to their positive habits, and learning how to manage unhelpful habits or reactions.

Julia, Lucy and Amir

Julia's facilitation of conversations between two of her team members, Lucy and Amir was introduced in Chapter 2. An element of Julia's approach was to invite each of them to talk about their personality profiles, based on reports generated by the psychometric, Lumina Spark. Lucy's profile showed that she was extraverted, people focused and imaginative. She was good at engaging and inspiring others, thinking boldly about new possibilities for her team and the business and, at her best, would keep her emotions out of the decision-making process. However, her enthusiasm could sometimes be too much for others, particularly those such as Amir who favoured a more controlled and subdued approach.

Amir's profile showed that his bias was for logic, reason and practical outcomes. He was known for staying calm in a crisis, sifting through the facts and resisting any impulse from those around him, such as Lucy, to dramatise issues. Even if Amir felt strongly about an issue, his preference was to consider the time and place to express his views. However, his preference for structure and discipline sometimes led him to being fixated on meeting targets, and so placing unrealistic demands on himself and colleagues. He also had the potential to be somewhat parochial in his loyalties, defending his own team members in the face of their manifest shortfalls, whilst attacking the performance of colleagues in other teams, including some of Lucy's team members.

Julia began by inviting them to share their profiles with each other, and to explore similarities. They were intrigued to discover how similar they were in terms of being outcome-focused, logical and tough. At this juncture Julia gave them each space to talk about these similarities, and in particular, for Amir to acknowledge that he had not thought about those qualities in Lucy, even though, having seen her profile, he could recognise them in how she managed her department. By holding the space for this acknowledgement, Julia supported Lucy and Amir to build rapport and to bring attention back to their mutual respect, rather than focusing exclusively on their differences and difficulties.

She then invited them to talk about their differences. (As I discussed in Chapter 2, Julia preceded this by introducing them to the concept of body-brain awareness, and to share their observations about what happened for them when they were triggered by each other into their RED body-brain states.) Amir confirmed the findings in his personality profile, showing that when he was triggered he was likely to become reactive around his low score on Agreeableness (MBTI – Thinking preference or Lumina Spark, Outcome-Focused preference), which took the form of him being dismissive, quarrelsome, and making off-hand remarks that were designed to undermine Lucy. He acknowledged that at these times his frustration got the better of him and he could see that his behaviour damaged trust and the potential for collaboration. Julia invited Lucy to reflect back what Amir had shared. Lucy reflected what she had heard, and Amir acknowledged that she had effectively captured what he had said. The honesty of Amir's self-disclosures reduced the tension between Amir and Lucy, and Lucy noted that she was feeling a sense of relief on hearing Amir owning and recognising the impact of his frustration. At Julia's invitation she went on to talk about aspects of her profile. She acknowledged that her enthusiasm, a part of her extraversion, would sometimes get the better of her, and she would find herself dominating conversations, interrupting others, or asking leading questions that she realised were not really questions but attempts to elicit confirmation of her views. She also acknowledged that when she was stressed, she would react by looking for the opportunity to expose areas of disagreement with logical arguments, and sometimes she would make impulsive, snap decisions. When Lucy had shared her self-observations, Amir reflected back what he had heard. Lucy qualified some aspects of Amir's reflections, and added that she was also pleased to see that she had scored highly on being practical and down-to-earth because she imagined that Amir and others may not so easily recognise that side of her. Amir acknowledged that he could be triggered by her apparently rash decisions and was reassured to see that her approach was usually anchored in sound, practical considerations.

Having shared their profiles, the areas of similarity, difference, and the aspects that could lead to reactivity in each of them, Julia then invited them to explore how they could use these insights to work more collaboratively together. First, she asked them to consider what they would choose to moderate in their own behaviour, and second, what request they would make of the other. Lucy said the personality profile, and the facilitated conversation, had shown her that her elaborative style of communication around new ideas needed to be moderated if she wanted to keep Amir engaged. She said that she would aim to be clearer about the practical aspects of her arguments, and that she would aim to get to the point more quickly. Amir confirmed that he would appreciate more fact-based and briefer communications from her. In terms of her request of Amir, Lucy noted that she responded best when the other person is optimistic and full of positive energy. She experienced Amir as sceptical and pessimistic, and she said she would appreciate him making an effort to being at least neutral, even if he didn't feel positive about an idea. She also asked that he listen with an open mind rather than detaching from conversations in groups and looking at his phone. Amir was a little defensive about the idea of being pessimistic, saying that there was too much 'grandstanding' in meetings, and that he saw himself as bringing a healthy dose of realism. Acknowledging this distinction, Julia asked Lucy to say what behaviours sent the message of pessimism rather than realism. Lucy said that she too wanted to be realistic and appreciated Amir's level-headedness and pragmatism. In her view the pessimism was not communicated through what he said, but rather in his manner, the derisory tone and the dismissive gestures. Amir received these qualifying observations constructively, acknowledging that his impatience did sometimes get mixed up with his realism, and that he had received feedback in other contexts about these reactive behaviours. Julia supported him to enact this distinction between realism and pessimism with Lucy, using direct language to communicate his challenge to the viability of a project, but sustaining a neutral tone and constructive body gestures. Lucy confirmed that this shift in communication landed positively for her, enabled her to stay engaged with the content of the conversation, and so be more able to address Amir's concerns.

Julia then asked Amir to say what actions he wanted to take as a result of the exploration of personality, and also to say what request he wanted to make of Lucy. He said that he recognised that he needed to be more active in his listening to her, especially in larger meeting contexts as well as one-to-one conversations. He could see that he inadvertently allowed his pragmatism and impatience to resolve issues to spill over into being curt and using cynical humour. He apologised for appearing disrespectful and reassured her that he did respect her views and ideas. Lucy appreciated these comments. In terms of his request, Amir said he would ask that Lucy would take more time to understand his challenges or objectives to an approach, rather than retorting so quickly with a long list of reinforcing arguments. When she did this, he said he felt like withdrawing from the conversation because he did not experience her as being open to his views. Lucy received this request in good spirit, acknowledging her tendency to fight her corner to the detriment of listening to the views of others. She

> said she would do her best to be more inquiring, and also invited Amir, in future interactions, to say something if she fell back into that old pattern.
>
> Exploring how interactive biases based on personality were impacting the conversations between Amir and Lucy formed an important part of improving their interactions and combined with other aspects of the *Breakthrough Conversations* approach, enabled them, with Julia's facilitation, to foster a much more collaborative relationship.

Personality provides a rich basis for examining conversational patterns, validating preferences and tendencies as being shaped in part by innate predisposition. A further basis for examining human relationships, attachment patterns, brings emphasis to certain learned biases in conversational behaviour that are substantially shaped by early, parent-child relational experiences.

Attachment patterns

Attachment theory was originally developed by Bowlby[9] in the study of early childhood relationships and later extended by Hazan and Shaver[10] to the study of adult and work relationships. The attachment process in humans closely resembles the largely instinctual process in animals whereby infants seek proximity to carers in the face of threat. Bowlby argues that in infancy the child develops an internal 'attachment model'; mental structures representing the degree to which others can be trusted, based on early experiences. If children experience responsiveness from parents – parents who are available and ready to respond when called upon to encourage or assist, but who do not intrude – they develop a 'secure base'. They have an internal sense of confidence that allows them, as children and as adults, to venture into the world, to show curiosity and openness to new experiences, and to form trusting and rewarding relationships.

However, if the early parenting experience is less reliable, attachments and emotional development are less secure. In addition to the secure form of attachment, two primary forms of insecure attachment have been identified.[11] Avoidant attachment occurs where parenting is experienced as unresponsive or rejecting; in these circumstances a child tends to be cut off, and this quality of distance can persist into adulthood. Anxious attachment occurs where parenting is experienced as inconsistent, sometimes ignoring and sometimes intrusive, and in these circumstances a child learns to be constantly alert to the caregiver's state of mind, clinging to his or her carer, with a tendency to be overwhelmed by emotions. In adulthood, anxious attachment is seen in the desire to please others, to cling to relationships, and to seek reassurance through recognition. A further insecure strategy that can develop from an experience of threatening or abusive attachment figures is essentially a combination of anxious and avoidant patterns. This arises because infants need to seek closeness to their attachment figure for survival, and yet, this closeness is steeped in threat and so the closeness is followed by fearful avoidance of closeness when it is offered. This strategy is usually referred to as disorganised in the child literature, and fearful avoidant in the adult literature.[12]

Although attachment patterns established in childhood can change, there is evidence that patterns of emotional attachment learned in childhood extend into adult relationships.[13,14] Two primary areas of research into adult attachment dynamics has been in the context of romantic relationships[15] and work relationships.[7] In romantic relationships[16] anxiously attached adults seem to experience separation from their attachment figure as a catastrophe, while more secure adults are more open to new information and able to revise beliefs in relationships, as well as being able to seek reassurance more effectively. Anxious partners are also more prone to strong anger. Avoidants tend to feel as if they are recipients of their partner's hostility and tend to feel distress when their partner expresses upset or seeks support. Avoidant partners can be socially skilled in general but avoid seeking or giving support when attachment needs arise within them or their partner.

In work relationships[7] securely attached respondents are least likely to put off work, least likely to have difficulty completing tasks, and least likely to fear failure and rejection from coworkers. In contrast, employees with an anxious attachment style report a greater fear of rejection from poor performance, while respondents with avoidant attachment tended to use work to avoid social interaction. Looking specifically at the impact of how leaders relate to followers, those with inconsistent leaders can become preoccupied with their own attachment needs,[17] hypersensitive to feedback and overreliant on affirmation, whereas avoidant followers are less likely to trust their leaders and may tend to distance themselves from their leaders.[18] Secure leaders are more likely to display a relational leadership style by expressing greater concern for the development of their followers, whereas avoidant leaders are more narrowly focused on rewards and recognition for task completion.[19]

Using attachment patterns to foster skilful conversations

An understanding of attachment patterns deepens our understanding of the relational needs and fears underpinning habitual and reactive conversational behaviour. By observing how clients speak and relate to us and to their colleagues, they reveal potential clues to their internal working models of relationships, both their belief in their self-worth in receiving support, and their belief regarding the accessibility and availability of other people in times of need.[20] So, if clients seem formal, distant, impatient or challenging, we might wonder if this way of relating is driven, at least in part, by an avoidant attachment style. If we ask those same clients to talk about their early experiences and receive bland or superficial responses with an unwillingness to elaborate, this might reinforce our initial hypothesis. These relational behaviours seen through an attachment lens suggest an underlying fear of failure, rejection, getting things wrong and of not being enough for others, with a core relational longing to feel safe connection or intimacy. The developmental challenge for the avoidant is to overcome shame or doubts about self-worth, and to risk interdependence in terms of the support they can offer and receive. Conversationally, the challenge is to be open in their self-disclosure and self-expression, to listen attentively to others and to meet the needs of self and others with warmth and consideration.

In contrast, if clients seem either overly friendly, pleasing or apologetic, or complaining, blaming or emotionally overwhelmed we might entertain a provisional hypothesis that their way of relating is driven by an anxious attachment style, and this may be reinforced if these same clients become overly elaborative and lost in details in recounting their early experiences. These relational behaviours seen through an attachment lens suggest an underlying fear of not mattering, being abandoned and having their interpersonal needs never satisfied by others, with a core relational longing to feel safe autonomy and independence. The development challenge for clients who are anxiously attached is to pay attention to their own needs, convictions and aspirations, and to understand and work against their fear of expressing differences. Conversationally the challenge is to speak with clarity, expressing their views even if they differ from others, and to nurture their capacity for independence, risk-taking and assertive influence.

If clients seem to be grounded and steady, open to engagement with us and also focused on their goals and expectations, we might hypothesise that they are securely attached, and this view might be reinforced when they provide a coherent autobiographical narrative in response to our invitation to talk about their early experiences. Conversationally secure attachment is flexibly assertive and responsive, and it is the cultivation of such agility that lies at the heart of *Breakthrough Conversations*. By supporting clients to recognise when their behaviours lean towards avoidant or anxious patterns and to acknowledge the fears and needs underlying these patterns, they have the potential to step out of their conditioned RED or AMBER styles and to develop their GREEN 'secure' capacities. The *Breakthrough Conversations* process offers this potential for transforming attachment behaviours by supporting clients to be more anchored in the reflective safety of body-brain awareness and so widening the windows of their emotional tolerance.

Attachment theory also offers insights for leadership development, and I have described avoidant, anxious and secure styles as underpinning three leadership positions, Defiant, Compliant and Authentic.[21] However, in using this framework my emphasis is not to define clients as sitting in one of these categories, but rather to invite them to consider how they might shift from one to another depending on the relational context. In practice most clients recognise that under pressure they have a tendency either towards defiance or compliance, but most also recognise that they can move to the other position in certain circumstances. (In the next chapter I discuss how I view these shifts, and the holding of the paradox between these extremes, as important developmental steps towards a more integrated, secure, attachment position.) In this framing it is also useful to recognise that each of the attachment positions offers certain adaptive habits, as well as self-protective reactions. So, like personality with its positive habits and over-extended reactivities, or character habits and their far enemies (Figure 5.2), we can view attachment positions as having qualities of habit and reactivity. Table 7.3 shows indicative habits and reactivities for the defiant/avoidant and compliant/anxious tendencies, deconstructed in terms of *ACES* (*Actions, Cognitions, Emotions, and Sensations*), together with indicative reflective (secure or GREEN) possibilities that are made available through self-regulation, inquiry and insight.

In a similar way to working with personality, clients are very receptive to attachment theory. I show them tables such as that in Table 7.3 and invite them to consider in which conversational contexts they occupy the defiant, compliant or more secure positions. Most readily identify contexts in which these indicative conversational behaviours arise and will share these observations in paired sessions. This technique draws on attachment theory for understanding conversational tendencies, but it does not necessarily require clients to look in detail at their early attachments with parents. However, some clients are very open to exploring the links between early learning and present-day behaviour, and a powerful way into this territory, is to draw on the Adult Attachment Interview.[22] I ask clients to consider each parent (or other caregivers) and to choose five adjectives or words that reflect their relationship with that person when they were growing up, capturing positive and more challenging aspects. Having done that I ask clients to describe a specific memory that illustrates that adjective or word. These descriptions readily yield clues to attachment dynamics and open the way for exploring how strategies learned early in life may be impacting present-day conversational tendencies. One caution is that this technique can quickly open up emotional territory for clients, and so we need to be ready to go slowly or to step back if the client is reluctant to unpack these feelings, or if the coach does not feel qualified to work with this material. The following case study illustrates the use of the five-adjectives approach to working with attachment patterns with a client pair.

142 Loosening habit and reactivity

Table 7.3 Indicative Habits and Reactions for Defiant and Compliant Attachment Positions

Defiant	Habit (AMBER)	Reactivity (RED)	Reflective (GREEN)
Actions	Decisive Challenging Task-focused Logical and practical Confronts differences	Withdraws or distant Dismissive of others Unexpressive/unemotional Hides behind intellect/logic Shames or belittles others	Listens and validates views of others Self-discloses Balances logic with emotional attunement
Cognitions	I must take control Others can't be trusted I will sort this out I need some space	I mustn't get it wrong I'll be rejected I'm not enough I will be judged	I can risk being open I can feel safe in connection We all make mistakes
Emotions	Controlled Numb Blank	Shame Inadequate Fear of failure/rejection	Compassion for self and others
Sensations	Habitual body tensions	Reactive body tensions	Soothes body tensions
Core needs	Safe intimacy/Security/Acceptance		Intimacy and autonomy

Compliant	**Habit (AMBER)**	**Reactivity (RED)**	**Reflective (GREEN)**
Actions	Seeks harmony Attunes to others Responsive Defuses tension Upholds processes/rules	Seeks reassurance Complains/blames Confused communications Makes demands Emotional outbursts	Asserts own views Clear statements Balances emotions with logic Assertive influence
Cognitions	We don't need to argue What do you want? I want to work together Let's follow the process	My views don't matter My feelings don't count I must push for a response I give up trying	I can risk expressing my views and convictions I feel safe being myself I can decide
Emotions	Concerned about others Empathising	Abandoned Ignored Lonely Angry	Compassion for self and others
Sensations	Habitual body tensions	Reactive body tensions	Soothes body tensions
Core needs	Safe autonomy/Connection/Engagement		Intimacy and autonomy

Liz and Fiona

Senior partners in their business, Liz and Fiona had built a successful organisation and had worked productively together for many years. However, in the previous 6 months to our work together things had become strained. Liz, who was more externally facing, felt that Fiona had lost focus on key business goals, whilst Fiona was feeling unappreciated for the effort she was making in managing staff and internal systems effectively. Their conversations, previously collaborative, had become distant and strained, with some angry confrontations, and they both said they had begun to lose trust in each other. In the second paired coaching session, following three individual sessions for each of them, Liz and Fiona agreed to talk about their respective attachment tendencies. Liz, whom I hypothesised as having avoidant tendencies in relation to Fiona, agreed in advance to share some aspects from our one-to-one conversations about her father and the five adjectives she had chosen to describe her early relationship with him. I was explicit with Liz that I thought this kind of self-disclosure would be a challenging but productive edge for her, since she rarely spoke about her personal feelings and background. She told Fiona that the adjectives she had chosen for her father were: Fun, Distracted, Ambitious, Disapproving and Scary. She spoke about these characteristics and, invited to elaborate on a situation that illustrated why she had chosen the words Disapproving and Scary, she described how fierce he could be if she was naughty. On one occasion she had accidentally smashed a pane of glass in the lounge door. Her father was furious and had shouted at her. She had answered back, saying it was an accident, but this had inflamed him further. As he approached, she rushed upstairs and locked herself in the bathroom, terrified that he was going to break down the door to punish her. She laughed about this experience, saying this had taught her a lesson.

I asked Liz to say what she had learned from this, and other similar experiences. She said it had toughened her up and that she did not let her emotions control her. Recognising she was describing an avoidant reactive pattern, I invited her to bring her mind back to the experience of fear when her father was outside the bathroom, and to tune into the body sensations that went with her fear. Inviting her to take her time, she gradually connected to the frightened child within her. She shared with Fiona that at that early age she had learned that it was best not to depend on others. Fiona reflected back what she had heard Liz say, and expressed her empathy and desire to be supportive. This led to a conversation about what was happening between them. Liz said she was not feeling supported by Fiona. As a consequence, she had withdrawn from contact and felt as if the success of the business depended on her alone. What she had not realised before, and had not communicated to Fiona, was how worried she was about the business, and how much she needed Fiona to carry some of the weight of

> responsibility for winning new contracts. Naming this need for support represented a profound shift for Liz from defiant reactivity to a responsive engagement with Fiona.
>
> Fiona met Liz's openness with sensitivity, and in response was able to step out of her habitual and reactive compliance. She talked about her frustration with herself for always being the 'good girl' – a characteristic she linked to her convent education with fearsome sisters – and her difficulty in standing up to Liz if she had a different opinion. She said she wanted to be involved more with clients but needed Liz to trust her to build relationships in her own way. Liz appreciated Fiona's candid comments and was relieved to realise that Fiona wanted to share responsibility with her for business success. Fiona, like Liz, had managed to step out of her implicit attachment bias towards compliance by stating her needs clearly and assertively. These attachment focused conversations enabled Liz and Fiona to understand how relational patterns developed early in their lives lay behind their current difficulties. Showing curiosity, self-challenge and ownership of their respective patterns, and being willing to talk about these together in paired sessions, they deepened their mutual understanding and trust, and went on to work more closely again in meeting their business challenges.

Cultural and social conditioning

Human beings are conditioned by experience, and I have already discussed how core needs, personality, and early experiences combine to play a central role in how we relate to others. A further important factor to consider in terms of its conversational impact is the conditioning that comes from our cultural or social contexts. Culture is typically defined as a collective phenomenon of share values and meanings. It is expressed in a multiplicity of ways including traditions, customs, ways of living, religion, manners, aesthetics, education and social institutions. There has been research into cultural differences over many decades, the most prominent being the work of Hofstede beginning at the end of the 1970s. He studied people who worked for IBM in more than 50 countries, initially identifying four dimensions that could distinguish one culture from another, and then later, in collaboration with other researchers, adding two more dimensions.[23] Another rich body of research by Trompenaars into business settings identifies seven dimensions of culture,[24] with some overlap and some differences to the six dimensions identified by Hofstede. So, for example, one cultural difference identified in both pieces of research was individualism versus collectivism. Do people regard themselves primarily as individuals or primarily as part of a group? Is it more important to focus on individuals so that they contribute to the community as and if they wish, or is it more important to consider the community first, since that is shared by many individuals? In the Trompenaars research, estimates of the average characteristics of managers in a given national culture are measured by asking them to respond to questions that contain a binary dilemma. For example, 80,000 managers across 100 countries were asked to respond to a question about the ways in which individuals could improve the quality of life:

A: Give individuals as much freedom as possible and the maximum opportunity to develop themselves
B: Emphasise the need for individuals to continuously take care of their fellow human beings.

Which of the two ways of reasoning do you think is usually best, A or B?

The results show that the highest scoring individualists are the Israelis, Romanians, Nigerians, and Canadians, closely followed by the American, Czechs, and Danish, all more than 65 per cent in favour of A. Those with the most collectivist bias are from Egypt, Nepal, Mexico, India and Japan, with more than 60 per cent in favour of B. The European country with the most bias towards collectivism is France (59 per cent). The authors note that this might be surprising until we remember that the French all take their vacations in August on the same date! Another intriguing result is that the Japanese are not significantly more group oriented than the French, whilst the Chinese are slightly more individualist than the Indians. Other dimensions with national biases include hierarchical (e.g. Latin American, Asian, African) versus participative (e.g. Germanic, Anglophone), assertive (Japan, Hungary, Austria) versus consensual (Norway, Sweden), open to change (Sweden, Denmark) versus conservative (e.g. Belgium, Germany) and enjoying life (Latin America, Africa, Nordic Europe) versus working hard (East Asia, Eastern Europe). A further interesting dimension for our focus on conversational bias first identified by Hall[25] is the distinction between direct, explicit and clear communication, most characteristic of Germanic, Scandinavian and American managers, and indirect, implicit and non-verbal communication, most characteristic of Asian, African and Arab managers.

This research suggests that cultural differences will impact how people to relate to each other. It encourages us to be curious about how the conditioning derived from our own cultural and social context shapes our values, assumptions and relationships. Unconscious bias refers to the idea that culture is like water to a fish. We can't see it unless we are challenged in some way to recognise it. I don't see my gender bias, my white privilege, my educational benefits, my economic security, unless for example I listen to others who can see them and can bring my implicit conditioning into conscious view. Something I emphasise to coaches and clients alike is that unconscious bias is inevitable – it is part of the human condition. The human brain is designed to learn from experience and to predict outcomes. This is the habit system automating routine aspects of our lives so that we can be more expedient in our interactions. If I see someone who looks and speaks in a similar way to me, I can make quick assumptions about them, without having to check out if they will be a threat or taking time to unpack the meanings behind the words and phrases that each of us is using. Our assumptions can be a shorthand for productivity. The survival parts of the brain – such as the contextual memory of the hippocampus (see Chapter 2) – enables us to predict or prejudge the safety of new situations, or in other words, to be prejudiced. Unconscious biases are the culturally and socially prejudiced tendencies built into our RED and AMBER body-brain systems, and these unconscious biases are manifested in how we relate to ourselves and others. The key antidote to such biases is the capacity to engage the conscious inquiry of the GREEN system.

The problem with stereotyping is that there is a tendency to take cultural and social differences at surface level and to see individuals solely through that lens. As the research above indicates, there are cultural differences in how people think about society and relationships. But, the researchers also emphasise that an understanding of cultural differences is not about how to understand the people of different nationalities. How any individual's cultural and social conditioning shapes their way of being and relating can only be discovered by inquiring and listening. In my experience coaches may sometimes avoid the whole question of unconscious bias, in themselves and in their clients, because it can feel like we are entering a political and moral minefield. But, in my view, if we can engage our own GREEN/reflective curiosity, both to our own biases, and to inviting clients to think about their biases, we have the potential to unpack an important domain of conversational breakthrough.

Exploring unconscious bias

I introduce the area of cultural and social conditioning as one of the four factors I consider as key shapers of conversational effectiveness: relational needs, personality, attachment patterns and cultural and social conditioning. Unlike these other areas, I don't offer a framework of cultural dimensions – although some clients are interested to learn more about the Hofstede or Trompenaars research – but rather I invite clients to tell stories that illustrate aspects of their personal experiences that they consider formative. So, they choose to explore one or more of many different areas: attitudes to family, to community, to race, to gender, to sexuality, to disability, to emotions, to equality, to money, to the disadvantaged, to achievement, to risk, to time, to the elderly and so on. My intention is to open up their curiosity to their own implicit biases and to explore how these biases impact the achievement of their goals and the quality of their conversations. Two case studies follow where reflection on cultural and social biases both led to those clients clarifying positive developmental steps that they wanted to take.

> Bina described how she was taught to be reserved and deferential in her interactions with men, whether her father, elders in her community and eventually her brothers. She saw herself as encultured to be indirect in her communication, accepting hierarchical structures and implicit inequalities, and having a strong work ethic. This cultural conditioning had an impact on how she conversed with others, especially men. She was an attentive listener, would seek to support the views of others, and although she was a creative person with many good ideas, she found it difficult to make space to speak up. Seeing these tendencies through the lens of culture supported her to challenge herself and to experiment with adopting a more assertive and influential stance. She decided to work with a female mentor whose own cultural conditioning emphasised gender equality and whose forthright and innovative style she admired.
>
> Another woman, Leah, described her upbringing, and in particular the type of schooling she received, as emphasising self-expression and individual freedom. She also recognised herself as highly assertive and competitive, combined with a strong work ethic. In many ways a successful manager known for her willingness to think radically and to introduce bold new initiatives, interpersonally many experienced her as transactional and driven, making little time to build relationships and overly focused on achieving short-term goals at the expense of longer-term strategies to build the breadth and depth of experience needed in her department. She said that she felt like she fitted the picture of a woman who had become successful by being as aggressive as her male counterparts. She felt that she needed to be twice as tough as her male colleagues for them to take her seriously but was nevertheless concerned about the impact on the motivation within her team. She chose to embark on a series of paired coaching sessions with her team members, with a particular focus on balancing her assertiveness with a more nurturing, facilitative interactive style. By actively choosing to listen, to ask questions and to build her sense of empathy for her team members, she reshaped her conversations in ways that were less governed by culturally embedded, or reactive patterns. Her team members appreciated her efforts at being more inclusive and supportive, even if they thought her efforts were a bit wooden at times. They could see that her intentions were positive, and

> this encouraged them to open up more with her. These conversations, based on considerations of cultural conditioning, enabled her to build a more motivated and mutually supportive team.

Sometimes we can see an interaction between cultures and one or more of the other factors. For example, someone who identifies a bias towards being indirect, participative and consensual from a cultural perspective may also score as having a more people focused personality with compliant attachment tendencies. In these circumstances our goal is not to decide how to apportion how much each factor has contributed to certain habits or types of reactivity. Rather, we are using one or more of these factors to bring these tendencies fully into awareness, so clients can make choices about their impact, and can set goals for how they wish to interact in future conversations.

When working with client pairs we can invite them to look at the similarities and differences in their self-assessment of cultural bias, and to explore together the ways in which these enable or hinder productive conversations. They may find that one uses direct communication and the other indirect communication. Or that one is relaxed about uncertainty and taking risks, whilst the other is more risk averse and conservative. Seeing these differences, we can then ask the question, how do these differences in bias impact the flow of conversations. Usually it is the unspoken aspects of these biases that causes problems. For example, when a direct person understands how a colleague has been encultured to be indirect and recognises how directness can be experienced as brusque or critical, they find themselves exploring how to flex their style. When the indirect person understands how a colleague has a cultural bias towards being direct, they are less likely to interpret comments as personal attacks, and to feel more empowered to express their own views. These insights are invitations into conversational agility. Similarly, when clients can see their different biases towards risk, rather than accusing each other of imprudence or resistance to change, they can explore together how their different perspectives can be the basis for a balance of risk and prudence.

Power dynamics in conversation

In Chapter 3 I touched on the impact that power dynamics can have on conversations as part of the *Context* aspect of the *Five-Eyed Model of Conversations*. For example, the majority of women I have worked with in organisations talk about their experience of gender bias. They report that even seemingly enlightened men are guilty of sexist comments or micro-aggressions – dismissive gestures, inappropriate jokes, patronising statements – even if they support equality in other ways. The conversational space is shaped by inequality, and the productivity of conversations is consequently limited. We see such power dynamics, conscious or unconscious, playing out in other areas of difference – race, sexuality, religion, education, disability or any of the numerous ways that people have been conditioned to see themselves as superior or inferior to others.

These can be delicate areas to explore because there is shame embedded in certain cultural biases, and the shame typically triggers reactive denials. 'I am not racist'. 'I am not sexist'. By examining these questions through the lens of cultural conditioning – and if in a pair, slowing things down with the *9-Minute Form* – we have the opportunity to normalise the reality that all human beings have cultural biases. No one is acultural. In this context the question is not, for example, a binary, yes/no question: 'Am I sexist?' or 'Am I racist?'. The question is: 'In what ways does my conditioning inevitably carry unconscious biases?' Or, thinking in terms of the three capabilities of *self-disclosure*, how can I use *self-inquiry* to explore my biases, *challenge* myself to recognise my blind spots, and take *ownership* for my biases so that I can consciously work against them in interactions with others. When clients address such issues in a pair it can lead to startling shifts in self-awareness and a quantum shift in mutual listening and understanding. It is these kinds of shifts in awareness that lead towards the next stage in the *Breakthrough Conversations* process.

Summary

In Stage 3 of the *Breakthrough Conversations* process the focus is on loosening habit and reactivity. By taking clients through a process of *self-inquiry*, *challenge* and *ownership*, we enable them to cultivate the capability of *self-disclosure*. Engaging others from a position of openness and authenticity encourages mutual openness and paves the way for collaboration and shared creativity. Four factors driving conversational tendencies are explored: core needs, personality, attachment patterns, and cultural and social conditioning. Three sets of interpersonal needs are identified based on the FIRO model, and the significance of one or more of these for clients is surfaced by a sensitive exploration of the emotions arising in conversational contexts. Personality models offer frames for understanding how innate biases, combined with environmental experiences, give rise to preferences in how people relate to each other, and seeing the habitual and reactive aspects of these preferences allows clients to manage their tendencies more consciously. Attachment patterns provide a way of understanding how early experiences impact adult relationships by identifying characteristic habitual and reactive conversational tendencies associated with defiant or compliant attachment styles. Recognising how these play out in different situations enables clients to make consciously reflective choices. The fourth area is concerned with how cultural and social conditioning create relational biases, conscious and unconscious. By exploring these through personal stories and observations

150 Loosening habit and reactivity

we create a space for understanding, and for bringing potentially limiting biases more fully into view.

Worksheet 7: Summary of underlying factors impacting conversations

The purpose of this worksheet is to summarise the behavioural tendencies arising from exploring the four factors of: core needs, personality, attachment patterns and cultural and social conditioning.

1. What are your core relational needs? Consider the degree to which it is most important for you to be:

    a. Seen, heard, recognised, accepted, or understood. To belong.
    b. Respected, appreciated, valued. To have safety and/or fairness.
    c. Connected, loved, close, trusted. To collaborate, play or co-create.

2. When these needs are not met our behaviour takes the form of AMBER/habitual or RED/reactive ways of relating, shaped by personality, attachment patterns, and cultural and social conditioning. Based on the conversations with your coach, summarise your characteristic tendencies in the following table, together with observations about how you would prefer to behave based on your GREEN/reflective capacities (Table 7.4).

Table 7.4 Summary of RAG Behaviours Shaped by Three Underlying Factors

	RED/Reactive	AMBER/Habitual	GREEN/Reflective
Personality			
Attachment Patterns			
Cultural and Social Conditioning			

3. Based on the summary above:

    a. What are your most common RED or AMBER conversational tendencies?
    b. What conversational behaviours do you display when you are in a GREEN state?

Notes

1 Rosenberg, M. (2003). *Nonviolent communication: A language of life*. Puddledancer Press.
2 Johnson, S. (1996). *The practice of emotionally focused couple therapy*. Routledge.
3 Schutz, W.C. (1958). *FIRO: A three dimensional theory of interpersonal behavior*. Holt, Rinehart, & Winston.
4 Lucas, R.E., Baird, B.M. (2004). Extraversion and emotional reactivity. *Journal of Personality and Social Psychology*, 86(3), 473–485.
5 Briley, D.A., Tucker-Drob, E.M. (2014). Genetic and environmental continuity in personality development: A meta-analysis. *Psychological Bulletin*, 140(5), 1303–1331.
6 Jang, K.L., Livesley, W.J., Vernon, P.A. (1996). Heritability of the big five personality dimensions and their facets: A twin study. *Journal of Personality*, 64(3), 577–592.
7 John, O.P., Srivastava, S. (1999). The Big-Five trait taxonomy: History, measurement, and theoretical perspectives. In L. A. Pervin & O. P. John (Eds.), *Handbook of personality: Theory and research* (Vol. 2, pp. 102–138). Guilford Press.
8 McCrae, R.R. (2002). Cross-cultural research on the five-factor model of personality. *Online Readings in Psychology and Culture*, 4(4), 1–12. https://doi.org/1 0.9707/2307-0919.1038 (Available: https://scholarworks.gvsu.edu/orpc/vol4/iss4/1)
9 Bowlby, J. (1969). *Attachment and loss: Attachment. V*. New York: Basic Books.
10 Hazan, C., Shaver, P. (1990). Love and work: An attachment-theoretical perspective. *Journal of Personality and Social Psychology*, 59, 270–280.
11 Ainsworth, M.D.S., Blehar, M.C., Waters, E., Wall, S. (1978). *Patterns of attachment: A psychological study of the strange situation*. Erlbaum.
12 Bartholomew, K., Horowitz, L. (1991). Attachment styles among young adults: A test of a four-category model. *Journal of Personality and Social Psychology*, 61, 226–244.
13 Ainsworth, M.D.S. (1989). Attachments beyond infancy. *American Psychologist*, 44, 709–716.
14 Main, K., Kaplan, N., Cassidy, J. (1985). Security in infancy, childhood, and adulthood: A move to the level of representation. *Monographs of the Society of Research and Childhood Development*, Serial No 209 50, Nos 1–2, edited by I. Bretherton, E. Waters. University of Chicago Press.
15 Brennan, K.A., Clark, C.L., Shaver, P.R. (1998). Self-report measurement of adult romantic attachment: An integrative overview. In J.A. Simpson & W.S. Rholes (Eds.), *Attachment theory and close relationships* (pp. 46–76). Guildford Press.
16 Brennan, K.A., Shaver, P.R. (1995). Dimensions of adult attachment, affect regulation and romantic relationship functioning. *Personality and Social Psychology Bulletin*, 21, 267–283.
17 Hudson, D. (2013). Attachment theory and leader-follower relationships. *The Psychologist-Manager Journal*, 16, 147–159.
18 Harms, P.D., Bai, Y., Han, G. (2016). How leader and follower attachment styles are mediated by trust. Human relations. *Studies Towards the Integration of the Social Sciences*, 69, 1853–1876.
19 Doverspike, D., Hollis, L., Justice, A., Polomsky, M. (1997). Correlations between leadership styles as measured by the least preferred co-worker scale and adults' attachment styles. *Psychological Reports*, 81, 1148–1150.

20 Mikulincer, M., Shaver, P. (2007). Boosting attachment security to pro-mote mental health, prosocial values, and inter-group tolerance. *Psychological Inquiry*, 18, 139–156.
21 Lee, G.J. (2003). *Leadership coaching: From personal insight to organisational performance.* CIPD.
22 George, C., Kaplan, N., Main, M. (1985). *The adult attachment interview.* Unpublished manuscript, University of California at Berkley.
23 Hofstede, G., Hofstede, G.J., Minkov, M. (2010). *Cultures and organisations. Software of the mind. Intercultural cooperation and its importance for survival.* McGraw-Hill Education.
24 Trompenaars, F., Hampden-Turner, C. (2012). *Riding the waves of culture: Understanding diversity in global business.* Nicholas Brearley Publishing.
25 Hall, E.T. (1973). *Silent language.* Bantam Doubleday Dell Publishing Group.

Chapter 8

Seeing the dance from the balcony

This stage of the *Breakthrough Conversations* process represents a fundamental shift in awareness. Arguably this is the stage at which breakthroughs are most likely to be realised. Freed from some of the shackles of long-held narratives and identification in Stage 3, there is the possibility of operating with more mental and emotional agility. Whether ourselves or our clients, we come to see that established patterns of habit or reactivity have been shaped by a blend of innate and environmental factors, and that, with awareness, we can step back and observe these tendencies with curiosity and non-judgement. The metaphor of *being on the balcony*[1] is another way of describing the capacity to be an observer or witness to one's own experience, whilst *seeing the dance*[2] is a metaphor for the ongoing cycle of co-creation that occurs within a conversation. Combining these, S*eeing the Dance from the Balcony* implies being able to observe the conversational dynamic and recognising the patterns that are being co-created – between ourselves and clients, between clients and their imagined conversational partners, or between a conversational pair.

The significance of this shift is central to *Breakthrough Conversations*. At this stage we come to see that the other person is not the source of the problem. The problem is the stuck conversational dance that is being unconsciously enacted by both parties. If we have insight into this dance ourselves, even if the other person doesn't, we are more likely to relate with compassion and understanding. If both parties can see that conversational dance and transcend it, they can be more open to difference, and to co-creating fresh solutions. In this chapter I begin by outlining the three elements of *agility* that support this stage, *disidentifying*, *attunement* and *both-and-thinking*. Then I frame the metaphor of *Seeing the Dance from the Balcony* in terms of the concept of vertical development and draw out the cognitive and behavioural possibilities this stage can foster. I explore how we can view a conversation as a potential space created by the poles of the self-other paradox, and that the sustaining of the tension between these poles promotes insight and vertical development. Building on this holding of tension between self and other, I then explore how we can picture

DOI: 10.4324/9781003054542-8

interactions as a cycle or dance shaped by the degree to which there is mutual awareness of underlying emotions and relational needs. Where underlying emotions and needs remain out of awareness the dance follows a RED or AMBER interactive cycle, but when we can bring underlying emotions and needs into awareness, we have the potential for GREEN/interactive cycles. Case studies illustrate the power of supporting clients to recognise these cycles.

Disidentifying, attunement, and both-and thinking

When we are most identified with our viewpoints, we are least available for shared sense-making. We believe our view to be the truth and if others disagree, we either want to persuade them of our view, or we move away from them and operate separately. It is our identifications with specific views that blocks curiosity and receptivity. Drawing together the accumulating cascade of capabilities of *motivation, managing state* and *self-inquiry* in Stages 1–3 of *Breakthrough Conversations*, in Stage 4 we complement these with *agility*. We can think of three elements that support mental and emotional agility, *disidentifying* from one's own viewpoint, *attunement* with the viewpoints of others and *both-and thinking*. *Disidentifying* requires us to observe our own identifications, or viewpoints. Cognitively this might involve a shift for example from an identification with the thought: 'I am being controlled by you', to a more observational, disidentified thought such as: 'I notice myself having the thought that I am feeling controlled by you'. The thought becomes an object of awareness that is open to review and challenge, rather than being an immutable fact. *Attunement* is concerned with understanding and empathising with another person's perspective. *Attunement* does not imply agreement. *Attunement* means understanding the logic of what another person is saying and being able to empathise with the accompanying emotions. By stepping fully into the other person's perspective, we aim to walk in their shoes and to see the world through their eyes. In the *9-Minute Form* our capacity to be attuned to another is displayed in how accurately we reflect back the meanings and feelings of the other person. Bringing together disidentification and attunement, the third aspect of agility is *both-and thinking,* which allows us to hold multiple viewpoints in mind. In a conversation, being able to hold two or more perspectives at the same time enables us to engage in conversation without flicking into reactive or unproductive habitual responses. Such agility is also central to vertical development, which describes the paradigm shifts that people can make in mindset or world view.

Vertical development

There are many theories proposing that adults have the potential to move through a number of developmental stages, whether in terms of cognitive development,[3] moral development,[4] psychosocial development,[5] ego development,[6] self-development,[7] or leadership development.[8] These theories describe the sequence of meaning-making frameworks that evolve over time. Each new level integrates the learning from the previous level into a new and larger frame of meaning making, allowing us to embrace more complexity, viewpoints and expanded time-horizons. Such development is called vertical to contrast it with horizontal development. Horizontal development typically occurs when we learn new skills, behaviour, or knowledge, and apply our skills in different situations. It is concerned with getting better at doing things within a specific stage of development. Vertical development involves a paradigm shift in how we see the world and is much harder to achieve. It refers to how we learn to see the world through new eyes, how we change our interpretations of experience, and how we transform our views of reality. It describes increases in what we are aware of, or what we can pay attention to, and therefore what we can influence or integrate. Our sense of identity is enlarged, and our ways of relating to others becomes increasingly agile and adaptive.

Much of the research seeks to identify seven or more stages that people can move through in a lifetime, from the earliest, childlike stages of being impulsive or opportunistic in one's relationship to the world, through to the highest stages of non-dual consciousness characteristic of sages and mystics. If someone is operating at the third stage, they have access to the first and second stages but the centre of gravity of their worldview is at the third stage. They do not have access to the expanded perspectives offered by the fourth stage or above. If we shift to a higher stage, we can think of our mental frames as 'transcending and including' all earlier stages. The vertical shift brings an expanded perspective, with the capacity to observe our own biases and their impact on our relationship with others. In the language of the *RAG* body–brain circuitry, our goal in *Breakthrough Conversations* is to use our GREEN, responsive capacities to notice when we are in the thrall of our habitual, AMBER or reactive RED tendencies. Indeed, the degree to which we can do this amidst the conversational experience is a key indicator of our stage of vertical development.

In terms of identifying the stage of vertical development in ourselves or others, it is useful to recognise that the mental and emotional agility of the majority of people operates at one of three stages,[9] which have been described as the Expert, Achiever and Catalyst stages.[10] I also label these stages in terms of what we might see as the central focus of our conversations: at the Expert stage we see our *skills* as the most important thing, at the Achiever stage it's our focus on *outcomes* and at the Catalyst stage it's using conversations as a space for *co-creating*. We can differentiate these stages in terms of how people approach and behave in conversations (see Table 8.1).

By emphasising the role of reflective awareness amidst the interactive experience, *Breakthrough Conversations* are explicitly seeking to support

156 Seeing the dance from the balcony

Table 8.1 Three Levels of Agility and Their Impact on Conversations

Skills/Expert	Outcomes/Achiever	Co-Creating/Catalyst
Views conversation skills as rules to be learned	Views conversation skills as a method for honing goals and agreements	Views conversations as a domain for discovery and co-creation
Strongly assertive or accommodating	Uses assertion and accommodation flexibly to influence others	Uses a balance of advocacy and inquiry to foster collaboration
Not aware of tacit mental frameworks and own subjectivity	Reflects on beliefs and values after the fact, but not aware of how views are conditioned	Reflects in action; recognises and names tacit feelings, assumptions and behaviours
Harsh judgements of self and others – avoids giving or receiving feedback	Values practical, behavioural feedback, but resists challenges to own mental frame or goals	Proactively seeks feedback and contrasting views to embrace more complexity and deeper meanings
Conversations are strongly governed by habit (AMBER) and reactivity (RED) with little responsive (GREEN) reflection	Some responsive (GREEN) reflection in conversations, but mostly habit (AMBER) and reactivity (RED)	Conversations are shaped by responsive (GREEN) reflections on impact and effectiveness of habitual (AMBER) or reactive (RED) tendencies

vertical development. If, reviewing Table 8.1, we recognise Expert tendencies in some of our conversations, we might ask ourselves what it would take for us to shift vertically to the Achiever stage. Similarly, if we recognise Achiever tendencies in our conversations we might ask ourselves what it would take to move vertically to the Catalyst stage. In fact, an inquiry of this kind, drawing as it does on our GREEN, responsive body–brain circuitry, is a vertically developed type of inquiry. By asking this question we begin to create the conditions for an expanded view of who we are and how this shapes interactions with others, and similarly, if we invite clients into such an inquiry, we are exploring their openness and capacity to embrace their potential for vertical development.

Conditions that evoke vertical development

A comprehensive review of vertical development[11] argues that there are three 'primary' conditions that support vertical development, *heat experiences*, *colliding perspectives* and *elevated sense-making*. Heat experiences refer to being in a situation that disrupts or disorients our habitual ways of thinking. Our body brain circuitry is on alert, our emotions are aroused, and there is some openness to the possibility of finding better ways of making sense of the challenge we are facing. Colliding perspectives arises when we are exposed to people with different mindsets, opinions, experiences and viewpoints. Our mental models collide with those of others to throw our certainties and mental constructs into question. Elevated sensemaking arises when we are able to integrate these different perspectives, and over time we establish a more elevated worldview, or stage of development.

Conversations have the potential to constellate all three of these conditions for vertical development. We know them as heat experiences when we connect with the motivation and courage to speak what is true for us in the face of our vulnerability, or when we open to hearing another's authentic expression. If we ask a client a penetrating question, we can feel the emotional temperature rise. Working with a pair, the atmosphere at the outset can feel electric with anticipation, each person sensing the potential for uncomfortable discoveries. Colliding perspectives arise in many ways. In the simplest sense, a conversation between two people always has the potential to bring differing viewpoints into contact with each other. As a coach our role is to invite an examination of mindsets – to support curiosity and new discoveries. We are looking to draw out colliding perspectives in relation to beliefs, interpretations and narratives about self and others. External colliding perspectives, manifested in one-to-one or paired sessions, usually point towards an internal collision between different parts of the mind, or what we might otherwise call internal conflict. We feel angry with the person we love the most, we aspire to being healthy but find ourselves eating a box of biscuits, we practice compassion much of the time but notice ourselves furious with others.

What we, or others, do with such colliding perspectives lies at the heart of whether there is elevated sensemaking, or, in my terminology, breakthrough. Habitual (AMBER) or reactive (RED) body–brain circuitry are most likely to constrain the capacity for vertical development, either processing new experiences as horizontal extensions to knowledge, or blocking receptivity to learning and entrenching us more in our existing mindsets. It is only if we can engage our reflective (GREEN) body–brain capacities and *disidentify*, *attune* and engage in *both-and thinking* that we can make ourselves available for elevated sensemaking, new insights and breakthrough to a higher developmental stage.

The potential space between self and other

The power of conversations is that they bring together the colliding perspectives of self and other, and, within our own minds, that includes the collision between the parts of the self that we own, and the parts of the self that we disown and make 'other'. I link this challenge of managing the tension between self and other to the concept of potential space.[12] Winnicott, a psychoanalyst specialising in working with children, coined the term 'potential space' to refer to developmental possibilities arising from the paradox of the infant's experience of 'I' and 'me' in the relationship with its mother. According to Winnicott it is through paradox that the infant experiences the illusion of omnipotence, of having created what is there to be found, and this is the basis for play, creativity and the use of symbols. The potential space between mother and baby, and the developmental possibilities it enables, is the forerunner to the richness of experience arising from sustaining the tension between what is 'me' and 'not-me', and the creative integration of these at a higher level of meaning making. Illustrating the central place of potential space to human development throughout the lifespan, Winnicott sees it as the basis for the experiencing that belongs to the arts, religion, creative scientific work and imaginative living. Our human potential is defined by this intermediate space and understanding how to sustain such spaces is fundamental to developing ourselves and others.

Generalising the concept of potential space, vertical progression is achieved through the ongoing renegotiation of the balance between adaptation; giving oneself over to receiving new knowledge from the external world and differentiation; making knowledge one's own and temporarily fixing the world according to one's self-definition. We can think of this movement back and forth as occurring between self-assertion and self-surrender,[13] or between autonomy and connection. It is this dialectical process that gives rise to what we can think of as a spiral of vertical development[6], where the potential space is held by the conversational dynamic between what is regarded as self, and what is regarded as other (Figure 8.1).

At any particular developmental moment for adults, self-identity will be defined in terms of the relationship between the poles of autonomy and connection. Sometimes the centre of gravity will be more towards the pole of autonomy, in which case self-identity is defined more in terms of interior experience and self-determination, with a reduced openness to exterior experience. At other times the centre of gravity will be more towards the pole of connection, in which case self-identity is defined more in terms of exterior experience and self-surrender, with a reduced attunement to interior experience.

In working with these dynamics within ourselves or our clients, our goal is to hold the potential space of inquiry. Supported by fostering GREEN body–brain circuitry and reflective presence, disparate and conflicting views can be embraced, and their creative integration can lead to breakthroughs in awareness and collaboration. However, if we are emotionally triggered by the challenge to self-identity presented by the conversation between self and other, there is resolution of the potential space, either in the direction of autonomy and defiance, or in the direction of connection and compliance[14]

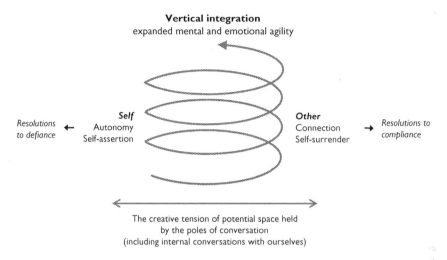

Figure 8.1 Spirals of Development Arising from the Conversational Space.

(see Table 7.3). Our goal in coaching is to create a space where such polarisations can be held in mind and explored experientially, so they can be gradually integrated into an expanded awareness and the basis for enhanced personal and relational agility. The following case studies show a practical approach for doing this when working in a one-to-one context.

Lara – Holding the Paradox between Defiance and Compliance

Lara's responsibility had increased substantially in terms of the size of her team. Overall, her department was considered to be producing excellent outputs, but many of her team members were stressed and threatening to leave. There was something about her approach from previous roles that was not working in this new role. Initially she could not explore what was going on without polarising into an attack on her team for not being competent enough, or an attack on herself for being a nasty person. I introduced her to the concept of body–brain circuitry and the *RAG* model, and we used some mindfulness practices to support greater equanimity and non-judgmental inquiry, and, as a method for supporting potential space. We would begin and end sessions with a short practice, and she used guided meditations at home.

The mindfulness had a profound impact on her capacity to regulate her emotions and so remain more open and reflective in her conversations with me. Once her mental steadiness was more established, we were able to look at her resolutions of paradox. At the defiant end of the spectrum she was at her most fierce because she believed that any errors or poor performance would imply that she was an incompetent manager. Consequently, she could be very harsh and shaming of staff if there was any possibility of work not meeting her high standards. In this mode she might use phrases such as, "What they need to understand is …" or "I can't believe that I have to do all the thinking". She justified this style by noting that, on many occasions, this approach did enable her and her team to achieve excellent results, even if there were casualties along the way. At the compliant end of the spectrum she felt she needed to be liked and loved by her team members as indication that she was a good person, and any suggestion that they were struggling with her management style left her shocked and ashamed. In this mode she would be intrusively concerned about others and their welfare, ringing them at home in the evening, or emailing during the weekend to send thoughtful comments. Her team members were experiencing her as flicking back and forth between these extremes, and many were feeling stressed, undermined, confused and angry.

When we looked at the co-existence of these defiant and compliant poles, she came to see that her harsh, internal drive to succeed was at the heart of the split. Her self-esteem was strongly attached to her professional achievements, and she trusted her own intellect and drive as the best guarantee of success. This approach worked when the sphere of her responsibilities was smaller, and she did not have a team to manage. But now, with a bigger remit and a sizable team, she needed to learn how to deliver results with and through others. This was a key developmental transition for her that required a reframing of how she viewed success. The combination of the use of the *RAG* frame, mindfulness and our coaching conversations provided her with the potential space to hold the defiance/compliance paradox; to bring compassion both to her own fear of not succeeding and her concern and support for others. It was in the potential space of this sustained paradox that she gradually developed a more integrated sense of how she could operate as a manager, supporting others to achieve to high standards.

Roger – working with internal and external paradox

For some clients it is useful to explore how the poles of the paradox of autonomy and connection are manifesting, both internally within the person's mind and their self-relationship, and externally in their relationships with others. For example, a very competent and experienced coach receiving coaching supervision with me spoke of his avoidance of assignments that made him feel out of his depth. I viewed this lack of self-belief as an anxious swing to compliance. He did not want to let others down and feared the consequences of his coaching being seen as having failed. This tendency was blocking his career development and limiting the richness of his coaching practice. However, at times, in particular in his personal relationships, he noted he could be completely fixed and intransigent; that is, when pushed to an extreme, he could swing to defiance in order to get his own needs met.

I saw the coaching supervision challenge as getting him to integrate his professional compliance with his more personal defiance. We framed the paradox in terms of how it was manifesting externally and internally. Externally his compliance took the form of staying firmly within his comfort zone and not taking risks. Internally this correlated with his sense of himself as not being academic and as believing that his clients would dismiss him for being ignorant. At the other pole, externally his defiance took the form of him holding his ground around certain issues with total intransigence, and internally this was underpinned by a sense of righteous outrage that others would dare to take advantage of him or not value his contribution. I worked with paradox by writing each pole of the paradox on to an A4 sheet of paper, placing them on the floor, and getting him to experience standing in each position, and then in the potential space between them. The floor had become the potential space holding the autonomy-connection dynamic. The idea was to encourage him to develop an embodied sense of what it was like to be in each of these positions.

He stood up and explored this space by stepping between the poles, inhabiting one extreme and then the other, and then stood back to get an overview of this external and internal dynamic. The use of potential space formed part of the work that marked a transition for the coach. He began to integrate his defiance and compliance into a more grounded, assertive position, enabling him to exhibit more courage and confidence in taking on more challenging assignments, as well as using more balanced and healthily robust methods for getting his own needs met.

Identifying the conversational dance

As the above illustrations show, holding the tension between emotionally driven polarities, such as between compliance and defiance, is a powerful approach for fostering expanded awareness and vertical shifts in sensemaking. We can apply this same notion – holding a space for exploring emotionally charged differences – to working with imagined or actual pairs.

The aim is to make explicit how the dance of emotions, thoughts and behaviours between two perspectives can get caught in a negative cycle. The RED pattern from one person is likely to evoke a RED pattern from the other, giving rise to a RED conversational dance. Conversely, if we can foster, through awareness, GREEN patterns in at least one, but ideally both members of a pair, we can support clients to step vertically into a GREEN conversational dance.

The reason RED or unproductive AMBER cycles occur is because core relational needs, and the vulnerable emotions associated with them are not being met. Our aim is to support clients to identify their relational needs and associated vulnerable emotions, and to show how their mutual, self-protective strategies are sustaining a negative cycle. To do this we need to draw out a distinction made in emotionally focused therapy between primary and secondary emotions.[15]

Primary and secondary emotions

In Chapter 3 I discussed emotions as part of the *PACES* (*Pause, Actions, Cognitions, Emotions, Sensations*) frame for deconstructing experience, and differentiated emotions along two dimensions, activated-deactivated and stress-flow (Figure 3.3). A further important distinction is between primary and secondary emotions. Primary emotions are immediate, implicit emotions that are often out of awareness. Secondary emotions are reactions to our primary emotions and the ones we can see on the surface. A key goal for us is to support clients to see how their secondary emotions arise as a protection against experiencing the vulnerability evoked by their primary emotions, and that these primary emotions are themselves directly linked to core relational needs. Before illustrating the richness of this dynamic I will distinguish these two types of emotion.

Primary emotions

Primary emotions are the initial, gut-feelings or visceral responses to a situation. We might feel primary emotions initially as sensations; perhaps as a lump in the throat, or in the pit of the stomach, a tightening of the shoulders, or a shortening of the breath. Unless we are practiced at noticing such sensations they remain largely out of awareness, but they are important because they usually indicate our vulnerable primary emotions. Common primary emotions are sadness, fear, hurt, anger, shame, joy, excitement or surprise. As you can see, primary emotions include those that evoke *stress*, such as sadness and fear, and those that evoke a sense of *flow*, such as joy and excitement. They are primary because they are the first emotions we feel in response to a situation, even though we often don't register them in awareness. Our goal is to support clients to notice their *flow* primary emotions as well as their *stressful* ones, since change occurs as much by nurturing *flow* states as understanding *stressful* states.

Less skilful conversations occur when stressful primary emotions associated with unmet needs trigger the RED body brain system and give rise to a RED conversational cycle – such as when a lack of respect (the unmet need) triggers a sense of hurt (primary emotion), which leads to the expression of anger (secondary emotion). In contrast, many conversations will be effective with an AMBER conversational cycle of habit. But we also need to recognise that habits are automatic and are not adaptable to new contexts, and so some AMBER behaviours lead to unproductive AMBER cycles, and indeed these cycles may gradually become RED cycles. Just think about how a partner's behaviour at first might seem interestingly individual, but how over time this same habitual behaviour can begin to grate and, if not discussed, may become a trigger for difficult interactions. In the case illustration with Julia, Lucy and Amir (Chapters 2 and 7), Lucy and Amir's relationship was effective for much of their routine work, but when out-of-the-ordinary issues arose their habitual interactive styles were ineffective and triggered a RED cycle. In summary, when conversations are difficult, it is the primary emotions associated with RED or unproductive AMBER cycles that we are seeking to uncover.

The GREEN primary emotions are positive emotions such as compassion, appreciation, love and joy, and these support us to bring observational curiosity to the experience of RED or AMBER states. As I have said already, it is as though GREEN states can co-exist with RED or AMBER states – based on a blending of the ventral vagal and sympathetic nervous system, or the ventral vagal and dorsal vagal systems (see Chapter 2) – providing the equanimity to tolerate difficult emotions and to investigate them with observational curiosity. In GREEN states the emotions are viewed as transitory states, some more challenging and some more enjoyable, but without them being experienced as overwhelming and so triggering the need for habitual or reactive strategies.

Secondary emotions

Typical secondary emotions include anger, frustration, guilt and defensiveness. When someone ignores us, we might react with anger, demanding attention or complaining. When someone blames us, we might find ourselves frustratedly retaliating, or perhaps feel guilty and blame ourselves. These emotions are secondary, because if we take time to introspect, we will discover that there are primary emotions underlying these secondary reactions. For example, when we get angry because someone ignores us this is a secondary emotion that might be underpinned by the primary emotion of hurt or sadness. When we feel guilt, this might be a secondary emotion underpinned by the primary emotion of fear or shame.

When we have the picture of primary and secondary emotions in mind, and recognise how key primary emotions are to shifts in awareness it can be tempting to invite clients to move too quickly from their secondary emotions to an exploration of the underlying primary emotions. When we see anger, we want clients to tune into their hurt or sadness. When we see withdrawal, we want clients to notice their shame or fear. However, it is crucial to validate secondary emotions fully first, otherwise we may find ourselves triggering further reactivity. Anger is a valid emotion indicating for example that we feel as if our boundaries have been cut across, or that someone is not respecting us. We are not trying to close down the potency of anger, but rather to honour and reflect its purpose. So, in the face of anger, we may say: *'I can see how energised you are about this issue ... I think this shows how much you care about this, and that you are prepared to fight for what you believe will work'*. If we validate secondary emotions in this way, we ensure that clients feel heard and understood. By interpreting the positive intent of secondary emotions and its associated behaviour, even if the behaviour itself is unskilful, clients feel validated. Such validation reduces the need for the protective secondary emotions and makes clients more available to explore their underlying primary emotions.

When we can see how our underlying needs and emotions are triggering us, we can make different relational choices. For example, when an unreliable friend cancels an arrangement with us at the last minute, we may notice our disappointment, but we may also notice an arising of anger. We find ourselves ruminating about the other person's unreliability and feel justified in our reaction. This is driven by our secondary emotion. If we speak to the friend from this state, we are likely to be unskilful, perhaps withdrawn or accusatory, and so trigger a RED cycle. But if we pause and listen to our bodies, we may notice a sense of hollowness in the belly that we associate with feeling hurt. We may tune into a deeper pattern of not feeling lovable, or of not mattering to others, and we may go further and associate this response to experiences in other relationships or stages of our lives. Seeing the rawness of these primary emotions, and the core relational need to feel seen and appreciated, we may choose to soothe ourselves, calling on our self-compassion. Having deepened our emotional awareness in this way, if we choose to talk with our friend about the impact of their last-minute cancellations, we can speak from a place of personal honesty and vulnerability, with our intentions for friendship to the fore. It is through self-inquiry and deepening awareness that we create the conditions for a more connecting conversation.

Having described the distinction between primary and secondary emotions and how they interact, we can return to the idea of a negative cycle, and consider how the interaction between primary and secondary emotions within two individuals can evoke mutually reinforcing cycles between individuals – either stress-inducing RED or AMBER cycles, or potentially, flow-inducing GREEN cycles.

Organising the interactive cycle

When we can support clients to make sense of the dance of emotions and needs between themselves and another, and so see how this dance is impacting their conversational effectiveness, they gain significant insight, and, arguably, make a vertical shift in awareness. They no longer see themselves or the other person as the problem but hold a systemic view of cause and effect. Their individualistic view of interaction is replaced by a sense of being part of a dyadic, interacting whole. Bringing together the power of making explicit the interactive cycle created by couples used in emotionally focused therapy, with the focus on *RAG* body–brain circuitry and its deconstruction in terms of *ACES*, we can offer clients a schematic picture of the distinction between RED/AMBER and GREEN interactive cycles (Figure 8.2).

Our aim is to show clients what happens in their RED or unproductive AMBER cycles, and, by supporting them to notice and name their primary emotions and needs, see how they can expand their awareness and shift to a GREEN cycle. We track the cycle, for each person, starting with the perception at the centre of the diagram, and then support clients to describe the feelings, thoughts and behaviours that arise. We can do this whether working one-to-one, getting a person to imagine another person's steps in

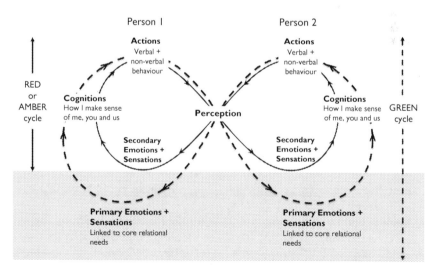

Figure 8.2 The *ACES* Aspects of RED/AMBER and GREEN Interactive Cycles.

the cycle, or with a client pair. The following case illustration is a continuation of a client pair introduced in Chapter 6.

Mick and Stuart

I have described work with Mick and Stuart to illustrate the use of the *9-Minute Form* to slow their interactions and to create the reflective space to explore underlying emotions, sensations and relational needs. I will return to this work to illustrate how we can track the cycle of interaction for pairs, drawing on the elements shown in Figure 8.2.

Mick and Stuart had become distant as a result of Mick not listening to Stuart's views or including him sufficiently in key business decisions, whilst Mick was feeling impatient with Stuart's lack of trust in his reasoning and good intentions. Deconstructing the RED cycle for Mick and Stuart in terms of *ACES*, the initiating trigger to the cycle occurred when they tried to discuss their different views about how to address business issues. For a long time, Stuart would invite Mick to meetings (*Action*) to thrash out their different views, but Mick's response (*Action*) had been increasingly to cut short such meetings or to rearrange them for a later date. Mick thought (*Cognition*) there were more pressing matters to attend to, and when he did meet with Stuart he thought their discussions were going around in circles without ever reaching a conclusion (*Cognition*). He thought Stuart was unhelpfully theoretical in his approach, and ironically Stuart thought exactly the same about Mick. Each of them would press their viewpoint on the other (*Action*) but neither would feel truly heard and understood by the other (*unmet need*), and they were consequently unable to find a collaborative win-win-solution. They were both immensely frustrated (*Emotion*) by the other but could not see a way to find common ground. In the face of such impasse Mick would make a unilateral decision (*Action*) without Stuart's buy-in. Stuart gradually gave up on trying to discuss issues with Mick (*Action, Cognition and Emotion*). Instead he offered his creative ideas and used his influence with other colleagues and took his own initiatives in a different direction to those of Mick. This divergence was causing confusion in the organisation and creating a partisan split in different departments.

After some resistance from Mick, they both engaged positively with paired sessions, appreciated the value of observing *RAG* body–brain states, and made positive use of the *9-Minute Form*. Holding the picture of the interactive cycle in mind, I supported each of them to explore the underlying emotions, sensations and needs driving their

RED cycle. For Mick, his core relational need was to be viewed as highly competent and that unconscious driver had largely served him well – he had achieved considerable success, he believed in his abilities, and he was ambitious to take on more senior leadership positions. His ambition meant he was especially focused on winning the approval of senior managers, and so he became impatient (*Secondary Emotion*) with Stuart if he impeded Mick's desire for rapid decision-making and results. In contrast to people who are more in touch with self-doubt – sometimes described as 'impostor syndrome' – Mick had a 'pride-based identification,'[16] and was not aware of his underlying need for approval and success. His apparent conviction, perceived sometimes as arrogance by others, was achieved by denying uncertainty and by being relatively impervious to those who opposed his views. However, he also cared about what others thought of him (*core need*), partly because he viewed himself as a person of integrity, and also because he knew that senior managers would question his future potential if he couldn't bring other colleagues with him. Working with Mick in a paired context brought out his internal conflict between the part of him that wanted to make quick decisions and prove his worth and so might railroad others (a Skills/Outcome bias in terms of vertical development – see Table 8.1), and the part of him that wanted to be intrinsically fair to others, that appreciated that his decisions carried uncertain outcomes, a consequent fear of failure (*Primary Emotion*), and a need for external recognition (*core need*). By holding these two parts of Mick's internal experience in tension with each other, he had the potential to shift vertically towards the possibility of holding more ambiguity, relationality, and so opening to the possibility of co-creating with Stuart and others.

For Stuart, his core relational need was to feel respected and for his opinions to be valued. In a one-to-one session we had explored his early cultural and attachment experiences in relation to his father. He described his cultural origins as one's which emphasised the authority of the father and the expectation that a son would not be challenging. He recalled how frustrating (*Primary Emotion*) it was when his father ignored him (*unmet need*) when he wanted to express his opinions, and from an attachment perspective we explored the tension between the part of him that had learned to comply in order to maintain harmony, and another part of him that felt defiant and would distance himself from his father in order to honour his individuality and self-expression. Making the link between the relational patterns with his father and the similarity with aspects of his relationship with Mick, Stuart recognised that he was particularly sensitive to what he perceived as Mick's dismissive attitude (*perception that triggers the cycle*). Seeing this link was itself a significant insight for Stuart and this motivated him to think it might be possible to find a different way of relating to Mick.

The underlying needs, emotions and sensations driving the RED cycle between Mick and Stuart were initially explored in one-to-one sessions, but it was when they could share together in *Seeing the Dance from the Balcony* that their relationship had a breakthrough. I described the full cycle, using the steps shown in the GREEN cycle (Figure 8.2) to acknowledge the RED cycle:

You each have strong ideas about the best way to approach your shared business challenges, but when your views are different, you struggle to find common ground between you. For you Mick, you have a sense of urgency about making decisions and you have strong beliefs in your preferred approach. You feel some exasperation (Secondary Emotion) that you and Stuart can't see eye-to-eye and, having tried to explain your position many times (Action), you decide to take a decision unilaterally (Cognition) and to progress things in a way that does not take account of Stuart's views. What Stuart can't see, is that underneath your confident decision-making, you have a fear of being perceived as failing (Primary Emotion), particularly by senior managers, which evokes a sense of potential shame or humiliation (Primary Emotion) about being perceived as ineffective (unmet need). So, what Stuart sees is your dominating style and confidence (Action), without realising that it is driven by underlying fears (Primary Emotion).

For you Stuart, you experience Mick as not being prepared to engage or listen to your views (triggering perception). This triggers your frustration (Secondary Emotion) and you tell yourself that you are being railroaded once again (Cognition about self). You try to engage with Mick with logic and reason (Action), explaining the rationale behind your thinking, but as you do this you perceive Mick as not really listening, or even if he does, he just responds by repeating his viewpoint rather than seeking to understand your perspective (triggering perception). You become argumentative sometimes, but more recently you have given up trying to engage with Mick (Action). What Mick sees is you either overwhelming him with logical arguments or becoming disengaged and distant, but what he does see is your underlying sense of being ignored by him (unmet need). You feel like he does not respect your views – that your input does not matter, and so beneath your secondary emotion of frustration is a primary emotion of hurt.

Mick and Stuart picked up this capturing of their cycle, elaborating on it, each giving examples of how it had played out in different circumstances, and with my support, expressing again the connection between the underlying, vulnerable primary emotions, the core relational needs, and the visible behaviours that were triggering for each other. Holding this picture of their conversational tendencies in view, they could look together at how to relate more effectively together. Mick could see the link between his denial of uncertainty and vulnerability and his fear of getting it wrong (Primary Emotion), with his reluctance to listen to others and to value radically different perspectives. He could see that he needed to be more comfortable with ambiguity and challenges to his convictions if he was to allow for the co-creation of robust solutions that he and Stuart could commit to. In short, he needed to shift vertically from an Achiever mindset to more of a Catalyst mindset. Stuart could see that his focus on reason and his relentless presenting of his arguments was ineffective. But he realised that if he spoke about his experience of being railroaded by Mick and the sense that Mick did not respect his views (unmet need), this was much more likely to engage Mick's attention. Stuart saw that when he owned his personal feelings (Primary and Secondary Emotions) around the need to feel seen and respected (core needs) by Mick, the response from Mick was to be genuinely sensitive and curious. Mick affirmed how much he genuinely valued Stuart's views, acknowledged that his own sense of impatience got the better of him sometimes, and committed to listen and probe for a deeper understanding of Stuart's ideas. The breakthroughs for Mick and Stuart came from a combination of their individual and paired sessions, but they both acknowledged that it was the enacting of these insights in the context of the paired sessions that had evoked the most significant shift in their relationship.

Summary

Stage 4 of the *Breakthrough Conversations* process draws on the emotional steadiness and insights gained at earlier stages and supports clients to view their conversational tendencies from a larger perspective. This change of perspective allows them to embrace broader aspects of their internal and relational experience, holding tensions between parts of the self, and between self and others and, by noticing potential triggers rather than reacting to them, they begin to integrate fundamental shifts in mental and emotional agility. Three aspects of *agility* are emphasised, *disidentifying, attunement,* and *both-and-thinking*. The development of these qualities provides the basis for supporting clients to make significant, vertical shifts in their ways of making sense of their interior, and their conversational dynamics. Drawing out areas of defiance and compliance – in such aspects as thoughts, feelings, needs, behaviours, values and intentions – and supporting clients to hold these in tension with each other, encourages them to embrace increased complexity and to view their own biases with curiosity and choice. A further technique for fostering vertical shifts and for *Seeing the Dance from the Balcony* is to support clients to identify distinct interactive cycles in conversations, tracking the cycle of *ACES* (*Actions, Cognitions, Emotions and Sensations*) in RED or AMBER cycles, and showing how these are driven by underlying needs, emotions and sensations. When the describing of a RED or AMBER cycle includes those underlying aspects, it has the potential to be experienced, simultaneously, as a GREEN cycle, where the body–brain circuitry supports broader awareness, responsiveness, and insight. When clients are able to converse with a GREEN interactive cycle, they are ready to move to Stage 5, the final stage of the *Breakthrough Conversations* process: *Harnessing Expanded Perspectives*.

Worksheet 8: Seeing the conversational dance

This worksheet enables clients to capture in words the elements of the conversational cycle represented in Figure 8.2. When both clients in a pair can identify the mutually reinforcing pattern of a RED or AMBER cycle and use their reflective awareness to also recognise the underlying primary emotions and core needs, they are in effect creating a GREEN awareness of their cycle, and so have the potential to come together as allies in seeing their co-created dance (Table 8.2).

In what ways, if any, does this description of the co-created nature of this conversational dynamic impact your understanding of how to work more effectively in future?

Table 8.2 Summary of Elements Driving RED, AMBER and GREEN Interactive Cycles

	Person 1	Person 2
Perceptions: What do you each perceive that gives rise to a RED/AMBER cycle?		
Actions: What behaviours do you each show in a RED/AMBER cycle?		
Cognitions: How do you each make sense of you, me, us, in a RED/AMBER cycle?		
Emotions/Sensations: What secondary E/S's do you each show in a RED/AMBER cycle? What primary E/S's and core needs do you each hide in a RED/AMBER cycle		

Notes

1 Ronald Heifetz and Marty Linsky describe operating in and above the fray as "... getting off the dance floor and going to the balcony," in Heifetz, R.A., Linsky, M. (2002, June). A survival guide for leaders. *Harvard Business Review*, 80(6), 65–74.
2 Johnson, S. (2011). *Hold me tight: Your guide to the most successful approach to building loving relationships.* Piatkus Books.
3 Piaget, J. (1954). *The construction of reality in the child.* Basic Books.
4 Kohlberg, L. (1969). Stage and sequence: The cognitive developmental approach to socialization. In D.A. Goslin (Ed.), *Handbook of socialization theory and research.* Rand-McNally.
5 Erickson, R.J. (1995). The importance of authenticity for self and society. *Symbolic Interaction*, 18, 121–144.
6 Cook-Greuter, S.R. (2004). Making the case for a developmental perspective. *Industrial and Commercial Training*, 36, 275–281.
7 Kegan, R. (1982). *The evolving self.* Harvard University Press.
8 Torbert, W. (1987). *Managing the corporate dream: Restructuring for long-term success.* Dow Jones Irwin.
9 Rooke, D., Torbert, W. (2005). Seven transformations of leadership. *Harvard Business Review*, p. 4.
10 Joiner, B., Josephs, S. (2006). *Leadership agility: Five levels of mastery for anticipating and initiating change.* Jossey-Bass.
11 Petrie, N. (2015). *The how-to of vertical leadership development – Part 2. 30 experts, 3 conditions, and 15 approaches.* White Paper, Centre for Creative Leadership.
12 Winnicott, D.W. (2005, first published in 1971). *Playing and reality.* Routledge Classics.
13 Angyal, A. (1965). *Neurosis and treatment: A holistic theory.* Wiley.
14 Lee, G.J. (2003). *Leadership coaching. From personal insight to organisational performance.* CIPD.
15 Greenberg, L.S., Johnson, S. (1988). *Emotionally focused couple therapy for couples.* Guildford Press.
16 Heller, L., Lapierre, A. (2012). *Healing developmental trauma: How early trauma affects self-regulation, self-image, and the capacity for relationship.* North Atlantic Books.

Chapter 9

Harnessing expanded perspectives

How do you know when you are operating from a GREEN body-brain state? Do you notice that your mind feels clear and your thinking is sharper? Do you register a sense of connection with others and the world around you? Do you feel a sense of your presence as a blend of groundedness and expansiveness? In seeking to cultivate a capacity for, and an awareness of, GREEN body-brain states in others, we need to know how to recognise and foster such states in ourselves. In my experience working with clients at Stage 5 is enjoyable because there is a sense of flow. It is as if the responsibility I have had up until now to spot unhelpful habits or reactions and to decide how to work with them is now owned more by clients themselves. Their reflective awareness and curiosity about their body-brain states allows them to recognise their own interior triggers, and they have come to see the value of taking time to pause and to name these reactions. When they are grounded in their GREEN body-brain state, they can observe the arising of RED body-brain reactions without being triggered into RED behaviours. So, in Stage 5 of the journey of *Breakthrough Conversations* there is an atmosphere of emotional steadiness – a calm motivation to understand and to explore. With an increase in mental and emotional agility earned through prior stages, clients have an expanded perspective about their challenges and relational tendencies. Our goal at this stage is to harness these expanded perspectives in the service of the practical outcomes that clients are wishing to address – to use their more trusting connections and capacity for collaboration to create new possibilities and to solve problems.

In this chapter I explore how we can work with clients to consolidate their learning from previous stages and harness it towards addressing practical outcomes. I first discuss *playfulness* as a key capability in Stage 5, then consider the focus for coaching at this stage, and finally explore how learning and development from the whole *Breakthrough Conversations* process can be transferred and generalised as enduring change.

DOI: 10.4324/9781003054542-9

The stage of playfulness

One of Winnicott's[1] insights was that the capacity to play in children depends on them feeling safe and secure. If they don't feel safe, much of their emotional energy goes into self-protective strategies – their body-brain systems become attuned to managing threatening RED states, and in these circumstances collaboration and creativity are constrained. As adults we are the same. We need a 'good enough' level of trust to 'play' with ideas, whether inside our own heads, or in interaction with others. It is when we can offer up ideas without fear of scorn or ridicule that we have the confidence to think novel thoughts, name intuitions or test out unformed or radical possibilities. Far from being an indulgence, play is essential to creative problem solving and, in conversation, it is the hallmark of collaboration and joint decision-making.

So, I am linking the capacity for *playfulness* to the GREEN body-brain system – the state we have been seeking to foster throughout the *Breakthrough Conversations* process. In relation to this stage I see *playfulness* as containing three elements: *creativity, collaboration* and *pragmatism. Creativity* can be defined as the capacity within and between individuals to develop ideas for the purpose of solving problems and exploiting opportunities. We know our own creativity when we see a solution to a problem that had previously evaded us, and if you are like me, you will notice that often such solutions emerge from chewing over a problem with others. In one-to-one coaching sessions new ideas emerge from the blend of introspection and discussion, and in paired sessions underpinned by safety and trust, clients can have the experience of discovering novel solutions together. Premature closure is the enemy of creativity, and so the first step is to support clients in resisting a rush to finding quick solutions. A manager using a rugby metaphor, described this as 'keeping the ball in the air' rather than 'bringing it to ground' – in other words, holding ambiguities and differences in awareness, tolerating the discomfort of uncertainty and allowing time for interactions to gestate and give birth to new ideas.

In our conversational approach we are explicitly inviting clients to collaborate, which you may recall is one of the four domains of conversation described in Chapter 1 (see Figure 1.1). *Collaboration,* the second aspect of *playfulness,* is concerned with a relationship-focus and a results-focus, and when these two directions of focus are combined, they support such aspects as: discovering, resolving, developing, creating and achieving. Collaboration allows two minds to work together, freed up from limiting habits or reactivity, so they can spark off each other and find synergies between differing perspectives. Whether in one-to-one or paired coaching contexts, there is a working alliance – individuals have a positive intention to work together, explicitly sharing their hopes, concerns and suggestions, and building on each other's contributions.

The third and perhaps surprising element that I propose we include in *playfulness* is *pragmatism.* I include it because, although conversations need to have freedom of exploration and expansiveness, creativity and collaboration are usually in the service of specific outcomes. Clients don't consult us solely for the joy of conversation. They want to address issues and to find solutions. So, when new ideas or solutions have been generated, we need to support clients to consider how they are going to turn ideas into practical actions. What will be achievable taking account of constraints and realities, what will be the tangible outcomes, what is optimal in terms of pace, scale and simplicity and how will progress be measured and reviewed? *Pragmatism* allows the collaborative generation of ideas to be translated into practical actions and positive outcomes. With the aim of fostering these capabilities in mind, I turn to the areas of coaching focus at this fifth stage.

Awareness amidst interaction

When clients have developed their body-brain awareness and their capacity to take a mental step back to observe their tendencies they gradually develop a more ongoing curiosity about their emotional states and how these are impacting their interactions. Just as the coach needs to sustain an embodied, emotional awareness amidst coaching conversations, we are aiming to support clients to develop this same capacity within themselves as they speak with us, or with a colleague in a paired session, and ultimately, to draw on this capacity amidst any conversation.

Here are examples of some useful questions that invite awareness amidst interaction:

As you talk about this, what are you noticing about yourself right now?

What feelings do you notice? What body sensations accompany those feelings? What thoughts or images are arising as you consider this situation?'

Our inquiry supports clients to access the elements of the *PACES* frame introduced at earlier stages, *Pausing* into self-inquiry, and then noticing the *Actions, Cognitions, Emotions* and *Sensations* that go with the issue under consideration. Such reflections bring body-brain states into awareness from a position of GREEN, reflective awareness. A client might say: '*In the past I would be in a RED state about this issue, and I would probably have reacted to colleagues in unhelpful ways. But, seeing those tendencies, I can take a moment to steady myself. The pause allows me to become more curious about how others are seeing this issue, and more attuned to my desire to address the issue assertively, but without blame or frustration'.*

An observation like this is evidence of the GREEN body-brain system being engaged as a means of reflecting on past RED reactivity. We are supporting clients to create a narrative of past ways of interacting and the emotional behaviours (RED/AMBER) that went with this, and to make explicit what it has taken to shift to more reflective (GREEN) states, and the new behaviours that go with this shift. Two illustrations follow that continue with clients introduced at earlier stages: one-to-one work with Julia, who is the manager of Lucy and Amir, and paired coaching with Mick and Stuart.

Julia

Lucy was pressuring Julia, her manager, to agree to a new recruitment choice for her area. Lucy felt that her preferred choice would bring fresh vitality to a team that had become somewhat complacent. However, Julia was concerned that Lucy's choice was risky. Lucy's department had already gone through substantial change over the previous year, and Julia felt that hiring someone with a track record as a bold change-agent might be unnecessarily destablising. Julia's concern was coupled with an existing question about Lucy's own willingness to decide when it was wise to be more cautious in her decision-making. There had been past instances of problematic team dynamics and a higher than average turnover of staff in Lucy's area. Julia acknowledged that she felt irritated by Lucy's single-minded determination to appoint her chosen candidate, despite Julia expressing her concerns and encouraging a consideration of other candidates.

In a one-to-one coaching session Julia raised this issue, and I noticed that as Julia spoke, she became animated, speaking quickly and with stronger emphasis. Already familiar with my way of working, I said to Julia: *'So, as you talk about this issue, can I invite you to take a pause ... to take a moment to notice what is arising for you ... what feelings do you notice ... what is happening in your body'.* Julia smiled, recognising this familiar invitation. She took a deeper breath and let herself settle into her body. She said she noticed tension in her belly, together with a tightness across her shoulders. She associated these with feelings of frustration, but also a worry that Lucy might be making a poor decision. The significance of this concern became apparent when Julia said that she was thinking that Lucy might be a future successor, but that hope was thrown into doubt when Lucy, in Julia's view, was failing to see that stabilising the team was more important than injecting further radical change. As Julia noticed these RED reactions she reflected on their familiarity. She recalled how we had explored similar reactions in the past, and how it had often led to her being impatient and critical of team members. She said that she was keen not to repeat this pattern. She believed Lucy had the potential to develop greater balance between prudence and risk-taking but could also see that her own bias towards prudence was triggering Lucy towards a more defiant, risk-taking stance.

> Drawing on her GREEN capacities, she saw that it was her disappointment and anxiety that were driving her reactivity. She needed to feel confident in Lucy, or someone else, as a viable deputy and successor, and Lucy's behaviour was triggering doubt and vulnerability for Julia. Owning the underlying relational need and associated feelings, Julia realised that speaking only about the recruitment choice with Lucy, without discussing her broader hopes for Lucy's future potential, would lead to a conversational impasse. She used the rest of the session to prepare for a conversation with Lucy. She wanted to show her support for Lucy's career development, and to highlight her desire to see Lucy being able to move more flexibly between bold and more cautious decisions, depending on the timing and context. She also decided she would share with Lucy that an absence of caution in Lucy evoked anxiety in Julia, and that this often manifested as impatience and criticism. Having rehearsed this conversation, with its GREEN observations about her RED reactive tendencies, she went on to have a highly productive conversation with Lucy. They quickly reached a more aligned, mutual understanding, and went on to make a different recruitment choice that satisfied them both and that proved to be an excellent match for what the team needed at that time.

Our aim is to support awareness amidst interaction, whether working one-to-one, as I did in the illustration with Julia above, or whether facilitating a pair. At this stage, when working with a pair, they experience less threat than at earlier stages. Areas of difference, rather than triggering AMBER or RED states and so habitual or reactive interactions, become sources of curiosity and exploration. The experience of a different view becomes an invitation to inquire: *'How am I experiencing this different perspective? What am I noticing in my body? What can I usefully communicate about what I am noticing and how is it impacting my listening and speaking?'* At this stage less energy is expended on handling threat, and so more energy is available for inquiry. There is a fluidity of movement between self-inquiry, attunement with the other person and the issue under discussion.

Mick and Stuart

I introduced Mick and Stuart in Chapter 6 to illustrate the use of the *9-Minute Form* and continued their story in Chapter 8 to illustrate *Seeing the Dance from the Balcony*. Mick had acknowledged his rush to decision-making and his poor listening that was borne from his impatience to get results and to be seen as successful, and, underlying this, a discomfort with ambiguity and uncertainty. Stuart had named his reactive withdrawal when he felt he was being railroaded by Mick and acknowledged his sensitivity to feeling that his views were not valued. Holding the elements of the RED cycle in view from the larger perspective of the GREEN cycle, Mick and Stuart embarked on a series of conversations focused on addressing a key business challenge. The organisation needed to find products to fill a medium-term gap between the decline of older products and the availability of new products in development. Traditionally the organisation had developed its own portfolio and there was a cultural reluctance to licensing external products, but there were some people who viewed product licensing as essential to maintain growth targets. Both Mick and Stuart saw the value of licensing options, but they differed in their approach. Mick was highly pragmatic, wanting to review three potential products and to make a decision within a couple of months. Stuart also recognised the need to move swiftly, but he favoured a more detailed analysis of the products available and the way they would fit with the organisation's current portfolio.

As Mick and Stuart discussed this business challenge there was the potential for them to slip back into their older patterns. Mick was concerned about the pace of progress and noticed how a sense of urgency was triggering some impatience when Stuart described his preferred approach. Invited to pause, Mick acknowledged these feelings, and said that he was worried that Stuart's approach might take so long that by the time they had decided, the products they were considering might be licensed by another company. Stuart appreciated Mick naming these concerns, admitting that he had felt some sensitivity to the impression that Mick was not really valuing his view on how to approach this task. Stuart also reassured Mick by saying that he too was eager to make a decision fairly quickly, but he was also concerned about the potential impact of cutting corners in their analysis. With the acknowledgement of their reactive tendencies in view, they became mutually curious about how they could use each of their strengths and experience in complementary ways. How could they harness Mick's pragmatic urgency with Stuart's analytic rigour and discernment? Reframing the challenge in this way they saw a potential to create a systematic process of product evaluation, drawing on the specialist resources from different areas of the organisation. They could see that in the past such systematic approaches were painstakingly slow because there was insufficient agreement about priorities. To achieve their goal of rigorous and rapid evaluation of new opportunities, they needed buy-in from senior managers and department heads about their timely contribution to the process. They could see that they would need to invest time in the short-term in influencing key stakeholders, but, if they did this, there was the potential to create a streamlined product evaluation process second to none. Mick and Stuart were very energised by their newfound sense of collaboration. They could see that bringing focus to their challenge across the organisation was not easy, but they also recognised that together they were a potent force. They agreed on a series of stakeholder meetings, agreed how to prepare their business case, and allocated a person from each of their areas to work together in building some supportive technology. As they took this change forward, they acknowledged that at times they could find themselves slipping into a RED or AMBER cycle. But they were now meeting regularly, and they made sure that part of their weekly one-to-one meeting included time to reflect on their relationship and how they were working together – they used their reflective awareness to re-establish a GREEN interactive cycle. A few months after this initiative had gained traction in the organisation, they had identified two new products for potential licensing, and a few weeks later had secured a deal for their preferred product.

Mick and Stuart used the *Breakthrough Conversations* process to identify their personal and interpersonal relational tendencies. By naming these and learning to manage how these tendencies impacted their conversations, they were able to work together more effectively. They found a new, creative approach to a shared challenge, recognised their complementary strengths and gaps, and collaborated in harnessing the buy-in and resources of their organisation. They translated their shared thinking into a pragmatic process and set of actions, and they were ultimately successful in delivering an important outcome for their organisation.

Celebrating positive cycles of interaction

When working with clients much of our focus is necessarily on areas of difficulty and reactivity. Clients look for help when something is wrong. Like most of us, they pay less attention to what is happening when things are going well. However, as we know from positive psychology and appreciative inquiry, focusing on strengths is an important part of fostering change. In relation to conversations, we are looking for signs that clients are operating from a GREEN body-brain state, indicated perhaps by them speaking calmly, listening attentively and naming their potential triggers and emotions. When we observe positive interactions like this it is an opportunity to bring these positive states more fully into awareness. Just as we might ask clients to pause and to attune to their body and emotions when discussing difficult issues in a RED state, it can be just as impactful to ask clients to pause and attune to their positive states. As for difficult states, I might say: *And so, as you speak to me about this, can I invite you to pause and to ask you what you are noticing?* By this stage in our work clients are familiar with our curiosity about their here-and-now experience and may readily offer reflections about their emotional state, their *RAG* state, or the nature of the interaction. But, equally, we may choose to prompt them, choosing to inquire into one or more of their domains of awareness: *What are you noticing in your body? What emotions are you aware of? What do you notice about the way you are speaking and listening? How would you describe your RAG state right now? How do you feel about the quality of interaction between the two of you right now?*

Some clients are surprised to discover bodily relaxation or an emotional settling that accompanies a productive conversation, whilst others may acknowledge those states in a cursory way. In either case our goal is to invite clients to pause and to dwell with this experience of positivity. We want clients to familiarise themselves with their embodied experience of resourcefulness – to inhabit their GREEN states – to savour them as though relishing a delicious flavour or gorgeous scent. By basking in these positive experiences for 20 or 30 seconds, we are supporting clients to rewire their brains towards the positive – towards the activation of their social engagement system, their prefrontal cortex and their positive hormones such as oxytocin and dopamine. We aim to celebrate these positive states and cycles and encourage clients to hold these experiences of positivity in awareness.

Neil and Rosa

In Chapter 11 I described how Neil and Rosa made use of a blend of individual and paired sessions to identify the body-brain states, feelings and relational needs underlying their interactive tendencies. At the outset Rosa, responsible for standardising organisational processes, had been struggling to engage Neil, the head of a large and successful region, in productive conversations. He had resisted her initiatives as inappropriate to his region, and she had complained to senior managers about his lack of cooperation. However, they both engaged productively with coaching. Neil acknowledged his preference for autonomy and admitted that he had blocked Rosa because he saw her as part of a head-office attempt to 'clip his wings'. Rosa had acknowledged her fear of failure following a previous redundancy, and recognised her tendency to be insensitive and controlling in her attempt to be seen as an effective change-agent. When Neil and Rosa explored their interactions, they saw how they tended to get into a reactive relational dance (a RED cycle). Held by the reflective container of coaching and their developing capacity to pause and inquire into their interior and relational states, they listened more deeply to each other, spoke more openly about their core needs and feelings, and based on a developing trust, began to see how their collaboration could be mutually beneficial. I thought their interactions were now characteristic of Stage 5 of the *Breakthrough Conversations* process.

In a paired session they were focusing on possible areas of collaboration. Rosa raised the question of a globally approved list of law firms approved for use by head office. These firms had been vetted in terms of depth and breadth of relevant experience, and favourable commercial terms had been agreed. But she noted that Neil's region was not currently using any of these firms, preferring instead to use their own choice of lawyers. Having learned the value of owning her potential reactivity, Rosa added that she could see that this issue was triggering some of her old frustrations, and she noticed a side of her that wanted to escalate the issue and to force Neil's region to comply. But, at the same time, she could see that this would undermine collaboration. She reiterated her overarching goal: that above all she wanted to find a way to work constructively with Neil because she could see benefit for both his area, and for the organisation as a whole. Neil appreciated Rosa's acknowledgement of her impulse to escalate the issue. Her openness encouraged him to be open about his own experience. He said that when she mentioned the idea of escalating things, he noticed himself tense up and to feel more rigid and defiant in relation to her. But he also noticed that when she emphasised the desire to support his region rather than to constrain it, he noticed himself become more relaxed.

It was at this point that I chose to pause their interaction and invited them to notice what was happening between them. Using the image of RED/AMBER or GREEN interactive cycles (see Figure 8.2), I asked them to consider what kind of cycle they were in. They both felt they were in a GREEN cycle, acknowledging the underlying factors that could drive their reactivity and so sustaining a more constructive interaction. I agreed with them and asked them to take a moment to talk about what they were doing that was sustaining a GREEN interaction in relation to a thorny topic. Neil spoke of his lack of defensiveness because he could see that Rosa was coming to him with her concerns rather than escalating to her manager, and Rosa spoke of her experience of Neil beginning to value her contributions and no longer feeling like he might be plotting to get her fired. They also noted that there was a sense of ease and even playfulness in their interactions. They could talk about sensitive issues and trust more in the resilience of their relationship. Each felt free to express their views openly and each felt the other was listening and receptive to a different point of view. By interrupting their business focus and bringing attention to their positive interactions I was seeking to reinforce and celebrate the significance of the developmental shift that they had made together. The conscious reflection on what has changed encourages clients to assimilate what is new and to begin to develop an internal anchor for engaging in more consciously constructive conversations.

It was the celebration of these positive cycles of interaction that led on to a productive conversation about the law firms being used in Neil's region. Rosa spoke about the benefits of identifying globally where regions had been most effective in satisfying regulatory requirements, leading to faster than average product approvals. Neil knew that approval times were key to profitability and acknowledged that the time for approvals in his region had been variable. However, Neil also spoke about his sense that the relationship between head office and the regions was unequal. There were initiatives from his region for which he had sought support from the head office, but he felt that his attempts to influence were falling on deaf ears. Rosa empathised with Neil. She could see that some of her head office colleagues were disconnected from what was happening in the regions and so were not as open as they might be to market-led initiatives. It was these honest, trusting conversations that led to them thinking creatively. They wanted to find a way of harnessing the best ideas from all of the regions. They could see that their was the potential for head office to be less focused on policing standards and instead become more of a facilitator of organisational collaboration. By combining their relationships with different stakeholder groups and thinking about how to present a case for managing things differently, they gained agreement to set up a relatively lean innovation group, with a selection of representatives from exemplary regions. This group, a direct product of a series of *Breakthrough Conversations* subsequently became a key source of innovation and competitive advantage for the organisation.

Fostering change and acceptance

Wilfred Bion, the psychoanalyst, famously described himself as aiming to approach sessions without memory or desire. He implies that if we are to be present to what is emerging in the room, we need to be open and receptive, without bias, expectation or agenda. If we can be steady and present with our clients, we model a quality of grounded acceptance and we create the optimal conditions for them to find their own presence and emerging insights. Although I find this way of thinking compelling in reminding me to be openly receptive and mindful in my role as coach, I also think we need to be attuned to our goals and outcomes. If we lean too heavily towards 'being', our acceptance of circumstances might look like passivity. On the other hand, if we hold too tightly to fixed coaching outcomes, we will be modelling a limiting focus on 'doing' over 'being', and we won't give clients the space to find their own truths. So, our challenge is to hold the paradox between bold intentions and realistic acceptance (*i.e.* the *Seeking* and *Spacious* cardinal directions of the *Character Compass*: see Figure 5.2 and Table 5.2). This same tension is captured in the serenity prayer: *May I accept the things I cannot change; the courage to change the things I can; and the wisdom to know the difference.* In terms of coaching we want to support clients to reach for stretching goals without collapsing into premature closure and acceptance. But on the other hand, we want to support clients to sustain a quality of acceptance that stops goals from becoming idealistic sources of stress.

This idea of finding the balance between stretching goals and acceptance can be placed in the context of the four stages of creativity:[2] *preparation, incubation, illumination* and *verification*. In this model, after we have prepared the ground, it is the spaciousness of *incubation* that creates the conditions for the spontaneous *illumination* of breakthrough. Our role as coach is initially to promote a GREEN cycle of interaction that is spacious enough for incubation to occur. When clients quickly propose a solution to a problem, I might encourage them to hold back and to be curious about the rush to closure. I am fostering what Keats described as negative capability, when clients are '… capable of being in uncertainties, mysteries, doubts, without any irritable reaching after fact and reason'.[3] I want clients to explore what it is like to dwell with ambiguities and uncomfortable emotions in the context of relationship. By sharing differing views and embracing divergences clients develop more expanded perspectives. Whether in a one-to-one session with me, or in a pair with a colleague, clients build a more enriched picture of their challenges and this enlarged picture contains more avenues for potentially creative outcomes. We sustain the conditions for illumination. Sometimes the illumination will feel like a creative breakthrough, such as occurred in the illustrations above. But in other cases, the illumination may be experienced more as acceptance. Sometimes the exploration of options and the holding of uncertainty does not yield a paradigm shift, but instead a grounded recognition that there is a need for compromise, cutting one's losses or finding the optimal way of handling a disappointing trajectory. In these situations, the expanded perspective yielded through conversational awareness is the basis for *pragmatism;* not as resignation, but rather as a healthy realism that enables clients to do their best in adverse circumstances. The following piece of paired coaching illustrates compromise and acceptance as pragmatic outcomes from the *Breakthrough Conversation* process.

Ellie and Hannah

The challenge facing the business that Ellie and Hannah worked for concerned the approaching decline of a product range that had been the basis for extraordinary growth over the preceding 10 years. New innovations were entering the market. The organisation had seen this coming, but it was unclear if the diversification strategy would address the impending shortfall against revenue targets. Ellie and Hannah were responsible for different areas of the previously successful product range, and their goal at the time of the coaching was to find ways of slowing the decline of these products. However, organisational anxiety was high and there was a tendency for different departments to blame each other when there was bad news about specific client opportunities. Ellie thought her area was shouldering the brunt of the work by having to tailor existing products quickly for specific client needs, and she thought Hannah's area were making this more difficult by over-promising on the changes that could be delivered in a short timeframe. Hannah felt that her area was showing great determination in finding ways to stem the loss of business but was disappointed by the lack of support and cooperation from Ellie's area.

Ellie and Hannah had each received some individual coaching sessions and had also engaged in a series of paired sessions. They had discovered that their personality styles were quite similar with a diligent dedication to high standards and a strong outcome focus. In terms of attachment patterns, they both showed a good deal of interpersonal composure and confidence much of the time, although in more stressful contexts Ellie was prone to compliance and would look for reasoned compromise. In contrast Hannah was prone towards defiance, with her controlling side manifesting as a lack of cooperation. Culturally, Ellie's previous organisation was highly collaborative, and she readily looked to form an alliance with Hannah. In contrast, Hannah was used to more competitive cultures and she viewed Ellie as a threat in terms of influence and opportunities. The paired sessions, grounded in body-brain awareness, had allowed these differences to be explored. Ellie had owned her impression that Hannah was intrinsically uncooperative, and Hannah had owned her assumption that Ellie was seeking to expand her area at the expense of hers. Recognising their potential to enact unproductive, RED or AMBER cycles of interaction, they were able to step back together and *See the Dance from the Balcony* (Stage 4). These shared insights led to more productive conversations. They acknowledged that both of their departments were struggling with the decline in the performance of the existing products. Hannah learned more about the pressures Ellie's team were facing in tailoring the approach to different clients, and Ellie learned more about the challenges Hannah's team were facing in persuading clients not to switch allegiance to new products from other companies. They recognised together that there was no magical breakthrough in creativity that would easily extend the life of their existing product range. But they also acknowledged that their teams were currently pulling in different directions and sending confusing messages to clients. They needed their teams to come together as a cohesive whole – to agree on priorities, to communicate consistently internally and externally, and to meet regularly in cross-functional sub-teams to discuss specific client challenges. The need for such collaboration had been obvious for several years, but previous attempts to broker collaboration had not been successful. However, this conversational process between the team leaders did lead to breakthroughs in their mutual understanding, which led to them jointly setting up a series of cross-functional team development events. They gathered feedback by surveying all of their team members about what was helping or hindering collaboration, and explored the findings together, agreeing areas for improvement.

The most sobering aspect of these discussions was the shared acceptance that whatever they did, the market for these products was declining. But this acceptance allowed them to shift focus to the competitive advantage that could be sustained through the quality of their collaboration. The more seamlessly they could work together, the more responsive they could be to their clients. Rather than fighting each other and feeling despondent, they could join in celebrating their successes in retaining clients. Reflecting with Ellie and Hannah after a couple of these team sessions, they spoke of the role that they were playing as role models to their teams. They realised that prior to the coaching they were unintentionally talking with their own team members as if the other team were a source of adversity, and these divisive attitudes were then being played out in multiple ways between junior members of their respective teams. They were role-modelling non-cooperation as leaders and creating non-cooperative teams. A key breakthrough of the coaching was the shift to collaboration between the teams, not so much as a basis for paradigm-shifting solutions, but rather as an optimal response to accepting a declining market opportunity. They saw that a GREEN body-brain state, and the

> GREEN interactive cycles these fostered, allowed them to respond well to their circumstances. Sometimes this yields a creative idea, and sometimes, as in this case, it yields a capacity to embrace a limiting reality with acceptance, and so respond with more agility.

Agreeing pragmatic goals

We typically support clients to think pragmatically about how to translate insights into tangible changes in behaviour by asking them what they are going to do differently, perhaps inviting them to set SMART goals by identifying a change that is Specific, Measurable, Achievable, Realistic and Time-based. I certainly find it useful to ask the following kinds of questions to draw out the pragmatism of clients:

Given this conversation and the ideas it has generated, what will you do to make this idea a reality?

If I was a fly on the wall, what would be the first signs showing me that something is different?

When is the next time you will be able to experiment with relating more skilfully – perhaps an upcoming meeting in the next few days, a team event, or a client opportunity?

How will you know when you are doing things differently? What can you do to review how things are going on a regular basis? (For a pair, to what extent do you want to review progress independently or together?)

Most clients find it helpful to have time at the end of coaching sessions to review what has been covered, and if appropriate, to explore what they are going to do as a consequence of any insights. Having said that, we also need to balance the need for pragmatic goals with the need for open-ended exploration. As I have said already, expansive, collaborative inquiry is the prize of reflective conversations, and we should be cautious about any bias we may have for pragmatic closure. But, equally, insights may never land in behavioural change if we don't encourage clients to ask the question: *So what? What will I/we do differently as a consequence of these insights? How can I/we plan to succeed in having more effective conversations?* Another, complementary way of exploring practical steps that sustains a sense of playfulness is to invite clients to explore not only how they plan to succeed, but also how they plan to fail!

Planning to fail

When we seek to change our behaviour it is inevitable that we will fail some of the time. However, many of us abandon our good intentions when we experience failures or setbacks. We give up on getting fit when we miss the gym, or we forget about losing weight after a night of fatty foods and alcohol. In a similar way, clients can feel guilty or self-doubting if they are not successful in following through on their intention of being more conversationally skilful. They might revert to their habitual patterns and pretend to themselves that it doesn't really matter, or they might be self-critical and become demotivated about their capacity to change. By inviting clients to plan how to fail we are asking them to consider the ways in which their conversational habits or reactive patterns are likely to recur. They create an if/then contingency plan: *if this happens, then I'll do that*. It's a mental plan for how to react to things that might trip them up, which then supports them to sustain their intentions. By embracing the possible steps to failure, they see more clearly the areas where they need to be most mindful, and also acknowledge the need to be forgiving when things don't go as well as they would have hoped. Planning to fail, far from being pessimistic, brings pragmatism to the challenge of change and supports self-compassion and perseverance in the face of our imperfect efforts.

Many clients find it fun to plan to fail. This paradoxical inquiry tends to be approached with a sense of playfulness – a humorous acknowledgement of the stickiness of our habits and the familiar paths they take us down. One client noted that he often starts a conversation with a sarcastic observation, even though he had learned that it tends to put others on edge. Another client noted that she tries to change the subject to avoid conflict, even though she recognises the need to address issues. By planning to fail, the pull of these tendencies, already identified earlier in the *Breakthrough Conversations* process, are recalled and highlighted as potential pitfalls. The sarcastic client begins meetings holding the intention not to be sarcastic more fully in mind because he has identified that behaviour as limiting when trying to create an atmosphere of trust. The conflict-avoidant client keeps the intention of engaging in the face of difference more to the fore because she sees changing the subject as central to how her interactions can be less effective. Planning to fail can be especially helpful with client pairs, where the generation of the ways they could fail to converse effectively together becomes a very useful listing of their limiting habits and reactions. An illustration of planning to fail with a pair follows, drawing on my work with Doug and Frasier first introduced in Chapter 5.

Doug and Frasier

After a number of productive individual and paired sessions, Doug and Frasier felt they had reached a deeper understanding of how their relationship became more distant at times. Doug's fear of conflict meant he avoided being direct about areas of concern, and as consequence Frasier retreated further into narrow, operational issues.

When Frasier tried to speak with Doug it was difficult to find mutually convenient times and so they tended to meet informally over a glass of wine at the end of the day. Such meetings were freeform, without an agenda, and their discussion would roam somewhat randomly across multiple issues. They had explored these patterns together and were committed to finding a new way forward, and so as part of our Stage 5 discussions I invited them to tell me how they would plan to fail in achieving their shared goals. After initial confusion about why I would ask them to do that they had a very playful, jokey conversation, trying to out-do each other in identifying the unhelpful things they would do. Their 'planning to fail' list included:

- Continually find reasons to put off our one-to-one meetings due to other priorities
- Meet at the end of the day when we are both exhausted
- Meet informally over a glass of wine and view that as an acceptable substitute for more formal meetings
- Don't have a meeting agenda
- Allow each other to embark on elaborative digressions
- Talk as obliquely as possible about issues and concerns, rather than stating them directly
- Ruminate in private about what is troubling about the relationship for each of us
- Complain to our partners about why this relationship is not working
- Be really positive until the pressure of frustration builds up, and then explode in uncontained anger or threats to resign.

Naming these tendencies helped Doug and Frasier to be effective at avoiding them. Six months after our work together, Doug and Frasier expressed their appreciation for the sustainable shift in their relationship. They each felt they understood their own interpersonal style more deeply, their relationship was more resilient and productive, and they were being successful in shaping new initiatives together.

Ongoing development

In practice clients do not move smoothly through the five stages of breakthrough described in this book. The work needs to circle back and forth, returning to Stage 1 to reconnect with purpose and core intentions, repeating techniques for managing emotional states introduced at Stage 2, reminding clients of links with personal insights at Stage 3, and supporting clients to view their interactions from a larger perspective in Stage 4. The *Breakthrough*

Conversation process provides clear developmental steps, but the journey is rarely linear. Even when we experience clients operating with the agility and playfulness indicative of Stage 4 and 5 in relation to one relationship, we may find them unable to transfer this learning to another context or relationship. In such cases I find myself circling back to the beginning, re-contracting around a new developmental goal, once again constructed in terms of one or more key relationships. These new conversational partners trigger different, and perhaps deeper, relational tendencies, and so offer an opportunity to deepen personal and interpersonal awareness still further. Repeated cycles of the five-stage process are connected together, Stage 5 leading back to Stage 1 and a new focus, so that ongoing development can be envisaged as a spiral of development, similar to that shown in Figure 8.1.

The strongest evidence of the sustainability and practical value of this approach occurs when clients talk about how they are applying the techniques. Many describe situations at home or at work where they noticed themselves being triggered into a RED state. Indeed, these concepts have become common parlance across many teams. They describe themselves as remembering to pause, to notice their emotional state, to take a mental step back to see the relational dynamic, and then choosing how to respond in ways that feel useful and skilful. Some clients are especially drawn to the *PACES* frame and will complete an *ACES* worksheet on their own as a way of structuring their personal reflections, whilst others like to remind themselves regularly about their intentions using the Character Compass. In addition to the personal use that clients make of their learning, I have also been impressed by how many choose to apply the techniques in supporting others to examine their interactions. Many leaders have chosen to address issues between team members by taking the role of the facilitator and using the *9-Minute Form* to foster more reflective conversations. They are surprised by how readily this technique deepens mutual understanding and creates the basis for increased collaboration.

Ultimately our capacity to apply these techniques depends on our own personal and interpersonal awareness. The more we can embody awareness amidst our interactions, the more we can model reflective awareness with clients, inviting them to deepen their insights, to attune more to others, to enhance their relational agility and to meet their challenges with wisdom, collaboration and breakthrough.

Summary

In the fifth stage of *Breakthrough Conversations* clients are able to sustain GREEN states of awareness and so observe and manage potentially disruptive RED or AMBER states. The key capability at this stage is *playfulness*, which consists of three elements: the *creativity* arising from examining different viewpoints and sustaining uncertainty, the *collaboration* to sustain a balance of listening and speaking, owning potential triggers, and moving between different perspectives and the *pragmatism* to translate ideas into tangible plans and actions. Our role at this stage is to support clients to sustain their body-brain awareness amidst interactions and to reinforce understanding of how previously similar contexts might have led to habitual or reactive tendencies. These positive shifts are further reinforced by guiding clients to pause and notice their body-brain states when there are positive cycles of interaction. This can be in the form of recognising the power of more skilful conversations to support shared reflection and the emergence of creative breakthroughs, or in other circumstances discovering insights leading to a new quality of acceptance and working with others to find the best accommodation to a limiting situation. When clients have generated new ideas or solutions, we support them to translate their ideas into tangible next steps. Planning to fail can be a lighthearted way of identifying potential obstacles to change and so reinforcing the enactment of new ways of conversing and collaboration.

Worksheet 9: Harnessing expanded perspectives

This purpose of this worksheet is to support clients to use their personal and interpersonal awareness to collaborate, solve shared challenges and agree on practical action plans. The worksheet can either be used as a preparation for a conversation or as a basis for reflection after a conversation.

1. What conversational behaviours do you tend to show in a RED, AMBER or GREEN cycle?
2. What is the first signal showing you that you have been triggered in some way? (Is it a body sensation, feeling, thought, something else?)
3. What supports you to observe potential triggers without reacting to them?
4. What is the impact of sharing your underlying emotional reactions and core needs with others during a conversation?
5. How can you pause to acknowledge and savour when a conversation is in a positive GREEN cycle?
6. What can you do to foster co-creation in relation to shared challenges?
7. How can you translate new ideas and solutions into practical action plans?

Notes

1 Winnicott, D.W. (2005, first published in 1971). *Playing and reality.* Routledge Classics.
2 Wallas, G. (2014, first published in 1926). *The art of thought.* Solis Press.
3 Bradley, A.C. (2016). The letters of Keats. In *Oxford lectures on poetry.* In H. E. Rollins (Ed.), (2 vols, pp. 193–194). Cambridge: Cambridge University Press, 1958.

Index

Note: Page numbers in *Italic* refer to figures; **bold** refer to tables; page numbers followed by 'n' refer to notes.

A
acceptance of circumstances 181–182; and compromise, case study 183–185
ACES worksheet 18, 57, 59, 60, **61**, 66, 73, 115, 188
Achiever stage 155–156
Actions, Cognitions, Emotions and *Sensations* 18
adrenaline 32
adult attachment, dynamics: romantic relationships 139; work relationships 139
Adult Attachment Interview 141
agility *16*, 17, 84; elements 153–154, 169; levels, impact on conversations **156**; mental and emotional 84, 153–155, 159, 169, 172
AMBER body–brain-system, signifiers 41–42; body sensations 42; non-verbal signals 42; verbal signals 42–43
AMBER or habitual 3, 36–37; conversations, defined 3–4; systems, in conversational domain 36–37, 163; unlikely, breakthrough source 4–5
anxious attachment 138–140
appreciation 126
attachment patterns 83, 129, 149; for business success, case study 142–144; in childhood, and adult 138–139; indicative habits and reactions 141, **142**; leaders 139; for leadership development 141; for skilful conversations 139–141

Attachment theory 138, 141
attunement 154, 176
avoidant attachment 138–140
awareness: amidst interaction, case study 174–178, 189; 'bottom-up' experience 53; defined 50–51; fostering and enhancement 10, 11, 52, 73; GREEN states of 188; models for enhancing conversational 50, 56–57; observer perspective 53–55; positive states 178–179; self-observation 53; space of 53, 56; and thinking 51, 73

B
basic emotions, theories 63
behaviour, and thinking 51
being on the balcony metaphor 153
being social, conversations: not results focused 7; sense of connection 8; social interactions, small 7–8; virtues of 8
Be Social domain 13; acknowledgement need 9; interactions, starting place 9; social media, approach to 8–9
best selves 93
biases: cultural and social, case study 147–148; implicit 147; ownership for 149; unconscious 145–148
Big Five factors of personality 133, **134**
Bion, W. 181
body–brain states 3, 18, 25, 109–110; attention to 44, 47; awareness, support

Index

emotional regulation 112–114; deconstructing using *PACES* 114–116; diagnosing *RAG* 38, *39*, 108–111; distinguish three 25–26, 46; identifying, worksheet 47–48; indicative sensations and behaviours 38; interactive awareness, increase 44, 47; primary sources of information 38–39; *RAG* approach to identifying 46; rationale for attending 26
body–brain systems: AMBER/habit system 35–37; distinction between, three 47; emotional states 46; understanding 32–33, 47; GREEN/reflective system 37–38; RED/reactive system 33–36; relational field impact 118; shape conversations, three *34*
body sensations, unawareness 37
both-and thinking 154
Bowlby, J. 138
brain: default mode network 51; primary structures of 28, 47; skull-based portion of 26–27
Breakthrough Conversations, and approach 2, 11, 18, 76; behavioural emphasis to 89; body-brain states 85; capabilities ladder *16*, 23; case studies of 1; coaching assignments, focus 13; collaborate domain 13; compassion 83, 108, 125; conversation, types 23; conversational purposes 14; critical elements 79; cultivation of emotional regulation 25; designed to facilitate 23; developmental steps, circle back and forth 187–188; distinctive elements 15; distinguishing, from others 3; enhancing awareness 50, 73; experience first-hand 18; five stages of 18, 81, 85, 187; illustrative, coaching piece 19–22; intrinsic motivation 82, 88, 93, 103, 106, 109; journey and destination as 2; ladder of capabilities for facilitating *16*; listening, importance 109; map, exploration and challenge stages 1, 18, 81 (*see also* Map of Breakthrough Conversations); need for 3; observer perspective 53–55, 67–68; origin, different frames 14, 23; pitfalls 186; potent constellating frame, conversations as 14, 23; pragmatic outcomes, case study 183–185; prefrontal cortex role 28; purposes 23; *RAG* categories 47; reflectiveness role 109; relational mindfulness, application 79; research evidence, no controlled 80; self-awareness 99; self-disclosure capability 83; self-observation 53; social engagement system 29; sustainability and practical value of 188; types of conversation 14; workshop setting in 104

C
capabilities ladder, for change *16*; agility, adaptability of mind 17; motivation to change 16–17; need for self-regulation 17; playfulness, creativity and collaboration sense of 17–18; self-disclosure 17
Catalyst stage 155–156
character 93
Character Compass 19, 82, 88, 93, *94*, 188; 12-character qualities 95–96, 99; case study 99–102; Grounded-Seeking dimension 95, 99; near and far enemies concept 96, 102; personalised 96; qualities and terms **97–98**; reactivity areas 102, 107; Spacious-Warm dimension 95, 99; vertical/horizontal dimension 94–95
character habits: defined 93; framework of (*see* Character Compass)
Chaskalson, M. 56
cognition, refer to 62
cognitive behavioural approaches 51–52
collaborate domain 12, 173
collaboration and co-creation, stage 17, 84–85, 173, 188
collectivist bias 145
colliding perspectives 157
compromise and acceptance: case study 183–185
conflict models 76–77, 79
connect domain: breakthroughs in 11–12; concerned with emotion 11; relational patterns in 12
conscientiousness 133
conversation: personality profiles 133, 135
conversational awareness, models: *Five-Eyed Model of Conversations* 50, 67, 68–73; *PACES (Pause, Actions, Cognitions, Emotions, Sensations)* framework 50, 57, 58–65
conversational behaviours, limiting/enabling **7**

conversational goals, and bias 91, 145; case study 90–91; successful conversation 92
conversational tendencies 129
conversations: biases, awareness 70; Character Compass 19; classified as 3; conflictual 76–77; consequences 1–2; crucial 77; cultural and social norms, influence 69; effective approach to, elements 80; emotional regulation during 116–118; facilitating change through 1–2; goals, multiple 91–93; habitual/AMBER 3–5, 8, 17, 23; limiting and enabling, behaviours **7**; power dynamics, influence 69, 148–149; productive/insightful or GREEN 2–3, 5; purpose construction, in terms 89–91; purposes of/types 5–6; reactive or RED 1, 3–4, 23; RED/reactive system in 37; relationship-focused 6–7; results-focused 6–7; setting, influence 70; stage, and capabilities 70; tennis match, metaphor 67
core needs 129
core relational needs 130, **131**, 132, 164
cortisol 32
couple therapy: Emotionally Focused Therapy for Couples (EFT) 77; Imago Relationship Therapy (IRT) 77
creativity: defined 173; illumination 182; incubation 85, 182; premature closure and 173; verification 182
cultural and social biases 83
cultural and social conditioning 129, 144–146, 149; case study 147–148
cultural differences 144–146
culture: bias 148–149; defined 144; dimensions of 144–146

D
debatre, refers 10
deeper self-inquiry 19
default mode network 51
defiance–compliance tension 161; case study 159–160
developmental stages 154–155
difficult conversations 77
disidentifying 154
dismissive gestures 148
Donaldson-Fielder, E. 56
dopamine 32

dorsal vagal system/freeze - shutdown 29–31; post-traumatic stress disorder (PTSD) 30

E
Ekman, P. 63
Ekman's six basic emotions 63
emotional attachment 139
Emotionally Focused Therapy for Couples (EFT) 77, 130; healing process, stages 78; long-term effectiveness 78; research evidence 78–79
emotional regulation: body-brain awareness support 112–114; during conversations 116–118; practices for 108, 124–126; relational field 117; systems 32; value, and practices 108
emotional states management 108; appreciation 83, 108, 126; case study, with RAG frame 113; compassion 83, 108, 125; GREEN state of awareness 112, 114; mindful inquiry, stages 110–112; mindfulness 82–83, 108, 124–125; RAG body-brain states, awareness 109–111
emotions 132; anger 164; defined 63; mapping *64*; negative cycle 162, 164; primary 162–163; secondary 163–165; and sensations, distinction between 65; two-dimensional classification of 64; two perspectives, between 161–162
Expert stage 155, 156
extraverted person 133

F
failures/setbacks *see* planning to fail
Five-Eyed Model of Conversations 18, 67, 73, 109; case study 68, 70–72; context, factors influencing conversation 69–70; conversation, goals of 71; Five-Eyes refer to 67; Me and you domain 68, 71; Observer Perspective 68–69; We domain 68, 72
flight/fight mode 29
Fundamental Interpersonal Relations Orientation (FIRO) 130, 149

G
Gandhi, M. 2
Getting to Yes 76
Gilbert, P. 32

GREEN body-brain states 157–158, 172–174, 178, 184
GREEN or reflective: breakthrough 5; conversations, defined 3, 5, 23; GREEN states experience 5; primary emotions 163; reflective awareness, capacity for 5, 174; systems, in conversation 37–38
GREEN/reflective body–brain system, signifiers: body sensations 43; non-verbal signals 43–44; verbal signals 44
grounded habits 94–95

H
habits, three-part habit loop 36
habits and reactive tendencies, loosening: factors responsible 83; self-disclosure, elements 83
habitual/AMBER conversations 3–5, 8, 17, 23
habitual narratives 109
habitual or reactive behaviour 130, 139, 157, 163, 176, 186; *see also* interactive cycles, RED/AMBER and GREEN
Hall, E.T. 145
Hall, L. 56
Harvard Negotiation Project 76–77
Hazan, C. 138
heart rate variability (HRV) 31–32, 47
heat experiences, refers to 156–157
Hofstede, G. 144, 146
horizontal development 155
hormones, and emotional regulation 32, 47
human, body-brain: defined, as interdependent whole 26; heart rate variability (HRV) 31–32; skull-based portion, of brain 26–27; survival circuitry 33; systems influencing emotional states 26
human change, archetypal stages 16–18
hypersensitivity 139

I
ideas application, case studies 19
Imago Relationship Therapy (IRT) 77, 118; principles, three-stage approach 77–78
inappropriate jokes 148
individualism *versus* collectivism 144–145
insecure attachment 138
Insight Dialogue 78, 116, 118

integrative bargaining, term 76
interaction, awareness amidst 174
interactive cycles, RED/AMBER and GREEN 163, 165–166, **179**; *ACES* aspects of *165*; case study 166–169, 180; elements driving, summary of **170**
internal and external paradox: case study 160–161
interoception 39, 49n9
introverted person 133

K
Kabat-Zinn, J. 79

L
labour-management negotiations 76
ladder of capabilities *see* capabilities ladder, for change
leadership development 141

M
Map of Breakthrough Conversations 1, 18, 70, 103; harnessing expanded perspectives stage 84–85, 172; looping and overlapping, stages 81; loosening habit and reactivity stage 19, 83, 129; managing emotional states stage 82–83, 108; preparing the ground stage 19, 82, 85, 88; seeing the dance from the balcony, metaphor 83–84, 153; stages, and capacities 76, *81*, 85, 103; worksheet 85–86
McKersie, R.B. 76
McMordie, M. 56
mental and emotional agility 84
mental contents 52
mental 'stability' and 'clarity' 110
mind, defined 26
mindful communication, keys 79
mindful inquiry 110–112, 125
mindfulness approach/practices 17, 51–52, 78, 82–83; attention as, muscle 55; body-scan 54–55; coaching context, application 56; compassion and appreciation 125–126; conversational agility role 53, 54; courses/apps 56; defined 52, 124; experiencing circuitry 53; guided 124; guidelines 78; mindful inquiry, stages 110–112; observer perspective 53–54; relational field 79; relationships, positive impact on 79–80; self-identity 55–56; spaciousness, and

reflectiveness 124–125; therapeutic presence 79; *see also* Character Compass
Mindfulness-Based Stress Reduction (MBSR) programmes 79
momentarily self-aware 53
motivation, to change 16–17, 82, 88, 103

N
narrative circuitry 53
national biases 145
nature of awareness 50
negative capability 182
negative cycle 162, 164
negativity bias 125–126
negotiations, and mutuality 76
nervous system: dorsal vagal system/ freeze – shutdown 30; sympathetic system/ fight/flight 29; ventral vagal/ social engagement 29
neuroplasticity 27
case study 120–124; combines with *RAG* diagnosis 118–119; one-to-one session 120; worksheet, outline 127
Non-violent communication (NVC) 77, 79, 130

O
'Observer' Perspective, concept 53–54; illustration, analogies 53–54; zooming-in and zooming-out 54–55, 73
Openness to experience, Conscientiousness, Extraversion, Agreeableness and Neuroticism (OCEAN) 133
operating in and above the fray, phrase 87n21, 170n1
oxytocin 33

P
PACES (Pause, Actions, Cognitions, Emotions, Sensations) framework 18–19, 57, 58–59, 82, 108, 126, 162, 188; access the elements 174; *ACES* worksheet, illustration 60, **61**; Actions 60, 62; body Sensations, focus 65; case study, ACES worksheet 58, 60, **61**, 66; Cognitions, *Now/About Now* phenomena 62–63; deconstructing states using 114–116; Emotions, two-dimensional approach 63–64; grounding, with sensations 59;

limiting and enabling patterns, deconstruction 60; Pause, to sensations 59–60; self-awareness 66; worksheet, deconstructing body-brain states 73–74
patronising statements 148
perceptual biases 51
personality 129; attachment theory 141; 'Big Five' dimensions 133, **134**; conversational patterns 138; interactive biases based on, case study 135–138; patterns of habit and reactivity 133, **134**, 135; research 133; role in shaping habitual and reactive tendencies 132–133
perspective shifts, and vertical development 83–84
planning to fail 185–186; case study 186–187; fun way, obstacles finding 186, 189; habits/reactive patterns, recurrence 186
playfulness *16*, 17, 84, 172–173, 188; collaboration 17, 85, 173, 188; creativity 17, 85, 173, 188; GREEN body-brain system 173; pragmatism 18, 85, 173–174, 188
Plutchik, R. 63
polyvagal theory 28, *35*, 47; nervous system, main parts 29–30; ventral, sympathetic and dorsal systems, links 30–31
Porges, S. 28
positional bargaining 79
positive cycles of interaction 178–179, 189; case study 179–181
positive states, awareness 178–179
post-traumatic stress disorder (PTSD) 30
potential space 157–159; case study 159–161; spirals of development *159*
power dynamics, in conversation 148–149
pragmatic goals 185
pragmatism 18, 85, 173–174, 188
premature closure, and creativity 173
primary emotions 162–163; *see also* emotions

R
RAG (RED, AMBER or GREEN): behaviours summary **150**; body-brain states, diagnosing *39*, 109–110; case

study 45–46, 113; conversations 3; frame 19, 46–47, 50; states, in terms of ACES patterns **74**; worksheet for identification, body–brain state 47–48
reasoning 145
RED body–brain system, signifiers 39–40; body sensations 41; non-verbal signals, characteristic 40–41; verbal signals 41
RED or reactive: conversations 3–4, 23; primary emotions with 163; system, in conversations 33–36
reflective awareness, reinforcement: case study 105–106
relational behaviours 140
relational mindfulness 56
relational presence *117*
relationship-focused conversations 6
results-focused conversations 6
Rogers, C. 79

S
Schutz, W. 130
secondary emotions 132, 163–164; *see also* emotions
Seeing the Dance from the Balcony metaphor 153
seeking habits 94–95, 96
self-assertion 158
self-compassion 83, 98, 108, 125
self-determination 158
self-disclosures *16*, 17; elements of 83, 129–130, 149 (*see also* self-inquiry); case study 131–132
self-identity 55–56, 158
self-inquiry 83, 129–130, 149, 154, 176
self-observation 53
self-other paradox 153; colliding perspectives 157–159; *see also* agility
self-regulation *16*, 17, 49n9, 82–83, 85, 98, 108, 126
self-surrender 158
sensation words 65
sense of self 55–56
setting expectations 9–10
sexist comments 148
Shaver, P. 138
Siegel, D. 26
SMART (Specific, Measurable, Achievable, Realistic and Time-based) goals 185
social engagement system 29
social media 8–9
spacious habits 95–96
stereotyping 146
strengths, fostering change 178
stretching goals, and acceptance 182
sympathetic system 29–30

T
thinking, defined 51, 53
threatening or abusive attachment 139
transact domain 10–11, 13; collaborate 12–13; connect 11–12, 13
transactional conversations 9, 13; explicit in transaction 10; key elements, setting expectations 9–10
Trompenaars, F. 144–145, 144–146

U
unconscious biases 145–148

V
values, refer to 93
ventral vagal system 29–31
vertical development 19, 84, 153, 155; conditions evoking 156–157; identifying stage of 155–156; spiral arising, conversational space 158, *159*
voicing of content 72

W
Walton, R.E. 76
warm habits 96
wilderness guide 1
Winnicott, D.W. 158, 173
worksheets: *9-Minute Form,* outline 127; areas covered checklist, preparing the ground 107; body–brain states, identification 47–56; conversational cycle 170; factors impacting conversations, summary 150; harnessing expanded perspectives 189; *PACES* framework 73–74; recognising conversational stages and capabilities 85–86; relational patterns understanding 23–24

Printed in the United States
by Baker & Taylor Publisher Services